# DISINFORMATION

# DISINFORMATION

## 22 Media Myths That
## Undermine the War on Terror

## RICHARD MINITER

Since 1947
REGNERY
PUBLISHING, INC.
An Eagle Publishing Company • Washington, DC

Library of Congress Cataloging-in-Publication Data

Miniter, Richard.
   Disinformation : 22 media myths that undermine the war on terror / Richard Miniter.
      p. cm.
   Includes bibliographical references and index.
   ISBN 0-89526-006-9
1. War on Terrorism, 2001—Press coverage.   I. Title.
P96.W36M56 2005
070.4'49973931—dc22

                  2005026756

Published in the United States by
Regnery Publishing, Inc.
One Massachusetts Avenue, NW
Washington, DC 20001
www.regnery.com
Distributed to the trade by
National Book Network
Lanham, MD 20706

Manufactured in the United States of America

10 9 8 7 6 5 4 3 2 1

Books are available in quantity for promotional or premium use. Write to Director of Special Sales, Regnery Publishing, Inc., One Massachusetts Avenue NW, Washington, DC 20001, for information on discounts and terms or call (202) 216-0600.

*For Richard F. Miniter, my father, Marine, police chief, marine biologist, historian, raconteur, manufacturing chief, deer hunter, author, mine owner, and father of six.*

# CONTENTS

# INTRODUCTION

*"You're entitled to your own opinion, but not your own facts."*

—SENATOR DANIEL PATRICK MOYNIHAN[1]

SITTING IN THE tiny television studio of a major American network, over-looking the U.S. Capitol dome, in the closing moments of a live interview, the host startled me.

She was a mild-mannered, nonpartisan presenter, with the kind of authoritative yet neutral voice that broadcasters covet. Thoroughly pre-pared, with a brick-thick stack of research heaped on the table before her, she had interviewed legions of experts on al Qaeda and global ter-rorism over the past four years. As the clock ran out, she offhandedly asked, "Why haven't we caught bin Laden yet? After all, isn't he dying on dialysis?"[2]

On national television, it doesn't do to let your mouth hang open. But I was surprised. The intelligence community had long since concluded that the early reports of Osama bin Laden's impending demise from kid-ney problems were both unreliable and untrue.

"No, actually he is *not* on dialysis."

She seemed thunderstruck.

The host was a cautious professional with sources and resources, yet she had been snookered. What about the average independent-minded American? How can he sort fact from factoid?

## A PARADE OF FACTOIDS

There are a lot of War on Terror myths masquerading as fact in the pages of respected newspapers, on the talk-radio airwaves, and on the World Wide Web. Some are cunningly disguised, others easily spotted.

They are usually admixtures of fact and fantasy with certain telltale elements: something secret (a plot, a flight), something out of context (a quote, an event), and something foul (usually a motive). Often a dose of anti-Semitism or anti-Americanism is added.

The acceptance of a myth gives the believer a sense of superiority, a delight of being "in" on the secret gears driving larger events. It is most savored by those who feel left out. Those who doubt the myth are written off as naïve, conned, or part of the plot. This was first noticed by political science professor Richard Hofstadter, who wrote an article called "The Paranoid Style in American Politics" in November 1964.[3] In those days, conservatives had little political power or influence. Hofstadter's essay appeared around the time that Senator Barry Goldwater, known as "Mr. Conservative," lost forty-four out of fifty states in the 1964 presidential contest—one of the largest political defeats in American history. At the time, many conservatives believed that international bankers or the Council on Foreign Relations or the United Nations were secretly controlling American politics. They pulled no punches. John Birch Society founder Robert Welch accused President Eisenhower of being either a traitorous Communist or the dupe of Communists.

Today, it is mostly liberals, antiwar crusaders, European intellectuals, and paleo-conservatives who truck in conspiracies. Many of these out-of-power activists have come to believe that a small band of "neo-cons" have made a puppet of the president, that the collapse of the Twin Towers was an "inside job," and so on.

Though Hofstadter was writing about what he called the "radical right," his words today could best describe the "Michael Moore Left":

Events since 1939 have given the contemporary right-wing paranoid a vast theatre for his imagination, full of rich and proliferating detail, replete with realistic cues and undeniable proofs of the validity of his suspicions. The theatre of action is now the entire world, and he can draw not only on the events of World War II, but also on those of the Korean War and the Cold War. Any historian of warfare knows it is in good part a comedy of errors and a museum of incompetence; but if for every error and every act of incompetence one can substitute an act of treason, many points of fascinating interpretation are open to the paranoid imagination. In the end, the real mystery, for one who reads the primary works of paranoid scholarship, is not how the United States has been brought to its present dangerous position but how it has managed to survive at all.[4]

So, too, with the War on Terror. Every error or incompetence in Iraq or elsewhere is produced as evidence of a neo-conservative conspiracy. All sense of proportion is lost. Senator Dick Durbin (Democrat of Illinois) can casually call America's terrorist holding pens "gulags" and compare U.S. soldiers to Nazis. (He later issued a half-hearted apology.) *Newsweek* magazine alleges that U.S. interrogators flushed a Koran down the toilet, in a spurious claim that touched off riots in Afghanistan. Uncorroborated stories from the Arab press of American "atrocities" are taken at face value. The "paranoid style" lives on.

## WHAT IS A MYTH?

The notion that bin Laden is on dialysis, which I treat at length in Myth #3, is one of many myths that have been thrown up in the wake of the horrific attacks of September 11, 2001. In many ways it is an archetypical myth. It is pleasing to believe (who wouldn't wish that the arch-terrorist was suffering in a dank cave, his dignity destroyed by a tangle of tubes linking him to a machine?), plausible, and hard to check. Like so many urban legends of the War on Terror, it has now been so often repeated that everyone knows it must be true. But it isn't.

For our purposes, a myth is a statement of seeming fact about the War on Terror that has become part of the conventional wisdom and is *provably false*. I have concentrated on myths that are widely believed by fair-minded people and ignored the more fevered and obscure conspiracy theories. I have also ignored contentions involving other people's motives (such as that Bush invaded Iraq to avenge his father) that might well be untrue, but are impossible to test. The many presidential memos that might shed light on the question will not be declassified for decades. Besides, who can say with certainty what drives other people? The real motivation could be unspoken or unknown even to the decision maker himself.

So in this book, we'll stick to what is widely believed yet *provably false*.

## WHY MYTHS DESERVE TO DIE

No myth is harmless and some are poisonous. One persistent rumor was that Jewish Americans who worked in the World Trade Center were warned to stay home by Israeli intelligence on September 11, 2001 (See Myth #6). Anti-Semitism is an old scourge that refuses to die; indeed, it seems to be refreshed by immigrants from lands where residents are subjected to hateful broadcasts by state-run media. This vile belief threatens American unity in the face of terror and it is based on a lie, which I hope will be dispatched by this book.

Many myths promote anti-Semitic, anti-American, or even anti-Islamic viewpoints while masquerading as fact.

Myths can also lead politicians, the press, and the public to take positions based on false evidence, to boldly go in the wrong direction. Judgments based on false or incomplete information can lead to tragedy or disaster, as our friends in the antiwar movement like to remind us about Iraq. So it really matters if terrorism actually is caused by poverty (see Myth #16) or if Iraq really is "another Vietnam" (see Myth #8), because enormous decisions will be made on or against these beliefs.

## THE INVESTIGATION

When I decided to investigate these myths, I quickly learned that I was wandering in a trackless territory. Few had investigated the half-truths of the Right and the Left or made a comprehensive attempt to set the record straight. Several magazines, such as *Foreign Policy*'s excellent "Think Again" series and *Popular Mechanics*' in-depth investigation into the claims of September 11 skeptics, and a few web sites, such as Salon.com and the invaluable buster of urban legends Snopes.com, have made vital, piecemeal contributions. Yet no book that I could find traced these myths to their sources and definitively debunked them.

As any prosecutor knows, it can take a lot of work to establish the truth or falsity of something. Whenever possible, I tracked down eyewitnesses who could speak authoritatively about the events in question. I interviewed CIA station chiefs responsible for funding the Afghan anti-Soviet resistance movement in the 1980s. I sought out Colonel Oliver North and asked him directly about his early "warnings" about al Qaeda. Their answers were surprising but solid.

Whenever possible, I went to the scene. I retraced bin Laden's last steps from a meeting hall in Jalalabad, Afghanistan, and then climbed into the cave complexes, bin Laden's last known bolthole up in the White Mountains near Tora Bora. In Baghdad, in 2003, I interviewed Paul Bremer and WMD hunter David Kay in the strange tranquility of the green zone. I also traveled to Brussels, Cairo, Dubai, Khartoum, Kuwait City, Kabul, London, New York, Paris, and Washington, D.C.

Sometimes it doesn't take a trip around the world to debunk a myth, just a stroll down the street. In government libraries, I surveyed tens of thousands of pages of court documents and agency reports, scrutinized academic studies and congressional testimony, and examined unpublished private papers. (The reader can examine some of the declassified documents in the back of the book, as well as an extensive bibliography.)

More importantly, I interviewed dozens of participants and experts, including active and retired members of the intelligence services of the United States, Western Europe, East Africa, Central Asia, and the Middle East. Many were helpful in providing documents, recollections, and insights. They had a profound desire to set the record straight, and this book would not have been possible without them. I did not simply accept the word of intelligence officers or other officials as gospel, but checked and cross-checked their testimony with information from other sources.

# WHERE DO MYTHS COME FROM?

There are essentially six sources of media myths:

## Honest errors

Upon small errors, myths are built. Some are garden-variety misquotes or misattributions. Others ignore or confuse some details. Here are some classic ones, drawn from Michael Moore's film *Fahrenheit 9/11*:

> ➤ President Bush didn't hold any meetings "with his head of counter-terrorism" (i.e. Richard Clarke) prior to September 11 to discuss ter-rorism. In reality, Clarke was a senior director at the National Security Council in the White House and did meet Bush, as Clarke makes clear in his own book *Against All Enemies*. But Clarke did not have a one-on-one meeting with the president, as he wished. Moore seems to have misunderstood Clarke.
>
> ➤ Terrorism funding was cut from the FBI budget prior to September 11. Actually, the 2001 spending appropriation for the FBI was not approved by Congress until weeks after September 11, 2001, and, when it was, it showed a massive increase. Counter-terrorism funding for the FBI was slashed in the closing years of the Clinton adminis-tration. Since 1999 is prior to September 11, 2001, Moore's statement is technically true but misleading. If Moore meant to imply that fund-ing for year 2001 was cut, he is wrong.
>
> ➤ President Bush was warned in the Presidential Daily Briefing of August 6, 2001, that Osama bin Laden was planning to attack the U.S. by hijacking airplanes. In fact, the only "warning" was in the title. As we shall see in Myth #5, the Presidential Daily Briefing did not con-tain any fresh or specific information at all. The reader can read the now declassified report in Appendix A.

## Spin by U.S. government officials

A classic case of government spin is the myth that the September 11 hijack-ers used "box cutters" to take control of the four planes. The tapes of calls from flight attendants and passengers, as well as the black boxes (when they were recovered) do not mention box cutters. In fact, there is a suggestion that other weapons—including acid and a gun—were used. But box cutters were a pleasing myth; these knives were approved for air travel prior to September 11. If the hijackers used them, it meant that the airports, airlines, private security, and the FAA all did their jobs. Al Qaeda used a loophole. If the terrorists used banned weapons, as some of the doomed passengers and crew said, then it means someone in authority failed.

Is this a dark conspiracy on the part of federal officials? Probably not. The transcripts that have been released to the press mention knives (which might have been box cutters) and the accounts that mention other weapons could be hysteria or hearsay, if the caller didn't see the weapon he described. Officials doubtlessly summarized the evidence in their favor. It certainly sounds better than "we are not really sure and may never know" and is more reassuring to air passengers than "airport security failed in Boston."

## Disinformation spread by foreign sources

Sometimes the media unwittingly picks up dubious information from foreign intelligence services, notably from Pakistan. (See Myth #1.) In other cases, the media is misled by foreign websites that are run by sympathizers to bin Laden. Consider just three websites. An Arab-language, pro-terrorism site called Islam Memo (www.Islammemo.cc) repeatedly floats "news accounts" that are *provably false*. The U.S. Information Service, a division of the State Department, calls it "perhaps the most unreliable source of 'news' on the Internet."[5] It frequently claims that many U.S. soldiers were killed in Iraq on a particular day, when, in fact, none were.

These claims are picked up and translated into English by Mohammed Abu Nasr, who co-edits the site Free Arab Voice (www.freearabvoice.org). Nasr is an Arab communist who is fiercely anti-American.

Nasr's translations are in turn picked up and pushed by Jihad Unspun (www.jihadunspun.net) which is run by a Canadian woman who converted to Islam *after* the September 11 attacks.

Here's how it works: Islam Memo published a letter from "Fatima," one of a group of thirteen girls claiming to have been repeatedly raped at Abu Ghraib prison. Nasr quickly translated the account and put it up on his site, on December 18, 2004. Jihad Unspun picked it up on December 24, 2004. In reality, six women and girls (not thirteen) were present at Abu Ghraib between July and December 24. None were named Fatima. None were sexually assaulted.

## Historical amnesia

It is often surprising how little recent history that reporters (and readers) know. While 1980s music might be popular on today's radio stations, 1980s history is vanishing from media memory. Take the oft-repeated claim that the U.S. funded the Taliban in the 1980s. The Taliban was not even formed until 1995, with the help of Pakistani intelligence. It is often confused with the mujihideen, the Afghan anti-Soviet resistance, which was founded in the 1980s. These are very different groups: The mujihideen were nationalists, the Taliban were religious extremists. Many mujihideen leaders joined what the Western press called the "Northern Alliance," the avowed enemy of the Taliban. These two armed movements warred in the high, cold mountain reaches of Afghanistan for years. Yet this didn't stop commentators and others from confusing the two or arguing that the U.S. funded the Taliban before it even existed. This confusion leads to dubious conclusions, such as "we funded the Taliban in the 1980s, and now they have welcomed bin Laden and turned against us." Critics call it "blowback." I call it historical amnesia.

## Leaks

Career civil servants are a major source of media myths. These bureaucrats, when they oppose administration policy, are major suppliers of scoops to hungry reporters. But not all of those scoops are entirely true, and few are proffered for disinterested reasons.

In "Did the Press Uncover Watergate?" a July 1974 article in *Commentary* magazine, journalist Edward Jay Epstein demonstrates that ace reporters Bob Woodward and Carl Bernstein were often weeks or months behind the grand jury, prosecutors, and congressional investigators. Not everything Deep Throat said turned out to be true. Epstein points out that the Woodward and Bernstein team spent months on a wild goose chase because of leaked FBI 302 reports. Unlike other arms of the scandal, this one produced no criminal convictions.

Epstein noticed something that transcends the Watergate scandal:

> Perhaps the most perplexing mystery in Bernstein and Woodward's book is why they fail to understand the role of the institutions and investigators who were supplying them and other reporters with leaks. This blind spot, endemic to journalists, proceeds from an unwillingness to see the complexity of bureaucratic in-fighting and of politics within the government itself. If the government is considered monolithic, journalists can report its activities, in simply comprehended and coherent terms, as an adversary out of touch with popular sentiments. On the other hand, if governmental activity is viewed as the product of diverse and competing agencies, all with different bases of power and interests, journalism becomes a much more difficult affair.[6]

Insiders and careerists can play reporters to advance their institutional interests, just as Deep Throat (now revealed to be Mark Felt) used the *Washington Post* and its now famous reporters. Indeed, in a front-page *Washington Post* article published in June 2005, Woodward worried whether he was Felt's "agent" and was treated the way a spy agency uses its human assets.

Of course, the greater good was served by exposing President Nixon's misdeeds. But that wasn't Deep Throat's primary motivation. He was passed over for a promotion at the FBI, when Nixon picked a longtime friend to head the bureau instead. Felt was the heir apparent and wanted to protect his beloved FBI from what he saw as White House meddling. He certainly had no moral or other objections to illegal break-ins for official purposes; he was later convicted (and still later, pardoned) for illegal break-ins he ordered in the early 1970s.

This pattern continues today. Mid-level bureaucrats at the State Department, Central Intelligence Agency, Defense Intelligence Agency, and elsewhere continue to air dubious claims. Usually, the press treats these sources as neutral professionals, not self-interested players. This touching faith in civil servants enables the press to turn policy disputes among departments into morality plays, rather than portray them as the raw struggles for power that they are. And always in these political struggles there is the lurking temptation to lie, to supply the half-truths that make media myths. Journalists need to be wary of being used by their sources, especially as the War on Terror rages.

Once a media myth, conceived in either ignorance or malevolence, makes its way into the public debate about the War on Terror, what happens next is critical. This brings us to "media failures."

## WHAT ARE "MEDIA FAILURES"?

Everyone from the 9-11 Commission to *Harper's* Lewis Lapham rightly frets about "intelligence failures." Yet we hear nothing about "media failures." We should.

The press is the people's intelligence service. Its reports guide voters' decisions in any democracy. When the media fails, is duped, tricked, used, played, or beguiled, more than just the media loses.

In the continuing conversation about the War on Terror, the media fails when it fails to be skeptical. And it serves no one when it spreads disinformation.

MYTH #1

# BIN LADEN WAS TRAINED OR FUNDED BY THE CIA

> *"The Pan-Islamic effort, whose fighters were funded, armed, and trained by the CIA, eventually brought some 25,000 Islamic militants, from more than fifty countries, to combat Soviet occupation of Afghanistan. The United States, intentionally or not, had launched Pan-Islam's first jihad, or holy war, in eight centuries."*
>
> —MARY ANNE WEAVER, *NEW YORKER*[1]

**FOR WHAT IT'S WORTH,** even Osama bin Laden denies that he was funded, trained or in any way helped by the CIA.

In 1993, an intrepid British journalist named Robert Fisk tracked down bin Laden in Almatig, a poor, small village in Sudan. Headlined "Anti-Soviet warrior puts his army on the road to peace," Fisk's report credits bin Laden with road-building and other good works. "He is a shy man," Fisk writes, who "brushes his teeth in the Arab fashion with a stick of *miswak* wood."

Fisk, who writes for the *Independent* (London), was the first Western reporter to interview bin Laden. And he is no ordinary reporter. He is so reviled on the Right that point-by-point debunking of his articles (or others) is known as a "Fisking." There are few anti-American criticisms Fisk does try to substantiate. So when he asked bin Laden directly about American assistance during the 1980s anti-Soviet war, he must have been disappointed when the arch-terrorist said: "Personally, neither I nor any of my brothers saw evidence of American help" in Afghanistan.[2]

If this was too oblique of a denial, Fisk had another chance to put the question to bin Laden. In 1996 he again interviewed bin Laden, this time in Afghanistan. He again asked about American support: "Did not the Americans support the mujihideen's war against the Soviets?"

"We were never at any time friends of the Americans," bin Laden said. "We knew that the Americans support Jews in Palestine and that they are our enemies."[3]

What is significant about these two interviews is they were conducted by Fisk, a columnist who would not go out of his way to defend the CIA or America, and that they occurred years before the September 11 attacks. The vast majority of the citations of the idea that the CIA or America funded, trained, or aided bin Laden appear after September 11.

Should the arch-terrorist be taken at his word? Well, over the past two decades, he has been remarkably consistent in both his anti-Americanism and his denials of CIA assistance. There is no evidence that the CIA ever paid bin Laden. No cancelled checks. No former associates of bin Laden or CIA officials or Afghan leaders or Pakistani officials have come forward to say, yes, I was there and we funded bin Laden. No news accounts from the 1980s published in English in any newspaper in the world make the claim. Indeed, the earliest article to mention bin Laden (or any variant spellings of his name) appears in a February 1992 edition of the *Guardian*—and it does not mention CIA funding. Subsequent congressional and media investigations have turned up nothing.[4]

In addition, nearly everyone who met bin Laden over the past two decades, from fellow terrorists to veteran reporters, dismisses the idea that he received CIA help.

Ayman al-Zawahiri is a medical doctor whose association with bin Laden stretches back to 1985. Today, he is al Qaeda's second in command. In 2001, under the fury of American bombs, he wrote a long tract called *Knights Under the Prophet's Banner*. Bear in mind that al-Zawahiri, in his tract and elsewhere, makes a common distinction between mujihideen (holy warriors) from Afghanistan and mujihideen from Arab lands, the so-called "Arab Afghans." As al-Zawahiri makes clear, the Arabs were funded by Saudi Arabia and other parts of the Arab world, while the real Afghans were funded partly by Arab donations and partly by American funds that passed through Pakistan's intelligence service. Al-Zawahiri concludes by mocking the idea that the Arab fighters were funded by the U.S. Here is what he wrote about the war against the Soviets in Afghanistan:

> While the United States backed Pakistan and the mujihideen factions with money and equipment, the young Arab mujihideen's relationship with the United States was totally different.
>
> Indeed the presence of those young Arab Afghans in Afghanistan and their increasing numbers represented a failure of U.S. policy and new proof of the famous U.S. stupidity. The financing of the activities of the Arab mujihideen came from aid sent to Afghanistan by popular [Arab] organizations. It was substantial aid.
>
> The Arab mujihideen did not confine themselves to financing their own jihad but also carried Muslim donations to the Afghan mujihideen themselves. Osama bin Laden has apprised me of the size of the popular Arab support for the Afghan mujihideen that amounted, according to his sources, to $200 million in the form of military aid alone in 10 years…
> [The Arabs] formed fronts that trained thousands of the Arab mujihideen and provided them with living expenses, housing, travel, and organization.
>
> If the Arab mujihideen are mercenaries of the United States who rebelled against it as it alleges, why is it unable to buy them back now? Are they not counted now—with Osama bin Laden as their head—as the primary threat to U.S. interests? Is not buying them more economical and less costly than the astronomical budgets that the United States is allotting for security and defense?"[5]

Other Arab Afghans agree. Abdullah Anas, an associate of bin Laden's mentor Abdullah Azzam, told the French television program *Zone Interdit* ("Forbidden Zone") on September 12, 2004: "If you say there was a relationship in the sense that the CIA used to meet with Arabs, discuss with them, prepare plans with them, and to fight with them—it never happened."[6]

Independent journalists also find the idea that the CIA funded bin Laden risible.

Ahmed Rashid, author of the authoritative book *Taliban*, writes that bin Laden's role in the 1980s was channeling money through the Makhtab al-Khidmat ("bureau of services"), which evolved into al Qaeda in 1989 after the pullout of Soviet troops. Funding for bin Laden's organization came from "Saudi Intelligence, the Saudi Red Crescent, the World Muslim League and private donations from Saudi princes and mosques," Rashid writes.[7]

Years before September 11, Peter Bergen, a bold CNN producer, arranged the first American broadcast interview with bin Laden. Before the September 11 attacks, Bergen turned in his manuscript for *Holy War Inc.*, which quickly became a bestselling book. Bergen concluded:

> While the charges that the CIA was responsible for the rise of the Afghan Arabs might make good copy, they don't make good history. The truth is more complicated, tinged with varying shades of gray. The United States wanted to be able to deny that the CIA was funding the Afghan war, so its support was funneled through Pakistan's Inter-Services Intelligence Agency (ISI). ISI in turn made the decisions about which Afghan factions to arm and train, tending to favor the most Islamist and pro-Pakistan. The Afghan Arabs generally fought alongside those factions, which is how the charge arose that they were creatures of the CIA.
>
> There was simply no point in the CIA and Afghan Arabs being in contact with each other. The Afghan Arabs functioned independently and had their own sources of funding. The CIA did not need the Afghan Arabs, and the Afghan Arabs did not need the CIA. So the notion that the Agency funded and trained the Afghan Arabs is, at best, misleading. The "let's blame everything bad that happens on the CIA" school of thought vastly overestimates the Agency's powers, both for good and ill.[8]

The CIA has also issued an official denial, saying: "For the record, you should know that the CIA never employed, paid, or maintained any relationship whatsoever with bin Laden."[9]

This is the rare case in which bin Laden, journalists, and the CIA agree.

Milton Bearden was the CIA station chief in Islamabad, Pakistan, from 1986 to 1989. He was responsible for supervising the funding of the Afghan resistance to the Soviets at the time. More than a year and a half *before* the September 11 attacks, Bearden was interviewed by the *New Yorker's* Mary Anne Weaver, a veteran journalist on Arab issues who is known for both her expertise and graceful style. Bearden told her that he did not know bin Laden during the Afghan war. "Did I know he was out there? Yes, I did, but did I say this tall, slim, ascetic Saudi was instrumental? No, I did not. There were a lot of bin Ladens who came to do jihad, and they unburdened us a lot. These guys were bringing in up to twenty to twenty-five million dollars a month from other Saudis and Gulf Arabs to underwrite the war. And that is a lot of money. It's an extra two hundred to three hundred million a year. And this is what bin Laden did. He spent most of the war as a fund-raiser, in Peshawar [Pakistan]. He was not a valiant warrior on the battlefield."[10]

Bearden oversaw the intelligence operations during the peak of American financial support for the anti-Soviet guerrillas. Under him, funding the Afghan resistance began in earnest; he was in charge of disbursing almost $500 million per year at its height. (The Saudis had been funding operations in Afghanistan since 1979. In 1980, at the urging of President Carter's national security adviser, Zbigniew Brzezinski, America agreed to supply limited funding to anti-Soviet forces. Britain, China, and Pakistan also began to underwrite the resistance. Later, in the Reagan years, the U.S. agreed to match Saudi expenditures dollar for dollar, which led to a huge increase in American expenditures in 1986. Significantly, under the arrangement, the Saudi funds went to the "Arab Afghans," including bin Laden, while the U.S. funds went to Pakistani intelligence, earmarked for actual Afghan fighters. "We put $500 million into Afghanistan in 1987 alone, and the Saudis matched the U.S. bill for bill," Bearden told the *New Yorker*.[11]

In an interview with me in a Reston Town Center restaurant, Bearden said scornfully: "I challenge anyone to give any proof that we gave one dollar to any of the Afghan Arabs, let alone bin Laden."[12]

There are many reasons to believe Bearden. He was in charge of all CIA funds at the time and knew where the money went. He retired from the CIA in 1995 to write books[13] and do some international consulting— he has no motive to mouth an agency line.

I also talked to Bearden's predecessor, Bill Peikney, who ran the CIA's operations in Islamabad from 1984 to 1986. Peikney strongly supports Bearden's account. He adds in an e-mail to me: "I don't recall bin Laden coming across my screen when I was there."[14] The CIA simply did not even know who bin Laden was in the mid-1980s. And when the agency knew who he was, from 1986 onwards, he was seen as only one of many Saudis active in the region.

Besides, the CIA preferred to finance Afghans fighting for their country, not extremist Arabs like bin Laden. The Arab Afghans rarely ventured up to the front. Indeed, many of these so-called holy warriors were killed by rival Islamist factions in Pakistan. Why invest in people who were not actively fighting Soviet troops?

Moreover, the handful of Americans who had heard of bin Laden in the 1980s knew him mainly for his violently anti-American views. Dana Rohrabacher, now a Republican congressman from Orange County, California, told me about a trip he took with the mujihideen in 1987. At the time, Rohrabacher was a Reagan aide who delighted in taking long overland trips inside Afghanistan with anti-Communist forces. On one such trek, his guide told him not to speak English for the next few hours because they were passing by bin Laden's encampment. Rohrabacher was told: "If he hears an American, he will kill you."[15] If a CIA operative had tried to recruit bin Laden, he probably would not have lived through the experience.

The CIA officers' case is bolstered by Pakistani officials. Brigadier Mohammed Yousaf headed the Afghan bureau of Pakistan's intelligence service, the ISI, from 1983 to 1987. In retirement, he wrote a memoir called *The Bear Trap*. According to a State Department translation, Brigadier Yousaf writes that "For every dollar supplied by the U.S. another was added by the Saudis . . . [The American funds] were transferred by the CIA to special accounts in Pakistan under the control of the ISI."[16] This is further evidence that the CIA did not directly fund any resistance groups and supports the case that the Saudis were funding one group (Arab Afghans) while the U.S., via Pakistan, was funding another (actual Afghans).

Finally, bin Laden simply did not need the CIA's money. He was awash in money from Saudi and Persian Gulf sources.

So again, all the evidence is this: The Saudis and the CIA *jointly* funded the war against the Soviet Union in Afghanistan. Osama bin Laden and the Arab Afghans came to Afghanistan with budgets from Saudi intelligence and other Gulf states and their own agenda. They didn't ask for CIA money and didn't get it.

To believe otherwise, one would have to conclude that everyone—bin Laden, his deputy, al-Zawahiri, other terrorists associated with bin Laden, independent journalists like Rashid and Bergen, and the CIA officials involved were all lying. That is quite a conspiracy. And one would have to believe that they were lying years before September 11, when it wouldn't have mattered much. And one would have us believe this without a single molecule of supporting evidence—no checks, no receipts, no memos, and no contemporaneous news stories.

So what did motivate bin Laden to fight the Soviets in Afghanistan? To understate that, we need to understand bin Laden's unique life story.

Osama bin Laden grew up mocked and isolated. He was the only son that Mohammed bin Awaz bin Laden, a Saudi construction magnate from Yemen, had with his least-favored wife, a Syrian beauty named Alia. Osama's mother made his isolation worse. When traveling in the West, she refused to wear a burqa over her Chanel suits, further alienating the bin Laden clan.[17] Rare pictures of Osama, taken in London in 1972, show a tall, awkward boy standing to one side as his two half-brothers put their arms around two girls. He is the only one not smiling.[18]

As his older half-brothers basked in their father's attention and were rewarded with well-paying jobs in the family construction firm, Osama retreated into books and religion. He soon gravitated to a severe form of Islam, which, in addition to traditional Islam's strictures against drinking and unveiled women, forbids all music, movies, television, smoking, dancing, and singing. By all accounts, his father approved of—but did not share—Osama's zealous form of Islam.

Osama had only two consistent ways of winning his father's attention: by speaking knowledgeably about the Koran after Friday night prayer services, and by gleefully forgoing all creature comforts during the family's annual two-week excursion into the Saudi desert. There, they camped in tents, without electricity or running water, in 110-degree heat. In time, these two traits—extreme religiosity and survivalism—would fuse to create the bin Laden we know today.

Radical ideology was the catalyst. While studying at King Abdul Aziz University in Jeddah, Saudi Arabia, in the late 1970s, bin Laden joined the Muslim Brotherhood, a radical Islamic group founded in Egypt in 1928. The group, which was banned at one time or another by all Arab governments, is believed to have cells across the Middle East. The Brotherhood specializes in recruiting university students and young professionals, many of whom later move on to even more radical and violent Islamist organizations. The Brotherhood believes that all Arab dictatorships should fall because they are insufficiently "Islamic," and that a return to the seventh-century values of Mohammed will raise the Arab world to global preeminence. These soon became the views of Osama bin Laden.

While still at university, bin Laden graduated to a more violent brand of Islamism. Sometime in 1978, he met a Palestinian firebrand named Abdullah Azzam. Azzam, a tall, charismatic man with arresting eyes, spoke with conviction and passion. His theme was jihad. He did not mean a spiritual struggle, but violence. Ten years later, a videotape of Azzam's fiery set speech on jihad surfaced at an Islamist conference in Oklahoma City. "The jihad, the fighting, is obligatory on you wherever you can perform it. And just as when you are in America you must fast—unless you are ill or on a voyage—so, too, must you wage jihad. The word jihad means fighting only, fighting with the sword."[19]

Such was Azzam's power as a speaker that a videotape of a single speech would persuade young men to abandon their studies, their families, and their jobs to train for war. Even Azzam's enemies came to respect his ability to recruit and inspire thousands of terrorists. Israel's former ambassador to the United Nations, Dore Gold, recently wrote: "It is difficult to overstate the impact that this Islamic radical [Azzam] had."[20]

Young bin Laden saw Azzam in person in 1978. The meeting changed his life. Without Azzam, bin Laden might have become a Saudi executive with a soft spot for radical ideas. With Azzam, he started on a path to become the most feared and hated terrorist of our time.

Less than a year later, two cataclysmic events at the frontiers of the Muslim world completed bin Laden's transformation from a radical into a *jihadi*. In 1979, Islamic extremists led a coup in Iran. The Iranian revolution showed bin Laden and his generation of Islamists that their dream of a Koranic theocracy was actually possible. They could change the world. Just as the 1917 Soviet revolution in Russia electrified Communists across Europe, the Iranian revolution galvanized radicals across the Muslim world.

The Iranian revolution taught bin Laden and his comrades-in-arms a second deadly lesson: not to fear the United States. Iranian militants took dozens of Americans hostage in the U.S. embassy in Teheran. America did nothing. As the months ticked by, President Carter seemed weak and ineffectual. Carter's feeble response surprised the Islamic radicals. According to their speeches and printed propaganda, militants became convinced that Allah was protecting the fundamentalist revolution in Iran and holding America at bay. They were elated and emboldened. No one could stop them now.

Then, in December 1979, the Soviet Union toppled a rival Communist regime in Afghanistan with a massive invasion of airborne special forces, paratroopers, tanks, and self-propelled artillery. On its eastern flank, Iran saw a threat to its revolution from its ancient enemy—the Russians—and was alarmed that its allies in Afghanistan were among the first gunned down by Soviet troops. The word went out: Islam is in danger. Azzam repeated the call to arms in his spellbinding speeches.

Bin Laden heard the call. "When the invasion of Afghanistan started, I was enraged and went there at once," he told Robert Fisk. "I arrived within days, before the end of 1979."[21] For what it is worth, bin Laden is probably lying. The Soviet invasion began December 25, 1979, and the Islamist effort took months to organize. But the lie illustrates bin Laden's reaction nonetheless: he was provoked and he would take action.

In neighboring Pakistan, bin Laden soon linked up with Azzam. There were thousands of other recruits—many drawn by Azzam's speeches—from around the Arab world. These were the Arab Afghans. They lacked guns, training, and coordination. Azzam busied himself trying to negotiate alliances among the various Arab factions—it would take unity to defeat the largest army in the world. But the unity rarely held and the Arab Afghans often fought among themselves. Bin Laden did not find a role until Azzam told him that an army also needs a quartermaster.

With Azzam's help, bin Laden opened the "bureau of services," the Makhtab Khadamat al-Mujahideen, in Peshawar, Pakistan. (In 1989, this organization was renamed al Qaeda, Arabic for "the base.") Bin Laden returned to Saudi Arabia to raise money and buy supplies. He returned with his family's construction vehicles to cut roads and build bomb-proof bunkers. He bought blocks of houses to quarter the holy warriors, the mujihideen. And, critically, he set up a central office to track recruits. Once registered with bin Laden's bureau of services,[22] a recruit was assured food, medical care, and, if he died in combat, a letter to his parents lionizing his martyrdom. Since the recruits came from as far away as Morocco and the Philippines, bin Laden ended up with a vast database of Islamic militants from around the world. That codex would enable him to set up cells of trusted terrorists in more than fifty-five countries in the 1990s.

As the Afghan jihad wore on, the Reagan administration decided to step up its financial support to something close to the funds provided by the Saudis and various Gulf state sheikhs (who had been financing the Afghan war for years). As a rule, America financed Afghan natives while Saudi Arabia funded Islamic extremists from outside Afghanistan. These were separate efforts funding separate groups; only a common Communist enemy united them.

The Reagan administration officials saw the war as a way of weakening and demoralizing the Soviet Union. A joke popular in conservative circles at the time captured the essence of the strategy: "How do you say Vietnam in Russian? Afghanistan." Ultimately, the Reagan administration pumped in more than $3 billion between 1985 and 1989.[23]

The Saudis saw the effort as a way of protecting their kingdom, spreading their severe version of Islam, and extending their influence to the non-Arab Muslim world. The Reagan administration was no more responsible for the anti-Soviet Arab Afghans than bin Laden and his fellow jihadis were responsible for Reagan's principled anti-Communism.

By February 1989, the Soviets had retreated and bin Laden joined the civil war to turn once-tolerant Afghanistan into a model Islamic state. But he used his own money, not the CIA's.

# BIN LADEN HAS A VAST FORTUNE AND IS ABLE TO FINANCE TERRORISM OUT OF HIS OWN POCKET

*"The war against terrorism is a war of accountants and auditors, as well as a war of weaponry and solicitors."*

—ATTORNEY GENERAL JOHN ASHCROFT[1]

*"There are two things a brother must always have for jihad, the self and money."*

—AN AL QAEDA OPERATIVE[2]

LIKE A JAMES BOND VILLAIN, Osama bin Laden is supposed to be a reclusive multi-millionaire with a ruthless ambition to murder millions and rule the (Arab) world.

Some have even imagined the arch-terrorist living in a vast, underground lair that would put Dr. No's to shame.[3] One British newspaper even published an illustration featuring elevators, armories, and control rooms.

When U.S. Special Forces and their Afghan allies won control of the mountain bunkers at Tora Bora in December 2001, they discovered small, squalid holes and limestone caves smeared with diesel soot and littered with spent cartridges. There were no air-conditioned underground warehouses or flood-lit control rooms.

For a long time, much of the American intelligence community thought that Osama bin Laden had a personal fortune of some $300 million. This figure still surfaces in news stories and slips from the lips of

cable commentators. Yet, upon examination, it turns out that lofty estimates of bin Laden's wealth are exaggerated.

The widespread perception of bin Laden's bottomless wallet were
based on two inter-related intelligence failures.

The $300 million figure first appeared in American intelligence
reports on November 17, 1998, according to the 9-11 Commission's
extensive investigation. The 9-11 Commission's *Monograph on Terrorist
Financing*[4] reveals, in footnote number 12:

> Reporting from November 1998 concluded that although the $300 mil-
> lion figure probably originated from rumors in the Saudi business com-
> munity, it was a "reasonable estimate" as a few years earlier, representing
> what would have been bin Laden's share of his family's business con-
> glomerate in Saudi Arabia. The intelligence community thought it had
> adequately verified this number by valuing bin Laden's investments in
> Sudan as well as what he could have inherited from his father's con-
> struction empire in Saudi Arabia. Finished intelligence supported the
> notion that bin Laden's "fortune" was still intact by concluding that bin
> Laden could only have established al Qaeda so quickly in Afghanistan if
> he had ready access to significant funds.[5]

In other words, it was a guesstimate.

The other, interlocking intelligence failure was ignorance: the CIA
and other intelligence services knew that bin Laden spent large sums on
terrorism and influence, but did not know where or how he was funded.
Since the intelligence community could not determine the sources of bin
Laden's budget, it was presumed to be his own pocket.

The conventional wisdom of the time is probably best summarized by
P. J. Crowley, former National Security Council spokesman and special
assistant to President Clinton. Crowley described the state of thinking
about bin Laden's finances inside the National Security Council following the August 7, 1998, embassy bombings. "The media repeated things
they were told by various government officials. It is a fact that bin Laden
had access to some portion of his share of the family fortune. He was
involved in various commercial enterprises in Sudan with the Military
Industrial Complex [that is actually what the Sudanese charmingly called

it], one portion of which we bombed in 1998. It was assumed that he was a financial backer for terrorist groups before his operational and inspirational role became more clear."[6]

As it would later emerge, bin Laden's portion of his family fortune was relatively small, and long since frozen. And his Sudanese investments were hardly what one foreign intelligence source called "money spinners."[7]

This ignorance of bin Laden's financial means persisted for years. The CIA, in an April 12, 2001, intelligence report, outlined how little was known about bin Laden's finances.

Gaps in our understanding contribute to the difficulty we have in pursuing the bin Laden financial target. We presently do not have the reporting to determine how much of bin Laden's personal wealth he has used or continues to use in financing his organization; we are unable to estimate with confidence the value of his assets and net worth; and we do not know the level of financial support he draws from his family and other donors sympathetic to his cause.[8]

Even after the September 11 attacks, the intelligence community's ignorance of bin Laden's finances continued.

The 9–11 Commission uncovered a November 14, 2002, e-mail from the head of the Treasury Department team tasked with disrupting al Qaeda's financing.

[S]ometime in the next 3 months a Congressional committee is rightfully going to haul us up to the Hill (or the President is going to call us into the Oval office) and ask us 4 questions:

1. Who finances al Qaeda?
2. How?
3. Where is it?
4. Why don't you have it (and stop it)?

Paul [O'Neill, secretary of the Treasury] could not answer [those questions] today.[9]

For some reason, the intelligence community failed to absorb the valuable work done by Clinton-era counter-terrorism czar Richard Clarke. Clarke led an inter-agency team of intelligence professionals to meet their counterparts in Saudi Arabia in 1999. In Riyadh, Clarke received far more precise information on bin Laden's finances.

Clarke was told that Osama most likely received $1 million a year from about 1970 to 1994 (a total of $24 million) from his family, according to Saudi intelligence and the 9-11 Commission reports. In 1994, the Saudi government forced the bin Laden family to sell Osama's share of the company and place his assets in a frozen account.

Clarke subsequently testified before the 9-11 Commission, which authoritatively dismissed the myth of bin Laden's vast fortune.

> For many years, the United States thought bin Laden financed al Qaeda's expenses through a vast personal inheritance or through the proceeds of the sale of his Sudanese businesses. Neither was true. Bin Laden was alleged to have inherited approximately $300 million when his father died, funds used while in Sudan and Afghanistan. This money was thought to have formed the basis of the financing for al Qaeda. Only after NSC-initiated interagency trips to Saudi Arabia in 1999 and 2000, and after interviews of bin Laden family members in the United States, was the myth of bin Laden's fortune discredited. From about 1970 until 1993 or 1994, Osama bin Laden received about a million dollars per year— adding up to a significant sum, to be sure, but not a $300 million fortune. In 1994 the Saudi government forced the bin Laden family to find a buyer for Osama's share of the family company and to place the proceeds into a frozen account. The Saudi freeze had the effect of divesting bin Laden of what would otherwise have been a $300 million fortune. Notwithstanding this information, some within the government continued to cite the $300 million figure well after 9-11, and the general public still gives credence to the notion of a "multimillionaire bin Laden.[10]

So what is bin Laden worth? Just for fun, I phoned a veteran financial planner and asked her to model an investment portfolio that earned 8 percent per year from 1970 to 1994, with $1 million added per year.

Assume all gains were automatically reinvested and no money withdrawn between 1970 and 1994. Also assume that bin Laden needed no money for living expenses, taxes, or other uses. (There are unrealistic assumptions, to be sure.) By 1994, that nest egg would be worth $73,105,939.95. If adjusted for inflation, that figure would be much lower, perhaps $40 million. That is the budget of a small public school district, not a global enterprise to rival Dr. No. And it is a lot less than $300 million.

This model is obviously a best-case scenario for bin Laden's fortune. To get a more realistic picture, we have to examine the quality of bin Laden's investments and the quantity of his expenses.

Virtually all of bin Laden's investments were money losers. He bought into an animal-hide dyeing factory in Sudan (not exactly a growth business), a highway that the Sudanese government never paid for, a bank that lost money—even a bee-keeping business in Yemen that didn't make sweet profits.

The 9-11 Commission is unequivocal on this point:

> Nor were bin Laden's assets in Sudan a source of money for al Qaeda. Bin Laden was reputed to own 35 companies in Sudan when he lived there from 1992 to 1996, but some may never have actually been owned by him and others were small or not economically viable. Bin Laden's investments may well have been designed to gain influence with the Sudanese government rather than be a revenue source. When bin Laden was pressured to leave Sudan in 1996, the Sudanese government apparently expropriated his assets and seized his accounts, so that he left Sudan with practically nothing. When bin Laden moved to Afghanistan in 1996, his financial situation was dire; it took months for him to get back on his feet.[11]

Whatever the value of these dubious Sudanese enterprises, their value to bin Laden is precisely zero—the government of Sudan seized them all. Bin Laden may have businesses in Afghanistan—accounts are sketchy—but these are also worth nothing to him today.

Now consider the expense side of the ledger: how much it costs bin Laden to support himself, his wives, his children, and his terrorist network—said to be active, before September 11, in fifty-five countries.

Terrorism is expensive. The 9-11 Commission estimates that the costs of the 1998 U.S. embassy bombings was $10,000, the September 11 attacks cost between $400,000 and $500,000, the Bali bombings cost $20,000, and planned operations against tankers in the Strait of Hormuz cost $130,000.[12] A 2004 report from the United Nations claimed that the Madrid bombings cost $10,000.[13]

These estimates, if anything, understate the costs of operating a terror network. They do not include the overhead of administering a network (salaries, benefits, supplies) as well as considerable expenses for air travel (al Qaeda requires a lot of face-to-face meetings), hotel charges, and other costs.

In practice, al Qaeda was perennially short of money. Detainees complained that bin Laden would not even pay for the C-section of a prominent operative's wife.[14]

Ramzi Yousef, the mastermind of the 1993 World Trade Center bombing, said he would have used a bigger bomb—but couldn't afford one.[15]

This is not the only time al Qaeda's funding problems limited its ability to carry out terror attacks. Consider a recent audiotape message by Ayman al-Zawahiri, bin Laden's deputy. Al-Zawahiri discusses why al Qaeda targeted the Egyptian—rather than the American or British—embassy in Pakistan for attack.

> A short time before the bombing of the [Egyptian] embassy the assigned group . . . told us that they could strike both the Egyptian and American embassies if we gave them enough money. We had already provided them with all that we had and we couldn't collect more money. So the group focused on bombing the Egyptian embassy.[16]

Jeffrey Battle was part of an al Qaeda terrorist cell broken up in Portland, Oregon. Shortly before Battle's arrest, the FBI recorded one of his telephone calls. It was a long rant about the cell's money worries.

> Because we don't have support. Everyone's scared to give up any money to help us. . . . Because that law that Bush wrote [the USA Patriot Act]. . . . Everyone's scared . . . he made a law that says for instance I left out of the

country and I fought, right, but I wasn't able to afford a ticket but you bought my plane ticket, you gave me money to do it.... By me going and me fighting, by this new law, they can come and take you and put you in jail.[17]

Both Battle and his former wife are now imprisoned.

Sheikh Qari Sa'id, who headed al Qaeda's finance committee, had a reputation for vetoing even small expenditures.

> Sa'id, a trained accountant, had worked with bin Laden in the late 1980s when they fought together in Afghanistan and then for one of bin Laden's companies in Sudan in the early to mid-1990s. Sa'id was apparently notoriously tightfisted with al Qaeda's money. Operational leaders may have occasionally bypassed Sa'id and the Finance Committee and requested funds directly from bin Laden. Al Qaeda members apparently financed themselves for day-to-day expenses and relied on the central organizations only for operational expenses.[18]

Sa'id reportedly vetoed a $1,500 expense for some of the hijackers to travel to Saudi Arabia, where they could get visas to fly to America. He had to be overruled by bin Laden himself, according to the 9-11 Commission.[19]

In two separate passages, the 9-11 Commission is quite clear that bin Laden had little money of his own.

> Contrary to common belief, bin Laden did not have access to any significant amounts of personal wealth (particularly after his move from Sudan to Afghanistan) and did not personally fund al Qaeda, either through an inheritance or businesses he was said to have owned in Sudan.[20]

And again:

> Contrary to popular myth, Osama bin Laden does not support al Qaeda through a personal fortune or a network of businesses. Rather, al Qaeda financial facilitators raise money from witting and unwitting donors,

mosques and sympathetic imams, and nongovernment organizations such as charities. The money seems to be distributed as quickly as it is raised, and we have found no evidence that there is a central "bank" or "war chest" from which al Qaeda draws funds. Before 9-11 al Qaeda's money was used to support its operations, its training and military apparatus, the Taliban, and, sporadically, other terrorist organizations. Since 9-11 al Qaeda's money supports operations and operatives and their families.[21]

Among the finance streams they say that al Qaeda *did not* use, according to the 9-11 Commission: drug money, contributions from the United States, "conflict diamonds," or fund-raising coalitions with other terrorist groups such as Hezbollah or Hamas.[22]

The list of purported al Qaeda funding sources is legion: counterfeit trade-marked goods, consumer coupon fraud, drug trafficking, insider trading, support from Gulf-area governments, and conflict diamonds are the most common. In many cases, one or two threads of information make such theories tantalizing; but after careful review of all of the evidence available to us, including some of the most sensitive information held by the U.S. government, we have judged that such theories cannot be substantiated.[23]

So where does al Qaeda get its funds?

Famed French judge counter-terrorism Jean-Louis Bruguiere declared that most terrorists get their money from "micro-financing" schemes, including credit and debit card fraud, rather than massive funding.[24]

Al Qaeda never had a "macro-financing" structure, said Judge Jean-Louis Bruguiere, the dean of Europe's anti-terrorism investigators. In fact, analyzing the clusters of activists, he found that there were never large flows of external money financing any attack. In nearly a decade of searching, all Bruguiere was able to find was "micro-financing" activists raising the little money they needed to survive and commit their crimes through credit card or debit card fraud. They turned out to be petty thieves, not grand gangsters.[25]

The 9-11 Commission concluded that the terror network relied on, aside from petty larceny and welfare fraud, covert fund-raising in Saudi Arabia and Persian Gulf states as well as on funds obtained from charities either directly or by illicit diversion.

Phony charities are an al Qaeda favorite, and include a U.S.-based nonprofit called Benevolence International. American corporations unwittingly supplied some of its funds. Among the donors, according to the daily *Asharq al-Awsat*, were Microsoft, UPS, and Compaq Corporation (taken over by Hewlett Packard in 2002). Some of these contributions may well have found their way to al Qaeda.[26]

The 9-11 Commission concludes:

Al Qaeda relied on fund-raising before 9-11 to a greater extent than thought at the time. Bin Laden did not have large sums of inherited money or extensive business resources. Rather, it appears that al Qaeda lived essentially hand to mouth. A group of financial facilitators generated the funds; they may have received money from a spectrum of donors, charities, and mosques, with only some knowing the ultimate destination of their money. The CIA estimates that it cost al Qaeda about $30 million per year to sustain its activities before 9-11, an amount raised almost entirely through donations.[27]

Al Qaeda's finances depend largely on abusing one of the central tenets of Islam, known as *zakat*, which requires that all faithful Muslims turn over a percentage of their annual income for charity.

As a result, al Qaeda's funding is neither stable nor reliable. "Al Qaeda fund-raising was largely cyclical, with the bulk of the money coming in during the Islamic holy month of Ramadan."[28]

To choke off bin Laden's funds, American and allied governments have killed or captured fund-raisers while Saudi security services have removed corrupt imams or charity officials. Some have simply been shot.

"Individuals such as Riyadh, an al Qaeda facilitator, and 'Swift Sword,' known for their ability to raise and deliver money for al Qaeda, have been captured or killed," the 9-11 Commission reports.[29]

Meanwhile, there has been an unpredicted global effort to seize the bank accounts of organizations that divert funds to al Qaeda. Assistant Attorney General Christopher Wray testified before the Senate Judiciary Committee in May 2004 that $138 million had been frozen before it could be used by terrorists.[30]

Al Qaeda may be eking out a bare existence, if the 9-11 Commission reports are correct. "Intelligence analysts estimate al Qaeda's operating budget may be only a few million dollars per year, although such estimates are only tentative."[31] This finding may well prove to be overly optimistic, but it underscores the point that both bin Laden and al Qaeda are in dire straits. Or, as one Australian intelligence official put it: "They are on struggle street."[32]

Bin Laden's wealth is a convenient myth for all concerned. American intelligence would rather that its failures be against an immensely wealthy arch-terrorist mastermind than against a strapped-for-cash criminal entrepreneur. More important, it allows bin Laden to say that he gave up a life of luxury to live in a cave, to sacrifice his worldly goods for the betterment of the *ummah*, the Muslim nation. It is a very important propaganda point, and we may come to regret giving it to him.

# BIN LADEN IS ON DIALYSIS

*"How hard can it be to find a 6-foot-8 [inch] Arab with a kidney prob-lem? Just find the camel with the dialysis machine, and follow it."*

—Comedian Blake Clark[1]

WHILE CLARK IS FUNNY, he is reiterating what is probably the most widely believed myth about bin Laden. Indian Muslims, Internet gurus, television anchors, and at least one prime minister have said that bin Laden has kidney trouble.

Even veteran *New York Times* columnist William Safire is apparently one of the believers. In 2001, Safire wrote that two Iraqi intelligence agents escorted Dr. Mohammed Khayal, a top kidney specialist in Saddam Hussein's regime, to a government car. When the doctor returned, three days later, "the building was abuzz with word that Saddam's Dr. Khayal had been to Afghanistan, where his patient was Osama bin Laden."[2]

Even Snopes.com, that famous debunker of urban legends, does not completely dismiss the story. "The truth of such whispers will be impossible to determine until bin Laden is captured and can be examined. However, at this point it would not be unreasonable to conclude that he is troubled by unspecified renal problems."[3]

So where is the evidence? Snopes.com's Barbara Mikkelson believes "the diversity of the sources provided... over an extended period of time lend credence to the premise that there is something wrong with the terrorist's kidney."[4] (Of course, a diversity of sources over an extended period of time have seen Elvis.) In short, there is no evidence, just a lot of chatter. Mikkelson notes that the sources are all anonymous, leaving open the possibility that the same person is "telling one reporter after another the same tale."[5] Indeed.

It is also possible that reporters are simply talking to each other. In different foreign locales, I've seen English-speaking reporters gravitate to each other and share their notes over drinks. This is, by and large, a healthy practice—it helps scribes come up to speed quickly and cross-check what officials have told them.

But it contributes to pack journalism and helps explain why so many news accounts from, say, Islamabad, sound the same. When the pack makes a mistake, the error shows up simultaneously in many different news accounts—and becomes much harder to correct. This is essentially a democratic model of truth—majority rule within the media. The problem is that truth is not a popularity contest. Either bin Laden has kidney trouble or he does not.

And, like any oft-told tale, the dialysis story takes many forms. In one account, a doctor went to India to buy a dialysis machine for bin Laden. In another account, Pakistani students offered to donate their kidneys to bin Laden. In yet another version, bin Laden went to a hospital in Dubai to get emergency treatment for renal problems. Still another account put bin Laden in a Taliban military hospital some time in 1998.

There is only one presumably well-informed source who has gone on the record to say that bin Laden was on dialysis: Pakistan's prime minister Pervez Musharraf. And he later changed his mind.

At first, General Pervez Musharraf seemed to strongly endorse the notion, in January 2002. "I think now, frankly, he [bin Laden] is dead for the reason he is a patient, he is a kidney patient," he told CNN. Musharraf added, "Pakistan knew bin Laden took two dialysis machines into Afghanistan. One was specifically for his own personal use."[6]

Over the next few years, bin Laden would appear alive and well in a string of audio and video tapes. In December 2004, when Musharraf again sat down with CNN's Wolf Blitzer, he all but reversed himself. Here is the key exchange:

**Blitzer:** Over the years, when we've spoken, you've suggested he was a sick man, Osama bin Laden, that he had kidney problems, he needed dialysis. Do you still believe that?

**Musharraf:** I'm confused, really. I thought that all the intelligence said that he suffers from kidney problems, that he got dialysis machines into the area, but since then, he is alive, that I'm sure of. I don't really know how much he's suffering.[7]

So the only on-the-record source for the dialysis theory has climbed down. There is no evidence that bin Laden is on dialysis.

By contrast, there is a mountain of evidence that bin Laden is not on dialysis.

No medical report has been produced that shows bin Laden is on dialysis. No reporter who has actually met bin Laden has seen the arch-terrorist hooked up to a dialysis machine or heard him talk about it. Robert Fisk, the only Western journalist to interview bin Laden three times, makes no mention of dialysis.

Peter Bergen led a CNN team into Afghanistan to interview bin Laden in 1997. He produced a segment for *Impact*, a CNN series that featured the first-ever American broadcast interview with bin Laden. It aired on August 10, 1997.[8] To see the arch-terrorist, Bergen, host Peter Arnett, and crew journeyed from Peshawar, Pakistan, overland to Jalalabad, Afghanistan, where they waited for days for bin Laden's "media adviser." He told them they could not use their camera, but had to use one that al Qaeda would lend them. At the time, al Qaeda had its own video production unit. (Years later, bin Laden's men would use a booby-trapped camera to kill Ahmad Shah Massoud, a Northern Alliance leader.)

Bergen and his party were driven for hours up mountain passes in a van with curtained windows. After passing through several checkpoints, they stopped in a village and were ushered into what Bergen described as a "shepherd's hut." Again, they waited. Finally, a tall, thin, slightly stooped man entered and introduced himself as Osama bin Laden. He appeared healthy and strong; neither the reporters nor bin Laden mentioned dialysis or kidney trouble.

Sitting on a restaurant terrace overlooking Washington, D.C.'s Connecticut Avenue, Bergen called the dialysis reports a "non-issue."[9] He completely dismissed the idea, and told me that when he saw bin Laden in March 1997, he noticed that the Saudi walked with a cane. "I don't think he is a guy in great health, owing to his poor diet," Bergen said, adding that bin Laden drank "a lot of tea." But he saw no dialysis machines and dismissed the reports as bunk.

It has been more than seven years since the dialysis reports first surfaced, Bergen notes. "He wouldn't still be alive if it were true."

Muslim reporters who have met bin Laden make no mention of any health ailment. One Arab-language account from the London-based daily *Asharq al-Awsat* tells of bin Laden spending hours at horse races with no visible discomfort (though he would put his fingers to his ears every time the racing horn sounded because he considered music "un-Islamic").

Even bin Laden's longtime associates dispute the kidney ailment meme. Saudi newspaper editor Khaled Batarfi has known bin Laden for two decades, ever since the two were neighbors in the Saudi port city of Jeddah. He told the *Sunday Tasmanian*, an Australian newspaper, that bin Laden "does not suffer from kidney disease."[10]

P. J. Crowley was the spokesman for the National Security Council during most of Clinton's second term, from 1997 to 2001 (except for a seven-month stint at the Pentagon). Did the National Security Council take the reports of bin Laden on dialysis seriously? "Was it taken seriously? Yes. Everything about bin Laden was taken seriously," Crowley told me.[11]

"There was a healthy skepticism of health reports of various world leaders" at the National Security Council at the time, Crowley said. He laughingly recalled reports that King Fahd of Saudi Arabia would die "in days" back in 1998. The king actually perished in July 2005. Crowley cited other examples, including Croatian dictator Franjo Tudjman, whose imminent demise was predicted for years before it came to pass. And, of course, Crowley added with a chuckle, there were all those estimates from Kremlinologists about the life of various Soviet leaders.

The dialysis reports had "no effect on policy whatsoever," Crowley said. "You go based on what you know, not what you surmised."

The dialysis business may have been a bit of what Crowley calls "circular reporting." The intelligence community learns something, it is picked up by the press, and then repeated in internal classified reports, each time, with more confidence.

Foreign government officials who have met bin Laden also insist that he has no problems with his kidneys. Bin Laden lived in Sudan from 1991 to May 1996. I interviewed political leaders and intelligence officials there who knew him. Gutbi al-Mahdi, Sudan's former intelligence chief, told me bin Laden had no health problems during his time in Sudan.[12] In fact, every Sudanese I spoke with denied that bin Laden had any health problems, let alone a kidney ailment requiring dialysis.

One Islamic radical whom I met in Khartoum had lived with bin Laden for six years in both Sudan and Afghanistan. He now teaches at Koran University in Khartoum. He met me for tea in the gardens of the Khartoum Hilton, near the confluence of the Blue and White Nile rivers. In a soft voice, he defended and praised "Sheikh Osama." When I asked him about bin Laden's kidney problems, he smiled. "He has no such problems."[13]

Bin Laden himself is of the same opinion. Hamid Mir, an intrepid Pakistani journalist who writes for the Pakistani daily *Dawn*, landed one of the only two authentic post–September 11 interviews with the world's most wanted man. (The other does not mention kidney or renal problems.) In November 2001, Mir was blindfolded and driven for many hours to a "cold place." He believed that it was Afghanistan. After waiting for hours, bin Laden arrived with a retinue of a dozen armed men.

In the course of the wide-ranging interview, Mir asked bin Laden about his kidneys: "A French newspaper has claimed that you have a kidney problem and have secretly gone to Dubai for treatment last year [2000]. Is that correct?"

Bin Laden responded: "My kidneys are all right. I did not go to Dubai last year. One British newspaper has published an imaginary interview with an Islamabad dateline with one of my sons in Saudi Arabia. All this is false."[14]

Is bin Laden to be believed? In the same interview with *Dawn*, he claims to have nuclear weapons and threatens to use them if the U.S. uses such weapons against him. He might assume that in concealing a kidney ailment he is hiding a weakness from his enemy. All that said, there are strong, independent reasons to believe bin Laden is telling the truth about his kidneys.

Perhaps the definitive account comes from bin Laden's doctor, who was arrested on October 21, 2002,[15] in Pakistan and held incommunicado for a full month. "It was a very extensive investigation, eight hours a day," he said. "It went on and on." He added, "I was not physically tortured; there was just mental anguish."[16]

Dr. Amer Aziz,[17] a British citizen born in Pakistan, was interrogated by eight CIA and FBI agents, as well as by Pakistani intelligence officers.[18] Strongly sympathetic to radical Islam, Aziz had treated bin Laden for years. He reportedly admitted to visiting bin Laden after the September 11 attacks. Upon his release, he talked freely to Paul Haven of the Associated Press in November 2002. The doctor said he had given bin Laden a "complete physical" in 1999 and treated him for back injuries after bin Laden was thrown from a horse. "His kidneys were fine," the doctor told Haven.[19] He said "If you're on dialysis, you have a special look. I didn't see any of that,"[20] and added that bin Laden "was walking. He was healthy."[21] Aziz was emphatic: "I did not see any evidence of kidney disease; I didn't see any evidence of dialysis."[22]

Aziz later discussed the dialysis issue with the *New York Times*. "When I hear these reports, I laugh. I did not see any evidence."[23]

He has good reason to laugh—legions of Westerners have bought the story that bin Laden is on dialysis, with no proof at all.

MYTH #4

# BEFORE SEPTEMBER 11,
# NO ONE HAD HEARD OF BIN LADEN

ONE OF THE STRANGEST, most persistent myths of Osama bin Laden is that he was unknown to the world until he burst into view by ordering the atrocities of September 11, 2001.

This view better describes the outlook of the average busy American prior to September 11 than the actual state of knowledge among government officials, the press, or members of the informed public.

In reality, the twin story lines of the 1990s were bin Laden's increasing ability to murder larger and larger numbers of Americans coupled with the press's consistently expanding coverage of the arch-terrorist.

Bin Laden's first attack on Americans targeted U.S. Marines billeted in two towering hotels in the port city of Aden, Yemen, on December 29, 1992. The Marines were in that desert republic to pilot humanitarian flights to feed the starving Muslims of Somalia, but that fact did not disturb bin Laden. A sharp-eyed security guard foiled one attack in the hotel parking lot, while the bombs hidden in the other hotel killed a hapless janitor and some Austrian tourists. No American casualties—and scant coverage back home. But the CIA began to track bin Laden.

Less than a month after President Clinton was sworn in, bin Laden's henchmen struck again—this time at the World Trade Center on February 26, 1993. The massive bomb was hidden in a rented Econoline van. Led by Ramzi Yousef, the killers hoped to use the internal geometry of the World Trade Center's parking garage to punch through the foundation pillars of the south tower and topple it onto the north tower— extinguishing some 250,000 lives. Fortunately, they miscalculated. The blast smashed through a concrete wall, killing a pregnant office manager named Monica Smith (and her unborn son), impaling a carpenter as he ate his lunch, and sucking a Windows on the World waiter into a yawning crater mouth more than six stories deep. All told, seven Americans died at the World Trade Center that terrible day.

The FBI investigation—code named "TRADEBOM"—quickly assembled the forensic evidence and nabbed several of the perpetrators. One fled to Iraq, where he was put on the government payroll and given a government house, according to documents seized by the U.S. Army from Iraqi archives in 2003. The mastermind, Ramzi Yousef, was captured in Islamabad, Pakistan, in 1995. In his possession was a picture of him posing with Osama bin Laden and a business card of Khalid Sheikh Mohammed, the eventual mastermind of the September 11 attacks. Bold as brass, Khalid emerged from a nearby hotel room and gave outraged interviews to the Pakistani press about the raid.[1]

The press can be forgiven for missing the story.

Bin Laden's involvement in the 1993 World Trade Center bombing was apparent only to the FBI investigators, but since they planned to bring criminal indictments, this information was not shared with the CIA or other government agencies—let alone the fourth estate. Rule 6E of the Federal Rules of Evidence and grand jury secrecy laws essentially kept the American public in the dark about Osama bin Laden from 1993 to 1996.

However, some reporters did see past the FBI blackout. Robert Fisk, a columnist for the *Observer* (London) who is known for his tireless opposition to mainstream American foreign policy, caught up with bin Laden in a small village in Sudan. His 1993 interview was the first interview with bin Laden published anywhere in the English-speaking world.

It wouldn't remain that way for long. By 1996, press coverage had begun a steady upward climb. Two incidents had put bin Laden on the radar screens of policymakers and the press. The first was his role in the Somali ambush of U.S. Army Rangers in Mogadishu (later popularized by Mark Bowden's bestselling book *Black Hawk Down*), which killed more than a dozen Americans and wounded more than four score. Second was bin Laden's masterminding of the November 7, 1995, bombing of the Office of the Program Manager of the Saudi Arabian National Guard in Riyadh, which took the lives of five Americans and two others. By 1995, the U.S. State Department and the Congressional Research Service published reports that warned of the gathering threat of bin Laden.

Meanwhile, Representative Bill McCollum, a Florida Republican who had stayed in touch with his Afghan contacts after the CIA tuned them out, launched a letter-writing campaign to alert President Clinton, CIA director James Woolsey, and national security adviser Tony Lake about bin Laden. His congressional task force turned out a string of reports about al Qaeda in the 1990s.

The June 1996 truck bomb attack on the U.S. Air Force barracks in Dhahran, Saudi Arabia—which was initially linked to bin Laden—only underlined the growing threat posed by al Qaeda.

Over the next two years, bin Laden would call press conferences to declare war on America five separate times.[2] When a Saudi millionaire turned Afghan survivalist declares war on the planet's sole superpower, even magazine editors smell a story.

Believe it or not, the first major American magazine to draw the nation's attention to bin Laden was *Reader's Digest*. Written by Kenneth Timmerman, the July 1998 article was headlined: "This Man Wants You Dead."[3] At the time, *Reader's Digest*—hardly an obscure publication—had more readers than *TV Guide*.

A month after the magazine appeared on supermarket racks and in readers' mailboxes, bin Laden's men blew up two U.S. embassies.

August 7, 1998, was the eighth anniversary of President H. W. Bush's announcement that he would send U.S. forces to the Middle East to expel Saddam Hussein's armies from Kuwait. Bin Laden did not want that anniversary to go unremembered. Although he had his ideological quarrels with Hussein, the arch-terrorist was resolutely opposed to the stationing of American soldiers on the holy sands of Arabia. The attack was daring and displayed heretofore unseen precision. Within nine minutes of each other, two bomb-laden trucks made their way to the gates of two U.S. embassies more than 500 miles apart. The blast was deafening. The explosive wave sliced through the reinforced concrete walls, ripping concrete floors from their moorings. Inside a sun-blotting dust cloud, the U.S. embassy in Nairobi tumbled down.

Moments later, a low-slung U.S. embassy in Dar Es Salaam, Tanzania, was eclipsed by an orange fireball.

Beneath the boulder-sized rubble in two African capitals, twelve American diplomats and hundreds of Africans were dead or dying. It was deadliest attack on diplomatic outposts in American history.

Over the next thirteen days President Clinton's advisers designed and developed the largest cruise-missile strike of the Clinton presidency. Meanwhile, magazine editors pumped up their coverage of bin Laden and his world-wide terror network.

After those attacks, there appeared a string of significant and sometimes prescient pieces about bin Laden. Within days of President Clinton's August 20, 1998, retaliatory strike on bin Laden's camps in Afghanistan and on a medical plant in Sudan, readers could peruse lengthy features written by journalists who had actually met public enemy number one. Robert Fisk wrote "Talks with Osama bin Laden"

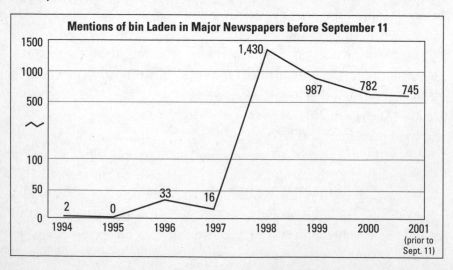

Mentions of bin Laden in Major Newspapers before September 11

for *The Nation* on August 21, 1998.[4] Peter Bergen and Frank Smyth contributed "Holy Warrior" to the *New Republic* on August 31, 1998.[5]

In the two years that followed, *Esquire* published "Greetings, America. My Name is Osama bin Laden,"[6] *Newsweek* printed a symposium called "Making a Symbol of Terror,"[7] and *Time* ran a story titled "Conversations with Terror."[8] Years before September 11, bin Laden was getting star treatment.

Computer records reveal that press coverage of bin Laden climbed steadily throughout the 1990s and surged to new heights following the 1998 embassy attacks. I did a Lexis-Nexis search for "Osama bin Laden" (along with the variant spellings of his name, including Usama) in the headline or lead paragraph of all news articles before September 11, 2001. On the opposite page is a chart displaying the results from the "Major Newspapers" file. Bear in mind, these are not all the stories that mention bin Laden, just the ones where he is mentioned in the headline or lead paragraph in large-circulation dailies.

Following the embassy attacks, magazine coverage shifted from "Who is bin Laden?" to "How can he be beaten?" Mary Anne Weaver's "The Real bin Laden," in the January 2000 edition of the *New Yorker*, argued that we are fighting bin Laden on his terms, in what she contended was a doomed strategy. "A War in the Shadows" in *U.S. News & World Report* pointed out the failings of America's policymakers and intelligence community.[9]

Below is a chart of major magazine articles in which Osama bin Laden appears in either the headline or lead paragraph.

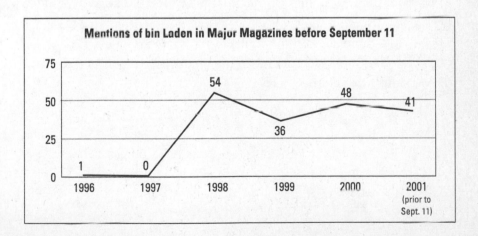

Mentions of bin Laden in Major Magazines before September 11

Did television reporters ignore bin Laden before September 11, 2001? Not according to Lexis-Nexis. Here are the comparable figures for the "News Transcripts" file, which includes all news programs on major American broadcast networks, cable television programs (including talk shows like *The O'Reilly Factor*), and local news programs seen in large metropolitan areas. Again, these are the references to programs with a headline or lead paragraph devoted to bin Laden, not all programs that include a stray mention of the arch-terrorist.

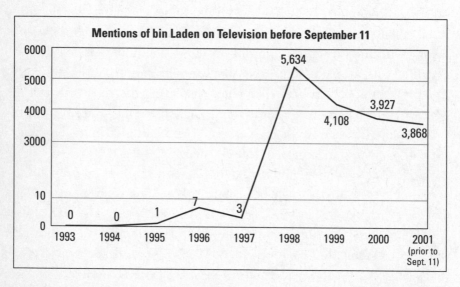

The evidence is simply overwhelming. Government officials and independent experts repeatedly told the public about bin Laden's deadly designs on America. Both the print and the broadcast media covered bin Laden extensively in the years leading up to the September 11 attacks. They sounded the alarm. But too many among the public and in public office did not listen. Bin Laden was not an obscure threat in the 1990s; he was simply one not decisively dealt with.

MYTH #5

# THE U.S. GOVERNMENT HAD MANY WARNINGS ABOUT BIN LADEN PRIOR TO SEPTEMBER 11 BUT FAILED TO ACT ON THEM

*"Bush Knew—Prez Was Warned of Possible Hijackings Before Terror Attack"*

—New York Post HEADLINE[1]

THE "SMOKING GUN" is supposed to be the August 6, 2001, Presidential Daily Briefing (PDB), a summary of vital intelligence prepared by the CIA. Its "re:" line seems to say it all: "Bin Ladin [sic] Determined to Strike in US."

It seems like a rock-solid case, but on closer inspection, it is as substantial as Charlie Rose's back curtain.

Exhibit A is the full text of the PDB. Recently declassified, the document is clearly not a warning at all, but a rehash of old news reports and outdated intelligence cables.

Here is the briefing paper, in its entirety, except for CIA redactions:

Bin Ladin Determined to Strike in US

Clandestine, foreign government, and media reports indicate Bin Ladin since 1997 has wanted to conduct terrorist attacks in the US. Bin Ladin implied in US television interviews in 1997 and 1998 that his followers would follow the example of World Trade Center bomber Ramzi Yousef and "bring the fighting to America."

After US missile strikes on his base in Afghanistan in 1998, Bin Ladin told followers he wanted to retaliate in Washington, according to a ... [redacted] ... service.

An Egyptian Islamic Jihad (EIJ) operative told an ... [redacted] ... service at the same time that Bin Ladin was planning to exploit the operative's access to the US to mount a terrorist strike.

The millennium plotting in Canada in 1999 may have been part of Bin Ladin's first serious attempt to implement a terrorist strike in the US. Convicted plotter Ahmed Ressam has told the FBI that he conceived the idea to attack Los Angeles International Airport himself, but that Bin Ladin lieutenant Abu Zubaydah encouraged him and helped facilitate the operation. Ressam also said that in 1998 Abu Zubaydah was planning his own US attack.

Ressam says Bin Ladin was aware of the Los Angeles operation.

Although Bin Ladin has not succeeded, his attacks against the US Embassies in Kenya and Tanzania in 1998 demonstrate that he prepares operations years in advance and is not deterred by setbacks. Bin Ladin associates surveilled our Embassies in Nairobi and Dar es Salaam as early as 1993, and some members of the Nairobi cell planning the bombings were arrested and deported in 1997.

Al-Qa'ida members—including some who are US citizens—have resided in or traveled to the US for years, and the group apparently maintains a support structure that could aid attacks. Two al-Qa'ida members found guilty in the conspiracy to bomb our Embassies in East Africa were US citizens, and a senior EIJ member lived in California in the mid-1990s.

A clandestine source said in 1998 that a Bin Ladin cell in New York was recruiting Muslim-American youth for attacks.

We have not been able to corroborate some of the more sensational threat reporting, such as that from a ... [redacted] ... service in 1998 saying that Bin Ladin wanted to hijack a US aircraft to gain the release of "Blind Shaykh" 'Umar 'Abd al-Rahman and other US-held extremists.

Nevertheless, FBI information since that time indicates patterns of suspicious activity in this country consistent with preparations for hijackings or other types of attacks, including recent surveillance of federal buildings in New York.

The FBI is conducting approximately 70 full field investigations throughout the US that it considers Bin Ladin-related. CIA and the FBI are investigating a call to our Embassy in the UAE in May saying that a group of Bin Ladin supporters was in the US planning attacks with explosives.

The bulk of the memo is a sexed-up history lesson. The mention of "hijackings" comes from foreign intelligence service reports dating back to 1998. Significantly, it does not mention flying hijacked planes into buildings, and it is uncorroborated. In other words, what the spooks call "chatter." Next it mentions "FBI information" about "suspicious activity"—but does not mention the FBI reports from field offices in Minnesota and Arizona of Arab radicals who wish to fly 747s—without bothering to learn how to take off or land. Finally, the "surveillance" of "federal buildings in New York" is nearly worthless. It is not connected to intelligence about hijackings and, of course, the World Trade Center towers were not federal buildings. Finally, the CIA notes that the FBI is investigating a possible plot involving "explosives."

Where is the warning here? A warning is a prediction about a future calamity. Yet not a single sentence in the PDB speaks of the future. Instead, every sentence is about the past or the present. A warning implies a degree of alarm. Yet every sentence is as passive as an encyclopedia entry. If the CIA had done its job properly and marshaled the pre–September 11 information that was later uncovered by the 9-11 Commission, then, possibly, this document could have turned into a warning. But as it stands now, it is not a warning, it is a status report. And not a very good one.

Next, let us consider how this "warning" came to be written.

In July, the CIA learned that Italian police had intercepted a cell phone call in Milan. Al Qaeda had long been active in Italy. Italian police and intelligence had foiled plots to attack the U.S. embassy in Rome and had uncovered terror cells in Turin, Milan, and elsewhere. Some were arrested, but many more were the targets of roving wiretaps. What the

Italians overheard surprised them. Al Qaeda seemed to be planning to assassinate President George W. Bush during a state visit to Genoa in July 2001.

Security was stepped up. The Italian military even supplied a battery of surface-to-air missiles to repel an air attack. The press treated it as simply overkill by the American Secret Service and did not probe any deeper.

President Bush was told about the al Qaeda assassination plot in his morning intelligence briefing. He wasn't happy.

The president said that earlier attempts by President Clinton to capture or kill bin Laden were simply "swatting at flies."[2] He wanted to "bring this guy down."[3] He wanted a realistic action plan for killing or capturing Osama bin Laden. When he was informed that the National Security Council was already leading an inter-agency effort to hit bin Laden in Afghanistan, Bush reportedly told Rice that he wanted something more imaginative than a cruise missile strike, which would cost millions "to hit a camel in the butt."[4]

Bush also demanded a thorough review of all intelligence about terrorist threats from al Qaeda, including the possibility of attacks inside the United States. That is why the PDB, which was delivered on August 6, 2001, was prepared.

At Bush's small ranch house among the scrub pines near Crawford, Texas, the CIA presented its findings. Rice tuned in via a secure teleconferencing link from her White House office.

Neither Bush nor Rice was happy with the briefing. Rice later described the briefing as "vague," a rehash of existing intelligence with no new analysis; it merely recited that bin Laden was dangerous, had plans to attack America, and that we should be careful. Not exactly a call to arms.

Little wonder that Rice (then the national security adviser) told the 9-11 Commission that "the country had taken the steps that it could, given there was no threat reporting what might happen inside the United States."[5]

Certainly, the intelligence community was abuzz with "threat reports," with no specifics about where, when, or how al Qaeda would strike.

Months before the September 11 attacks, the CIA Counter-Terrorism Center—known as the "CTC"—distributed a classified memo headlined "Threat of Impending al Qaeda Attack to Continue Indefinitely." CIA director George Tenet dismissed it as "maddeningly short on actionable details."[6] The report was not distributed outside of the CIA.

Richard Clarke, the hard-driving "counter-terrorism czar," testified before the 9-11 Commission about pre–September 11 intelligence. He said that the number of "al Qaeda threats and other terrorist threats was in the tens of thousands—probably hundreds of thousands."[7] But none of them contained specific information that could be used to stop the September 11 plot. Clarke is even more emphatic in his book *Against All Enemies*: "Had we had any chance of stopping it, had we the knowledge we needed to prevent that day, those of us sitting as members of CSG [Counter-terrorism Security Group] would literally have given our lives to do so; many of those around the CSG table had already put their lives at risk for their country."[8]

What was lacking was "actionable intelligence." To prevent the September 11 attacks (or any terrorist attack), intelligence officials need to know the target, timing, and type of attack, what counter-terrorism researcher Kevin Michael Derksen calls "the three Ts of tactical intelligence."[9] Without knowing *all* three elements—when, where, and how—an attack cannot be stopped. If you knew that al Qaeda was going to attack the World Trade Center on September 11, but assumed it would be a truck bomb attack, you would be inspecting cars while the planes crashed overhead.

A State Department intelligence officer once described the analytic side of the spy business this way:

> Imagine your boss . . . placing a lunch-size brown bag twisted at the top on your desk and asking you to tell him what the contents mean. Dutifully, you untwist the bag and spill the contents on your desk. The contents are some sixty pieces of a puzzle. As you look over the puzzle pieces you immediately notice that about one-third of [them] are blank, and another third appear to have edges that have been cut off. As you look at the pieces that have some part of a picture on them, you sense that this

is really a mixture of about four different puzzles. Now keep in mind that you have no box top to tell you what the puzzle should look like and you do not know how many pieces are in the puzzle....Welcome to the art of terrorism analysis. We rarely see a majority of the pieces of a terrorist threat puzzle. When we do, action is taken.[10]

Did the president—or any member of the intelligence community—know enough to have prevented the September 11 attacks?

Both the 9-11 Commission and the U.S. Congress's Joint Inquiry into Intelligence Community Activities Before and After the Terrorist Attacks of September 11, 2001, exhaustively investigated this question. Both used professional investigators to comb through the public record, took sworn testimony from officials, and enjoyed access to reams of classified material. Both identified dozens of intelligence failures, mostly relating to information sharing, bureaucratic infighting, computer problems, and boneheaded decisions. Still, both bodies came to the same conclusion: The intelligence community did not know the timing, the target, or the type of attack. The president had no actionable intelligence.

For those who are tempted to dismiss the reports of both the 9-11 Commission and the congressional joint inquiry as a "whitewash," remember that the hijackers themselves did not know the three Ts. A December 2001 raid on an al Qaeda safe house in Afghanistan turned up a videotape featuring a lengthy speech by Osama bin Laden:

> The brothers, who conducted the operation, all they knew was that they have a martyrdom operation and that we asked each of them to go to America, but they didn't know anything about the operation, not even one letter. But they were trained and we did not reveal the operation to them until they are there [in the United States] and just before they boarded the planes.
>
> Those who were trained to fly didn't know the others. One group of people did not know the other group.[11]

The hijackers, until the morning of September 11, did not know the target or the type of attack. And the timing was not disclosed to them until a few days before the attack, according to the 9-11 Commission. (Indeed, it was originally slated for May,[12] then for July, before bin Laden chose September 11—the five-year anniversary of the 1996 conviction of Ramzi Yousef, who planned the 1993 World Trade Center bombing.)[13] If the hijackers had been apprehended before September 11, there is very little they could have said—even if they had wanted to cooperate.

So how would it be possible for the president to know something that the terror cell members did not?

Those on the Right and Left—everyone from the *Washington Times'* Bill Gertz to filmmaker Michael Moore—who cling to the idea that the U.S. government had enough foreknowledge of the attacks to stop them usually cite a handful of reports. Let's examine each of them.

Gertz, in his book *Breakdown: How America's Intelligence Failures Led to September 11*, notes an interview with Kie Fallis, a onetime Defense Intelligence Agency analyst. Fallis told him, "I obtained information in January of 2000 that indicated terrorists were planning two or three major attacks against the United States. The only gaps were where and when."[14] That is akin to saying that you will win the lottery, and the only gaps are the winning numbers and the day on which to play them.

It turns out that Fallis did not even know that al Qaeda planned to hijack planes and ram them into buildings. All Fallis knew is that some al Qaeda operatives, some of whom were tied to the October 2000 attack on the USS *Cole*, had met in Malaysia in January 2000—and that they were up to no good. What exactly is the president supposed to do with this information?

Others point to two September 10 phone intercepts of the National Security Agency. The NSA overheard two Arabic speakers say, "The match begins tomorrow" and "Tomorrow is zero hour."[15] These seem to be coded conversations about an upcoming attack.

The intelligence community was not told about these intercepts until after the September 11 attacks. This looks like a dramatic example of foreknowledge, but it isn't.

NSA director Michael Hayden was called on the carpet in June 2002 during the congressional joint inquiry. He pointed out that the agency gathers some two million intercepts *per hour*. Analysts must make snap decisions about which ones to translate and pass on. The two intercepts were put aside as "unactionable" because they did not contain information about a target or a type of attack. All the NSA knew is that tomorrow, somewhere in the world, al Qaeda was hoping to strike somehow. Again, nothing to go on. Messages like this are intercepted routinely and analysts know that many such intercepts are al Qaeda disinformation, when there is no attack in the works.

Still others point to the arrest of Zacarias Moussaoui, the so-called "twentieth hijacker." Even now, terrorism analysts cannot agree if Moussaoui was supposed to be part of what al Qaeda high command called "the planes operation" or part of a planned second wave of attacks.

Here are the facts that are not in contention: A Pan Am International Flight Academy instructor became suspicious of Moussaoui because he wanted to learn how to pilot a 747, but not how to take off or land. A concerned instructor had to phone the Minnesota FBI four times and, even then, only got the attention of a special agent by blurting out, "A 747 loaded with fuel can be used as a bomb."[16]

Moussaoui, whom the FBI linked to an al Qaeda affiliate in Chechnya on August 26, 2001, refused to cooperate. When he did talk, months after the attacks, it became clear that he had no knowledge of the target or timing of the attack. It is unclear whether Moussaoui thought he was part of a conventional hijacking. Again, no actionable intelligence.

What about the famous "Phoenix memo"?

Kenneth Williams, a veteran policeman turned FBI special agent, interviewed some Arab men who were taking flight lessons in Arizona, men who had aroused his suspicions. One had a picture of bin Laden in his living room. Others were tied to an al Qaeda group in London. On July 10, 2001, he e-mailed the FBI's Osama bin Laden unit and the FBI's New York field office, which often takes the lead in counter-terrorism investigations. The so-called Phoenix memo was quietly shelved—until after the attacks.

Did it contain information that could have tipped off the federal government to the killers living among us?

The 9-11 Commission did not think so: "If the memo had been distributed in a timely fashion and its recommendations were acted on promptly, we do not believe it would have uncovered the plot."

Kevin Michael Derksen of the University of Winnipeg investigated pre–September 11 intelligence for the specialist journal *Studies in Conflict and Terrorism*. He concludes that "security agencies should not be held responsible for failing to forestall what was an impenetrable terrorist plot. An examination of the evidence has shown that security agencies did not have the actionable intelligence they needed to prevent the attack or the means to obtain it."[17]

Even so, the intelligence services performed poorly. Here is a partial list of some of the intelligence failures uncovered by investigators:

> ➣ The very high barrier placed by the Foreign Intelligence Security Act prevented FBI and CIA counter-intelligence operatives from working together or sharing information.[18]
> ➣ The FBI's computer system was antiquated. When the Phoenix FBI office issued a warning about the possibility of fundamentalists entering the United States to train on airplane simulators, Phoenix agents had no way of searching the FBI's internal database to see if there were any other reports about fundamentalists taking flight training in the U.S.[19] Some FBI offices could not even send e-mail to other offices.
> ➣ For more than two years, the National Security Agency had tapped the phones of an al Qaeda safe house in Sana'a, the capital of Yemen. The NSA analysts had the ability to trace some (but not all) of the calls made from the safe house. In particular, they were suspicious about an al Qaeda operative named "Khalid." But they couldn't determine Khalid's last name or where he was headed. As *U.S. News & World Report* detailed in 2004, only after September 11 did the NSA discover that the Khalid in question was Khalid al-Mihdhar, who hijacked the plane that crashed into the Pentagon. The safe house belonged to al-Mihdhar's father-in-law.[20]
> ➣ British restaurant worker Niaz Khan told the FBI in 2000 that al Qaeda was planning to attack the U.S. He even explained that he was

taught the interior of a Boeing airplane. The FBI let him go and took no action (except to put Khan on the list of people banned from flying into the U.S.). After Khan returned to Britain, he tried to contact British intelligence, but they didn't want to hear from him. Only after he contacted *Crimestoppers*, a British television series, did anyone pay any attention to him.[21]

> The FBI had several tips about a mosque in San Diego where some of the September 11 hijackers had worshipped. Yet the bureau had no idea that the plot was under way, even though they had extensive wiretaps on some of the activities there.[22]

Even if intelligence officers could have followed up on these leads, it is doubtful they would have uncovered "actionable intelligence" about the target, timing, and type of attack. Remember, the hijackers themselves did not know all of these details until the morning of September 11.

The only way that the president could have been warned prior to September 11 would be if American intelligence had an "asset" among bin Laden's inner circle in Afghanistan—and it did not.

Stubborn believers that the CIA warned the president assume that the CIA is omniscient. But as historian David McCullough, speaking in another context, told the *Christian Science Monitor*, "You can't ever judge why people did things the way they did in the past unless you take into consideration what they didn't know. Looking back, we say: 'They should have known, or listened to him or to her. It's never that simple.'"[23]

Why does this conspiracy theory linger? Historian Joseph E. Persico argues that it is simply human nature. Persico is an acknowledged expert on the last surprise attack on the American homeland: the Japanese assault on Pearl Harbor. He notes that President Franklin Delano Roosevelt had some inkling of Japan's dark designs before the December 7, 1941, attack. Relations between Washington and Tokyo had been souring for years, and the U.S. was opposed to Japan's bloody invasion and occupation of eastern China. So FDR knew that Japan might attack at some point. But there was no intelligence suggesting that Japan would attack at Pearl Harbor, or when it would attack, or how. Still, FDR's critics and many others continue to suspect that he knew all along and that he allowed Pearl Harbor to happen as a "backdoor to war."

"Why do conspiracy theories keep sprouting?" Persico asks. "Neat, suspenseful plots create high drama, while the truth is often messy, contradictory, even dull."[24]

The same is true today. And Bush's critics are as misguided as FDR's.

MYTH #6

# WARNED BY THE MOSSAD, THERE WERE NO JEWS AT THE WORLD TRADE CENTER ON SEPTEMBER 11

*"Israelis remained absent [on September 11] based on hints from the Israeli General Security Apparatus, the Shabak."*

—AL-WATAN, A JORDANIAN NEWSPAPER[1]

*"4,000 Jews did not go to work at the World Trade Center on September 11."*

—*INFORMATION TIMES*, CITING LEBANON'S AL-MANOR TELEVISION[2]

**ACTUALLY, THE FIRST MAN TO DIE** in the September 11 attacks was an Israeli commando turned Internet billionaire. And he died a hero. His name was Daniel Lewin.

While Lewin's last moments were extraordinary—he was the only September 11 victim who had the chance to slug Mohammed Atta—his life was equally extraordinary. It is worth telling because it helps refute one of the most poisonous myths of our time: that Israel warned Jews that the World Trade Center would be destroyed on September 11.

Born in 1970, Lewin grew up in South Chester Court, a firmly middle-class suburb of Denver. It was quiet neighborhood of doctors, professors, and other professionals. Yet young Danny was a hell-raiser. He hated rules and loved risks; his dreams, according to a childhood friend, were of skiing, motorcycles, and fast cars. His father, Charles Lewin, was trained as a psychiatrist and believed the best way to discipline his rebellious son was to talk to him for hours. Although the elder Lewin used his full psychiatric powers, the "talking cure" didn't take.

Then, at age fifteen, Daniel's life irrevocably changed. His father announced that he was moving the family to Jerusalem. Daniel was shocked. He didn't want to leave his friends or his Colorado high school. And, at the time, he was not particularly religious. Making *aliya*, the decision to live in the Jewish homeland, meant little to him.

Things did not get any easier for Daniel when he arrived in the ancient Jewish city. Unlike in Tel Aviv, with its beachfront bars and discos, the denizens of Jerusalem live on a windy ridge and tend to be strictly religious. In many neighborhoods, all activity ceases by sundown Friday night, the start of the Jewish Sabbath. The roads empty as cars, taxis, and buses head home. Stores close. Nearly everyone goes to dine with their families—not exactly a teen-age boy's idea of fun. According to Gil Rudawsky, a longtime friend, Daniel longed for anything American, a baseball cap or t-shirt.[3]

Within a year, however, Daniel began to adapt to Israel's unique rhythms. Then came another transformational moment. He took up bodybuilding, and his changing body changed his life. He took to weight lifting with the zeal of a convert; soon the obsessive weight lifter began entering bodybuilding contests. And started winning. Eventually he was crowned with the bodybuilding title "Mr. Teenage Israel." A new confidence arrived, and for the first time, Daniel realized that he was in control of his life, that hard work could transform his circumstances. For the rest of his days, he would never cease working all-out toward a goal.

He next applied his athletic discipline to scholastics, and won a place at Technion, Israel's prestigious technology university. He studied hard at hard subjects—and his grades showed it. He earned undergraduate degrees in science and mathematics. IBM hired him to work as a full-time researcher at its labs in Haifa, an old port city on the Mediterranean.

Then, as required by Israeli law, he set aside his research and joined Israel's armed forces. Again he excelled. He was recruited into the Sayeret Matkal, a special forces unit equivalent to America's Delta Force. In that elite unit, he carried out covert counter-terrorism campaigns in the West Bank and Gaza Strip, and eventually rose to the rank of captain.

After four years serving in burning deserts and murderous neighborhoods, Lewin returned to science. His academic work impressed the admissions committee of the Massachussets Institute of Technology (MIT), which invited him to join its Ph.D. program. His life was about to change again. One of the co-creators of the Internet, Tim Berners-Lee, challenged MIT graduate students to develop a way to overcome the web's many bottlenecks. Lewin worked night and day. He came up with a new method for moving information on the web, based on a complex (mathematicians would say elegant) set of algorithms.

With mathematical formulas that could help web sites deal with unexpected traffic spikes, Lewin and his professor started Akamai, a rare Internet outfit that actually made money. By 2001, Akamai had a staff of more than 1,000 and operated 12,000 servers in 63 countries.[4]

Akamai went public in October 1999 and the share price climbed almost 500 percent. For a time, Lewin's shares were valued at some $3 billion. After the Internet bubble burst, Lewin was worth a mere $100 million. Still, he bought his motorcycles and fast cars.

Then Lewin boarded a Boeing 767, marked as American Airlines flight 11, bound for Los Angeles. It was September 11, 2001.

In the first-class section, Lewin sat one row behind Mohamed Atta and Abdulaziz Alomari, the two hijacker "pilots." At 8:14 a.m., they rose and menaced two flight attendants on their way to the cockpit. Lewin, according to a recently released government report, moved to stop them.[5] He had special forces training and a bodybuilder physique. Friends describe him as "absolutely rock solid and thick."[6]

Lewin may have gotten a few blows in before he was fatally stabbed in the back. He did not know that Satam al-Suqami, another hijacker, was seated right behind him. "If anyone was going to get him, they were going to come from behind," Todd Dagres, a longtime friend, told the *New York Daily News*. "Nobody who approached him from where he could see them would ever get the better of him, ever."[7]

At 8:46 a.m., Atta and Alomari steered Flight 11 into the north tower of the World Trade Center. In an explosion of glass and steel, ninety-two people vanished—including the first hero of September 11.

As it happened, Lewin left a legacy that made the atrocity of September 11 slightly easier to bear. His algorithms meant that dozens of Internet news sites that had leased Akamai's technology, including

CNN.com, did not crumble under the tsunami of web traffic that day. That meant that millions who feared that a loved one was trapped in the Twin Towers at least had access to the latest news. In those first bitter hours, that was no small consolation.

What makes Lewin's story worth recounting is that it simultaneously reminds us of the shocking losses of September 11 and demolishes the idea that no Israelis died that day. If Israeli intelligence really was issuing warnings, wouldn't it have warned a former top commando cum Internet billionaire?

Nor was Lewin the only Israeli casualty.

According to the Israeli government, five Israelis died in the September 11 attacks. In addition to Lewin, these victims ranged from Alona Avraham,[8] a passenger on United Airlines Flight 175 whose parents thought she would be safer visiting America than staying in Israel; Leon Lebor,[9] a deaf janitor at the World Trade Center who left Israel because he had trouble learning Hebrew; Cantor Fitzgerald employee Shay Levinhar,[10] a former Israeli air force officer; and business executive Haggai Sheffi,[11] an Israeli computer consultant who died eating breakfast at the Windows on the World restaurant.

Another 500 Jews also died in the doomed towers of the World Trade Center, according to estimates by Abraham Foxman of the Anti-Defamation League. He added, "The figure would have been even higher had it not been for the fact that many Orthodox Jews went to work an hour later than usual because they had to recite Selichot prayers recited in the days before the Jewish New Year."[12] (It is highly unlikely that the Israeli government told them to delay work to say those prayers; the Orthodox have been saying them for centuries and listen to no one but G-d. Explanation: The Orthodox do not spell out God, but write "G-d.")

Foxman's estimate is broadly supported by other authorities, though estimates can vary widely. *Jewish Week*'s analysis of official records found that there were "at least 400 victims either confirmed or highly likely to be Jewish."[13] The *Wall Street Journal*, on the other hand, reported that about 10 percent of the World Trade Center victims, whose 1,700 families listed a religion, said they were Jewish. That amounts to 170 Jews who died in the Twin Towers. Of course, some 1,000 victims' families did not declare a religion at all.

No official register of September 11 victims by religion exists. And for good reason. Tabulating a precise number is not a matter of counting bodies, but interrogating souls. To know how many Jews died would require answering one of the oldest and most vexing debates in politics or religion: Who is a Jew? It is a debate that continues in Israel at this very moment and simply cannot be answered with finality and authority.

So exactly how many Jews were murdered on September 11 will remain uncertain. But that hundreds of Jews died in the attacks is beyond doubt.

Allied with the notion that "no Jews died in the World Trade Center" is the idea that "4,000 Jews were warned about September 11 and failed to show up for work." The 4,000 number seems to come from a news report that the Israeli embassy in New York had received roughly 4,000 phone calls regarding missing loved ones, most of whom were not truly missing or were multiple calls regarding the same person. The most benign interpretation of how this news story—since denied by the embassy in any event—was spun into 4,000 Jews staying home was that it was poorly translated into Arabic. There is no evidence that Jews were advised to stay home and a wealth of evidence that many Jews died on September 11.

Another spur of this anti-Semitic conspiracy theory is that Israel was able to warn Jews about the attacks because the Mossad carried them out. Remember that bin Laden, not the Mossad, repeatedly took credit for the September 11 attacks.

Bin Laden released a videotape on October 30, 2004, in which he clearly and convincingly claimed responsibility for the atrocities:

> I shall talk to you about the story behind those events [the September 11 attacks] and shall tell you truthfully about the moments in which the decision was taken.

He confirmed his direction of the details of operational planning, stating:

> For the record, we had agreed with the Commander-General Muhammad Atta . . . that all operations should be carried out within twenty minutes, before Bush and his administration notice.[14]

U.S. forces found another al Qaeda videotape in Afghanistan in November 2001. On that tape, the arch-terrorist describes how he planned the attacks:

> We calculated in advance the number of casualties from the enemy, who would be killed based on the position of the tower. We calculated that the floors that would be hit would be three or four floors. I was the most optimistic of them all. (Inaudible) due to my experience in this field, I was thinking that the fire from the gas in the plane would melt the iron structure of the building and collapse the area where the plane hit and all the floors above it only.... We had notification since the previous Thursday that the event would take place that day."[15]

Yet the poisonous slander that thousands of Jews stayed home on September 11 thanks to a timely warning from Israeli intelligence will not die. From where did this foul slander slither? The trail of this myth begins with a clutch of radical Islamic websites in North America, jumps to a terrorist-controlled television station in Lebanon, fans out into the angry streets of Pakistan, and finally returns to the American continent. The web site Slate.com traced its strange progression:

> Within days, the story appeared in newspapers around the world. A remarkably similar version appeared under the byline of Irina Malenko in Russia's *Pravda* on Sept. 21. *Pravda* removed the article from its web site a few hours after posting, calling it a "great and foolish mistake," but it can still be accessed. On Sept. 21, the *Chicago Tribune* reported that a Pakistani paper, which it did not name, had published a similar account. In his Sept. 23 *Slate* "Dispatch" from Islamabad, Peter Maass reported that a local pro-Taliban politician repeated the 4,000 Jews claim at an anti-U.S. rally. On Sept. 26, Pakistan's *Business Recorder* printed the story about 4,000 Jews in language almost identical to the original *Al-Manor* article as a letter to the editor under the name "Hakeem." The same day, the *New York Times* reported that the allegation had appeared in a newsletter published by an Islamic charity and in lesson plans prepared by Egyptian middle-school teachers. On Oct. 4, the *Chicago Tribune* spotted the

allegation in a Saudi paper, which it did not name. In the Oct. 8 issue of *Time*, Tim McGirk reported from Pakistan that the story had swept through the country's mosques and the Urdu newspapers.

On Sept. 28, *USA Today* repeated the claim in the context that "Muslims the world over" had tried to pin the attack on Israel. *USA Today* did not explain the origin of the charge. The *Village Voice* did the same on Oct. 2. The hoax-debunking site Snopes.com assailed the story, as well. With the Web as a weapon, a lie spreads quickly and easily. With the Web as a corrective tool, the same lie becomes much easier to bat away.[16]

Eventually this slander received a kind of immortality in the illiterate verses of the taxpayer-supported poet laureate of New Jersey, Amiri Baraka. (He was appointed by Democratic governor James McGreevey.) Baraka writes in "Somebody Blew Up America": "Who told 4,000 Israeli workers at the twin towers to stay at home that day…"

Indeed, blaming Israel for terrorist attacks is a reflex action in some quarters.[17] No proof required. Consider the July 23, 2005, car bombing of a resort hotel in Sharm-el-Sheikh, Egypt. Eighty-eight people died. Within a day, Egypt's state-run television network, as well as al Jazeera and al Arabiya, were claiming that Israel's intelligence service was behind the blasts. The more things change…

# THE POST–SEPTEMBER 11 WORLD IS MORE DANGEROUS FOR AMERICANS THAN EVER BEFORE

*"Thousands of dangerous killers, schooled in the methods of murder, often supported by outlaw regimes, are now spread throughout the world like ticking time bombs, set to go off without warning . . . In a single instant [on September 11], we realized that this will be a decisive decade."*

—PRESIDENT GEORGE W. BUSH, 2002

PRESIDENTS KNOW THE POWER of their words and usually filter them through layers of careful advisers and cautious bureaucrats before pouring them out into the public domain. Yet in his 2002 State of the Union address, before the Congress and the world, President Bush succumbed to a commonplace myth: Since the September 11 attacks, the world is more dangerous for Americans than ever before.

This legend, often dispensed in stronger doses, can be heard from both elected Republicans and Democrats as well from the pundits and the press. It may even be the unconscious assumption of many people. But is it true? The fear is that the September 11 attacks, or in other variations, the Bush administration's reaction to them, have made all of our lives riskier than ever before. At any moment, you could hear the hum of engines overhead or be rocked by blasts on the ground. One of America's great writers summed up this sense of formless dread in a memorable way:

The subtlest change in New York is something people don't speak much about but that is in everyone's mind. The city, for the first time in its long history, is destructible. A single flight of planes no bigger than a wedge of geese can quickly end this island fantasy, burn the towers, crumble the bridges, turn the underground passages into lethal chambers, cremate the millions. The intimation of mortality is part of New York now: in the sound of jets overhead, in the black headlines of the latest edition.

All dwellers in cities must live with the stubborn fact of annihilation; in New York the fact is somewhat more concentrated because of the concentration of the city itself, and because, of all targets, New York has a certain clear priority. In the mind of whatever perverted dreamer might loose the lightning, New York must hold a steady, irresistible charm."[1]

These words were written by E. B. White, in his book *Here Is New York*.[2] What is interesting, now, about White's words is that they first appeared in 1949.[3]

That simple fact—the date of White's reflections—suggests two things: that this aura of shapeless anxiety is not new, but periodically descends on New York and the nation, and that it is possible that the world really was more dangerous in the past than it is now.

Indeed, the Cold War era *was* more perilous than today. With its thousands of nuclear missiles pointed at the homeland, the USSR had the capacity to destroy the U.S. many times over. Nuclear annihilation, lest we forget, haunted the Western world for almost fifty years. The Cold War was not the mythologized happy time of stable co-existence at all. At one point during the Cuban missile crisis, only one political officer stood between a Soviet submarine commander and his desire to launch a nuclear torpedo. The Cold War was a period of dangerous instability, with endless proxy wars, coups, insurgencies, revolutions, counter-revolutions, and state-sponsored terrorism. When Communism fell, most of these activities came to an end.[4]

Nor was nuclear holocaust the only nightmare hanging over the free world. The Soviet Union was also a major manufacturer of chemical and biological weapons. Damocles, an ancient Greek courtier, once switched places with the king, Dionysius I. To demonstrate the peril he lived with every day, Dionysius hung a sword over Damocles' head, suspended by a single strand of hair. During the Cold War, a figurative sword hung over the head of every human being on Earth. Al Qaeda, or any other terrorist group active today, simply does not have the same destructive power.

Communist forces were also responsible for provoking two wars with the United States, in Korea and Vietnam. Together, these two conflicts cost more than 70,000 Americans their lives and injured more than 400,000. Many of these injuries left soldiers or civilians permanently crippled or disfigured.

By contrast, al Qaeda has killed fewer than 4,000 Americans since 1992. And while the Soviets and their allies could field a mechanized army of millions, al Qaeda numbers in the thousands. The International Institute for Strategic Studies, an independent research organization in London, estimates bin Laden's total force at 18,000. Department of Defense estimates range as low as 3,000.[5] "Today we have seen the enemy," writes Russell Seitz, a former fellow of Harvard's Center for International Affairs, "and he has, at most, one division under arms."[6] The Soviets deployed as many as six divisions near the Fulda Gap in East Germany alone. As Colin Powell writes in his biography, "As I took over V Corps, in 1986, four American divisions [including the U.S. VII Corps] and nineteen Soviet divisions still confronted each other over a border bristling with even deadlier weaponry."

Across Asia and Africa, as the colonial empires of Britain, France, and other European powers retreated, millions more died in civil wars inspired by Communist guerrillas. When the false dawn of peace finally came, millions more suffered and died under the ruthless rule of dictators allied with either the Soviet Union or the United States. Have we forgotten China's "Cultural Revolution," when the Red Guards sent millions to die in faraway fields, sometimes for the "crime" of owning a pair of eyeglasses? They were but few of the seventy million murdered by order of Mao Tse-tung. Or the some forty million worked to death in the chain of sub—Arctic Circle concentration camps known as the "gulag archipelago," vast islands of misery set up on permafrost wastes? Let us not forget the millions who were murdered by Communist revolutionary Pol Pot's regime in Cambodia. Among the "political enemies" executed by machete were crying infants and illiterate peasants. I walked through one of the killing fields, outside of Phnom Penh, in 1999. Amid the open pits, one can see still bits of bone poking out between the blades of grass.

Even the risk of terrorism was higher in the end years of the Cold War. The Soviet Union and China provided an ideological justification, extensive small-arms and bomb-making training, and cascades of cash for terrorists around the world. From the Shining Path in South America to the Red Army Faction and Red Brigades in Europe, these self-described revolutionaries kidnapped, killed, and bombed throughout the 1970s and 1980s. Only the fall of the Soviet Union brought an end to their reign of terror.

Even Near Eastern terror had its roots in Soviet strategy. The Palestine Liberation Organization (PLO), founded in 1964 to oppose the 1948 creation of the state of Israel, received its doctrine, training, and weapons from the Soviets and their captive satellites. The PLO soon released a wave of assassinations, kidnappings, hijackings, and bombings that plague the Middle East to this day. Their allies, Black September, would murder American diplomats in Khartoum, Sudan, and Israeli athletes in Munich, Germany, in 1972. By the late 1970s, the Soviet Union would lose control over its Arab terrorists, who increasingly embraced a radical Islamist ideology. Other nations, including Iran, Iraq, and Syria, would take the Soviets' place as terror sponsors—and it is the Russians, from Moscow to Chechnya, who are now bedeviled by the demons they created.

With the disappearance of the Soviet Union, many of the terror groups outside Arab lands have withered or turned to kidnapping and drug sales to survive. Communist terrorists in Europe and South America, which were known to target American executives, officers, and diplomats, have disappeared. Americans, especially in Germany, Italy, and Greece, are safer as a result.

But hasn't the risk from terrorism risen in the wake of September 11? Not according to any valid statistical measure.

One political scientist who is a recognized expert in analyzing risks from terrorist attacks is Todd Sandler, the Dockson Professor of International Relations and Economics at the University of Southern California in Los Angeles. By any measure, he is a distinguished scholar. Sandler has written or has contributed to nineteen books, published numerous peer-reviewed academic articles and newspaper op-eds, and won awards and grants from the National Science Foundation.

Sandler is no pro-Bush shill. He sparked a controversy in 2004 by claiming that the Bush administration was substantially underestimating the deaths from terror attacks, apparently, he contends, for election-year reasons.[7] The State Department's annual survey of world-wide terrorism showed 208 terrorism acts for the year 2003. Sandler, who maintains his own extensive database of global terrorist incidents, recorded 275 attacks—a 32 percent difference. Such a discrepancy between the official State Department figures and his own did not appear in previous years, leading Sandler to suspect the worst. "It would seem someone who is controlling the figures is acting more out of politics than recording statistics," he told the press.[8] He charged that the Bush administration was undercounting to leave the "false impression" that the U.S. is winning the War on Terror.[9] (The State Department later updated its figures. The dispute did not turn on the number of al Qaeda incidents, which were essentially the same by both the State Department's and Sandler's reckoning.)

So it is significant that Sandler published data that challenges the widely held belief that the threat of terrorism has worsened since September 11, 2001. In Sandler's paper, co-authored with Walter Enders, titled "After 9-11: Is it all different now?" he finds: "While there is no doubt that perceptions changed and deep-seated fears arose that fateful day, there has been no data-based analysis on how transnational terrorism (i.e. terrorism with international implications or genesis) differs, if at all, since 9-11."[10]

Sandler's data reveals that the September 11 attacks were unprecedented and unusual, not part of a pattern. The almost 3,000 deaths on that September morning were "as great as all deaths from transnational terrorism from 1988–2000. Prior to 9-11, no terrorist incident, domestic or transnational, resulted in more than 500 casualties."[11] To date, no terrorist atrocity anywhere in the world has caused as much carnage as September 11. Indeed, terrorist incidents of all kinds "displayed no changes after 9-11. Incidents remained at their pre–9-11 levels."[12]

As surprising as it may seem, the number of terrorist attacks has declined since 1990 while the death toll per attack has climbed slightly. Twenty-nine percent of all terror strikes since 1968 occurred since 1990. But 46 percent of all deaths from terrorism have happened since 1990.[13]

While casualty rates increased slightly in the 1990s, and remained steady in the years after the September 11 attacks, the risk of terror-related death is still low and is in line with pre–September 11 trends, according to Sandler. "Since 1968, there have been 14,440 international terrorist attacks, an average of 425 a year. Even including September 11, the average number of casualties [which includes both deaths and injuries] per incident was just 3.6, while the average number of deaths was below one."[14]

Why is terrorism more deadly since 1990? Several factors are at work. Terrorists as a whole have increasingly moved away from hostage-taking and hijacking plots, which are hard to execute and usually take few lives. This change is at least partly ideological. Communist terrorists hoped to drive public opinion, not alienate it through mayhem and slaughter. That is why these groups focused on hijackings and hostages. By 1990, many of these Communist groups began to disappear, while radical Islamic crews continued to rise. In 1980, religious international terror cadres accounted for only two of sixty-four active terror bands. By 1995, religious terrorist groups made up twenty-nine of fifty-eight terror outfits active world-wide.[15] These Islamist radicals embraced a doctrine that allowed them to extinguish the lives of unbelievers (and even faithful Muslims) on religious grounds and on the firm belief that high death tolls would persuade Americans to withdraw from Muslim lands.

Their strategy may be sinister, but it is not irrational; it has proved successful in Lebanon and Somalia and it is not hard to find people in the Middle East who think that it will eventually succeed in Iraq and Afghanistan. As the composition and ideology of terror groups mutated, the deadliness of these organizations changed too. But that change began in 1990, not 2001.[16]

Sandler's work is squarely in the center of research in this field and is backed by the independent findings of many other scholars. John Mueller, the Woody Hayes Professor of Political Science at Ohio State University, specializes in studying public opinion and risk. The author of an array of peer-reviewed articles and pieces for the *Wall Street Journal*, *New York Times*, and *Washington Post*, he has won fellowships from Guggenheim and grants from the National Science Foundation. In a short article in *Regulation* magazine[17] and an academic paper prepared for a conference at Harvard University,[18] Mueller points out that the risk of perishing in a terror attack is quite small. "Until 2001, far fewer Americans were killed in any grouping of years by all forms of international terrorism than were killed by lightning, and almost none of these terrorist attacks occurred inside the United States."[19]

And since September 11? "Although there have been many deadly terror incidents in the world since 2001, all (thus far, at least) have relied on conventional methods and have not remotely challenged September 11 quantitatively."[20] There have been no attacks inside the United States since 2001 and the many attacks outside have not yielded death tolls anywhere near the attacks on New York and Washington, or even the number of deaths following the 1988 bombing of an aircraft over Lockerbie, Scotland, which killed 270. The Madrid bombings, as horrific as they were, took some 200 lives.

Mueller, citing the work of University of Michigan transportation researchers Michael Sivak and Michael Flannagan, points out that there would have to be a September 11–style attack *every month* before terrorism killed as many Americans as car crashes do.[21] Or to put it another way, the chance of an American dying on one nonstop airline flight is one in 13 million—the same level of risk that one suffers driving just 11.2 miles on a rural interstate highway.[22]

So Michael Moore was quite right when he pointed out on CBS's *60 Minutes* program that "the chances of any of us dying in a terrorist incident is very, very, very small."[23]

But his interviewer, broadcaster Bob Simon, clearly understood public opinion when he rejoined: "But no one sees the world like that."[24]

The threat of terrorism should not be shrugged off, but actively fought. One reason that the United States and many of its allies have been free of terror since 2001 is that President Bush has prosecuted the

War on Terror with vigor. Indeed, if the goal of terrorists is to terrify, then the best way to fight back is to refuse to be terrified.

Still, against all evidence, fear remains. Brendan Miniter, my brother and a staff columnist for the *Wall Street Journal*'s editorial-page website OpinionJournal.com, sums it up best in a 2002 column:

The other night I realized Osama bin Laden had taken away the innocence of a perfectly good rainstorm. I was standing on the corner of Clinton and Joralemon streets, in a Brooklyn neighborhood directly across the East River from Ground Zero, watching commuters sense a change in the air. A downpour was coming. Everyone wanted to get home before getting wet.

Lightning flashed across the sky. I waited for the thunder. The seconds ticked by. A man about my age crossed the street, looked at me and said: "Lightning?" His underlying question was obvious. It was a few days after the news broke of Jose Padilla's arrest; dirty bombs and nuclear blasts were on everyone's mind. Was that the flash that precedes a nuclear shockwave?

Then the thunder cracked. The boom was loud. So loud that the man, barely done with his question, hit the ground.

I really hate bin Laden. There are anywhere from 3,000 to a million reasons to hate that guy. And with each passing day, I seem to find a new one.

The other day, I'm sure it was him, Osama held up my subway train. I had raced to catch that train, only to hear the conductor's announcement: "All trains are being held in the stations due to smoky conditions at Park Place." The car fell silent. No one said it out loud, but everyone had to be wondering: *Is this how we'll first hear of a chemical or biological attack?*

I had boarded the subway at the same stop on Sept. 11, minutes *after* the towers were hit. The conductor that fateful morning made a similarly innocuous announcement: "Due to an emergency at the World Trade Center, this train will not be stopping at Park Place." Minutes earlier I was on the Brooklyn Promenade looking across to lower Manhattan when the second plane hit, so I already knew. But many that morning were on autopilot, including the conductor who drove the train into lower Manhattan. I wish he hadn't, for I never would've gotten close to the burning towers, felt the heat and heard the roar of the flames.

So, on this recent morning, I couldn't have been the only one wondering if the smoke up ahead was the beginning of another attack. We're not on autopilot anymore; we're on constant alert. The train continued on, through Park Place. Everything was fine."[25]

Of course, this reaction is human, perhaps all too human. Yet to the extent that we surrender to it against all reason, terror succeeds.

# THE IRAQ WAR IS ANOTHER VIETNAM

*"The parallels between what we did in Vietnam and
what we're doing in Iraq now are unbelievable."*

—GEORGE LUCAS, STAR WARS CREATOR[1]

THUNDERING SOUTH from Baghdad in a Black Hawk helicopter in November 2003, I was strapped into the rear seat closest to the door.

There was nothing to do except watch the brightly lit landscape speed by. As we approached the landing zone near the ruins of ancient Nineveh, the helicopter passed over a boy herding goats. He looked up—and waved.

Belted in to my left was a reporter from a major American daily. He leaned over to shout into my ear. "Vietnam!"

With the helicopter engine at full throttle and wind roaring in, conversation was impossible. I couldn't ask him what about Iraq reminded him of Vietnam. So I searched the ground for some sign of Vietnamese terrain. I had been in Vietnam only a few years earlier and was instinctively looking for a broad, muddy river crowded with boats, a thick canopy of trees whose trunks were hidden in shade even at noon, or the colossal red-brick ruins of French colonialism. I saw none of that.

Instead, there were flat-roofed, single-story buildings sprouting new satellite dishes, dots of green vegetation carefully fed by irrigation, and a hot expanse of boulder-strewn sand. Even the crewman at the machine gun, just forward of me, was in desert camouflage, not Vietnam-era jungle fatigues. Perhaps the reporter meant that the shadow of the helicopter, now undulating over the parched croplands and silvery irrigation ditches, was reminiscent of Vietnam. But there were no Black Hawks in the skies of Vietnam.

On the ground, the reporter told me that he had no real memory of Vietnam. (In fact, he had graduated from Yale in 1994.) All that he knew of the Vietnam War was *Apocalypse Now*, *Platoon*, and a series of television documentaries featuring helicopters, rice paddies, and the music of the Rolling Stones. Now, in Iraq, he said he felt like he was "living inside a movie."[2]

That same movie seems to be running inside the heads of scores of foreign correspondents, television pundits, think-tank experts, and armchair historians. It is a misconception at home on both the Left and the Right; everyone from Senator Ted Kennedy (Iraq is "George Bush's Vietnam")[3] to Pat Buchanan ("While U.S. casualties in Iraq, five dead a week, do not approach the 150 we lost every week for seven years, in Vietnam, the home front does call to mind 1968 and even the early Nixon years.")[4] has raised the specter of an Indochinese quagmire.

Although both terrain and technology couldn't be more opposite, this tired comparison between Vietnam and Iraq lives on.

Perhaps the comparison is unavoidable. The Vietnam War was a formative experience for the baby boomers, the largest generation in American history. It dominated the newscasts of the three television networks nearly every night for *eight* years, from the 1964 Gulf of Tonkin resolution to 1973 negotiations in Paris. Even when the war was popular—and, yes, it was popular in the early years—it dominated the national conversation. "The Ballad of the Green Beret," a pro-war song, was a chart-topping hit in 1966.[5] Later, when the draft divided America and antiwar protesters filled the streets, Vietnam remained Topic A. For the people who were of voting age during the war, allowing it to slide gently into history is difficult. Now they are perched in high positions—guiding news coverage, shaping the agenda in Congress, and setting the curriculum in classrooms across the country—and can ensure that the Vietnam War is never treated like the Korean conflict, a vital piece of Cold War history with limited lessons for today.

Even the officer corps of the American military, even those who were born after the last helicopter lifted off the roof of the U.S. embassy in Saigon, are haunted by Vietnam.[6] It was the last time that the U.S. military fought a protracted war against insurgents and the first time the press and the public turned against a military operation overseas. Officer training reflects the "lessons of Vietnam" and, in private conversations, officers tell me that they worry about "another Vietnam."

What exactly is "another Vietnam"? While hard to define precisely, the specter of it appears whenever the U.S. military is sent overseas. Remember when the war in Afghanistan was supposed to be "another Vietnam"?

Less than three weeks into the ground war in 2001, the legendary *New York Times* columnist R. W. Apple asked: "Could Afghanistan become another Vietnam? Is the United States facing another stalemate on the other side of the world? Premature the questions may be, three weeks after the fighting began. Unreasonable they are not."[7]

The *Los Angeles Times* warned: "The United States is not headed into a quagmire; it's already in one."[8]

In Britain, the *Financial Times* ran a two-part article on the war in Afghanistan titled "Ghosts of Vietnam." The *Guardian,* Britain's center-left daily, summed it up with this headline: "This is our Vietnam."[9] One of the icons of American liberalism, Arthur Schlesinger Jr., wrote "Are We Trapped in Another Vietnam?" in the *Independent* (London): "Evidently our leaders gambled on the supposition that the unpopularity of the regime would mean the bombing would bring about the Taliban's rapid collapse. And they also seem to have assumed that it would not be too difficult to put together a post-Taliban government. This was a series of misjudgments."[10]

Even the Australians—whose nation sent troops to Vietnam in the 1960s—thought they were in a time warp. "The war itself in [Afghanistan] has already begun to create a certain déjà vu of the Vietnam variety," Mike

Carlton wrote in the *Sydney Morning Herald*. "You can almost hear the hoots of laughter from Hanoi."[11]

Then there was the former spokesman for the Australian Defense Department, Adrian D'Hage, who warned that the campaign against the Taliban had "an eerie echo of Vietnam, when Australian soldiers were sent to fight the Vietcong." The war, he complained, was "being planned by generals who have learned little, if anything, from history."[12]

All of these learned gentlemen completely overlooked the many essential differences between the Vietnam and Afghan wars. The Vietnam War was a contest of superpowers. In 2001, all the leading powers were united against the Taliban and bin Laden. The Taliban had no superpower (or even regional power) to train, arm, fund, or defend themselves. "The differences between the Soviet Union's situation and ours are dramatic," Defense Secretary Donald Rumsfeld explained. "The Soviets wanted that country. We don't. They lived in the neighborhood. We don't. They had a superpower opposing them. We don't."[13]

Finally, the war in Afghanistan had an unquestionable legitimacy because the United States had suffered an unprovoked and surprise attack that slew thousands of innocents. Even today, four years into the global War on Terror and the nascent antiwar movement, the legitimacy of the war in Afghanistan is rarely questioned. (Indeed, a major argument against the Iraq War contends that it is a distraction from completing the Afghan War.)

Afghanistan, while still a troubled and violent land, has not become another Vietnam. It should stand as a warning to all of those who see "another Vietnam" in every foreign fight. Yet, like so many warnings, it went unheeded.

Then, in 2003, it was Iraq's turn to be the next Vietnam.

Of course, there are some striking similarities between the Vietnam conflict and the war in Iraq. Both were marked by terrorism against civilians and local government officials, featured massive counter-insurgency operations, and were multi-year wars in which final victory seemed elusive. Both conflicts were characterized by attempts at nation-building in cultures and countries where democracy had yet to firmly take root and faced significant opposition by an antiwar movement at home. And that is where the parallels end.

Perhaps the definitive side-by-side comparison of the Vietnam and Iraq wars appears in a monograph published by the Strategic Studies Institute (SSI), a Defense Department think tank. In "Iraq and Vietnam: Differences, Similarities, and Insights," Jeffrey Record, a professor at the Air Force's Air War College in Montgomery, Alabama, and W. Andrew Terrill, a former Army officer and Middle East specialist at SSI, made an exhaustive study of the Vietnam and Iraq wars.

The two authors are uniquely qualified. Record served as an assistant province adviser in the Mekong Delta during the Vietnam War and as a national security adviser to Democratic senators Sam Nunn and Lloyd Bentsen. He is the author of six books and a dozen monographs, including "Why We Lost in Vietnam." Terrill was a lieutenant colonel in the U.S. Army Reserve in the Middle East and is an acknowledged expert on the Iran-Iraq War and terrorism.

Drawing historical comparisons between Vietnam and Iraq is tricky, as Record and Terrill note:

> Summarizing by historical analogy is an inherently risky business because no two historical events are completely alike and because policymakers' knowledge and use of history are often distorted by ignorance and political bias. In the case of Iraq and Vietnam, extreme caution should be exercised in comparing two wars so far apart in time, locus, and historical circumstances. In fact, a careful examination of the evidence reveals that the differences between the two conflicts greatly outnumber the similarities. This is especially true in the strategic and military dimensions of the wars. There is simply no comparison between the strategic environment, the scale of military operations, the scale of losses incurred, the quality of enemy resistance, the role of enemy allies, and the duration of combat."[14]

Drawing on their monograph and an array of published material, as well as a recent trip of my own to Iraq, let's investigate whether Iraq is really "another Vietnam."

## The battlegrounds are different

Vietnam and Iraq are vastly different societies. The Vietnamese nation
has existed for centuries; its people have a long history and well-formed
national identity. Vietnamese nationalism was hardened and sharpened
in wars against the Japanese and French empires.

On the other hand, Iraq was born when the colonial powers of Britain
and France decided to stitch together three Ottoman Empire provinces
in the aftermath of World War I. Many Middle East specialists wonder,
even now, if the Sunni, Shi'ite, and Kurdish populations really see themselves as Iraqis. Iraq has long been riven by ethnic and religious strife.
Certainly Iraqi nationalism seems to diminish the farther one travels from
Baghdad. In the western hinterland, many of Iraq's residents freely
migrate across borders, and loyalty is still to family, tribe, and Islam—not
Iraq.

Iraq's nationalism, which is quite real in the major cities, did not
emerge naturally from the Arab people inhabiting Mesopotamia. Instead,
it was forged by Saddam Hussein as a top-down tool to hold the nation
together. Whatever the qualities and merits of Iraqi nationalism, it is dis-
tinctly different from its Vietnamese counterpart.

## The progression of the war is different

In Vietnam, American troops met a guerrilla force that developed into a
mechanized, regimented army capable of fielding as many as 80,000 men
in a single campaign.

Iraq is Vietnam in reverse. Saddam Hussein's tanks were abandoned
and his predominantly Shi'ite conscripts fled to their homes, replaced by
an insurgency that rarely deploys more than four men at a time.

## The Vietnamese and Iraqi insurgencies are different

The Vietnamese Communists advanced a clear economic, political, and
military program supported by a complex ideological dogma. The enemies of Iraqi democracy do not attempt to indoctrinate their fellow
Iraqis, but only kill, maim, and terrorize them. The Communists offered
a utopian goal for the war: after a final victory, peasants would enjoy a
more prosperous, more equal life in a united and independent homeland.

The Iraqi guerrillas seem to want nothing beyond the exit of America and its allies and promise nothing. The insurgents do not even promise peace, if they should prevail.

The Vietnamese insurgency was tightly controlled through a rigid hierarchy directed by a central authority, while the one in Iraq is segmented into three clusters. The largest faction is staffed by former intelligence officers and Ba'ath Party loyalists; a second faction is a motley collection of Shi'ite front groups, identifying with Muqtada al-Sadr and most likely run by Iranian intelligence officers; and a third strand, probably run by Abu Musab al-Zarqawi, is made up of elements of al Qaeda who have journeyed into Iraq to wage jihad. So the Iraqi insurgency is not a centralized tool of an enemy power, but three separate movements run by agents of three different powers. This may not be good news for the U.S. military, but it is not a repetition of Vietnam.

In Vietnam, the insurgency was largely rural and peopled by peasants. In Iraq, it is largely urban and waged by well-schooled sons and daughters of the middle class. As a result, the manpower pool for insurgents was greater in Vietnam than it appears to be in Iraq today. The Communists could count on recruits from the peasantry, which accounted for roughly 80 percent of the total population in 1965. With a total membership of fewer than two million in 2003, the Ba'ath Party amounts to less than half of 1 percent of the total Iraqi population. It is a minority even among the roughly 20 percent of Iraqis who call themselves Sunni Arabs.[15] Al-Sadr's forces and other radical Shi'ite militias number less than 5,000. The al Qaeda fighters—apparently led by al-Zarqawi—are foreigners and number less than 2,000, according to allied estimates.

The size of the enemy forces in Vietnam was much greater. The total number of North Vietnamese regulars and Viet Cong grew from 300,000 in 1963 to 700,000 in 1966 and peaked at roughly one million in 1973, the year the U.S. decided to withdraw.[16] Even the largest estimates of the total number of insurgents in Iraq put their strength at between 5,000 and 20,000 people.[17] Currently, the U.S. alone has more then 130,000 troops in Iraq.

In Vietnam, the enemy was willing and able to take immense losses. The Vietnamese government announced, in April 1995, that their nation had lost 1.1 million dead in their war against the Americans. The military dead alone accounted for 5 percent of the North Vietnamese population and the pockets of South Vietnam controlled by the Communists.[18] As Record and Terrill note, "No other major belligerent in a twentieth-century war sustained such a high military death toll proportional to its population."[19]

The entire Iraqi insurgency doesn't even amount to 5 percent of the population. To sustain losses equivalent to that of the Vietnamese Communists, the Iraqi insurgents would have to sacrifice many times their total number, which is impossible unless the insurgency finds a way to grow.

## This time the gloves are off

In the 1960s, the U.S. was constrained by two great powers, the Soviet Union and Communist China. Any move to invade North Vietnam or dramatically escalate the conflict risked provoking the ire of the Soviets. The nightmare scenario: a tidal wave of Chinese army regulars flooding across the border, as they did in Korea.

Today, the U.S. is the world's sole surviving superpower. The best outside help that Iraqi insurgents can count on comes from Iran and Syria. To date, Iran and Syria can offer only the car bomb, not the A-bomb. And now it is Iran and Syria who dare not escalate too quickly—lest they incite America's retaliation.

## The big battles are over

The duration of major combat operations—defined as combined air and ground operations involving thousands of troops—is another striking difference between Vietnam and Iraq. The Vietnam War lasted fourteen years, more than eight of which were consumed by intense combat against an organized foe. By contrast, U.S. forces smashed the Iraqi army in less than three weeks in 2003.

## The quality of the enemy is different

The enemy in Vietnam was well drilled, with a seemingly limitless supply of modern Soviet- and Chinese-made weapons. Some of these Soviet weapons, especially small arms and anti-aircraft guns, were frankly superior to America's military technology. In Saddam Hussein's Iraq, ground forces were poorly trained and equipped with outmoded weapons. Enemy discipline evaporated under fire. Worse still, from the perspective of Saddam Hussein, Iraq had lost its superpower patron with the collapse of the Soviet Union in 1991. It received very little new equipment in the decade preceding the war—while the U.S. was fielding new smart bombs and stealth aircraft. Even in engagements with small numbers of insurgents, America has new technology to disrupt the signals used to trigger roadside bombs.

In Tikrit, Saddam Hussein's hometown, I met Lt. Gen. Barbeio, who showed me new imaging technology that allows tanks and dismounted troops to deploy more closely and more rapidly than ever before—a deadly development for anti-democratic forces. Simply put, the enemy in Iraq does not have the discipline and technological edge that it did in Vietnam.

### The war aims are different too

In the 1960s, U.S. officials merely hoped to contain North Vietnam. In Iraq, the goal was a complete "regime change." In the 1960s, America's goal was essentially negative, to defend its embattled ally in South Vietnam, to defend the status quo. Today, America's goal is positive, to bring a new democracy into being in Iraq. As Record and Terrill note, "In the 1960s, the United States was the counter-revolutionary power in Southeast Asia; it sought to preserve the non-Communist status quo in South Vietnam. . . . In 2003, the United States was the revolutionary power in the Middle East by virtue of its proclaimed intention to democratize Iraq for the purpose of providing an inspirational model to the rest of the Arab world."[20]

In the 1960s, U.S. policymakers feared a "domino effect" that would topple allied governments in the region and replace them with Communist dictatorships; today American officials are openly hoping for a "domino effect" in the Middle East that will replace tyrants with democrats.

### The two wars have differing policy and moral justifications

Secretary of State Dean Rusk repeatedly justified the Vietnam War by arguing that America had to stop Communist aggression and by citing moral obligations to honor commitments to allies. "If that commitment becomes unreliable, the Communist world would draw conclusions that would lead to our ruin and almost certainly catastrophic war."[21]

Rusk's Cold War calculation simply has no parallel in Iraq. The U.S. was not allied with Iraq before the war, therefore, defending the integrity of America's treaty obligations is simply not an issue.

The Iraq war was sold on a very different basis. If the United Nations Security Council resolutions were to have any credibility, President Bush argued, they would have to be enforced. President Bush argued that the safety and security of Americans turned on removing Saddam Hussein from power. The argument was simple. Iraq was developing weapons of mass destruction and sponsoring terror groups. Before the threat to America's cities became imminent, the president contended, the nation had to act. If not, the dictator might give catastrophic weapons to al Qaeda or other Islamic radicals. Hussein might even use them directly on U.S. bases in the region, as he had against the Kurds. Whatever the merits of Bush's claims, they amount to a very different rationale for war than the ones supported by the Kennedy, Johnson, and Nixon administrations.

### American casualties were far higher in Vietnam than in Iraq today

America lost a total of 55,750 dead from 1965 to 1972—a death toll of nineteen servicemen per day.[22] The U.S. has lost fewer than 2,000 dead from June 2003 to June 2005—a rate of fewer than two servicemen a day.[23] Indeed, the number of accidental and other non-battle deaths in Iraq continues to outpace the number of deaths from combat.

### The antiwar movement is weaker now

In the 1960s, America was beset by a large, well-organized antiwar movement. Today, the antiwar movement is fragmented and marginalized and that fact appears unlikely to change any time soon. Indeed, the movement seems to exist as a nostalgia vehicle for some and a dating service for others.

One reason for marginalization of the antiwar crowd is the absence of a draft. "The major reason you don't see colleges up in arms about the

Iraq War is that we no longer have conscription," Northwestern University sociologist Charles Moskos told *National Journal*. "If you stared drafting students again, you'd see protests start up in a hurry.[24]

Without conscription, there is no debate about who serves and who does not. No one resents "privileged" college students lolling in gothic quadrangles while unfortunates are sent to serve in humid fields of fire. Service is voluntary and simply one of a set of choices in a free society.

Nor is there a debate about those who shirked national service or fled to Canada or about the injustice of the draft, an issue that still burns among some baby boomers.

In September 2004, television host George Stephanopoulos asked then secretary of state Colin Powell about a passage in his memoirs, where he reveals that he was "angry at the preferential treatment" given some draft dodgers, while disadvantaged young men were pressed into uniform. "That system was disturbing to me. That's why I was such a supporter of the voluntary army when it came," said Powell.[25]

And when it came, the voluntary army looked more like America. *National Journal* noted in May 2004 that the U.S. population was 69 percent white, 12 percent black, and 11 percent Hispanic. Deaths in Iraq and Afghanistan were 71 percent white, 12 percent black, and 11 percent Hispanic.[26] (The balance was Pacific Islanders, Native Americans, foreigners who volunteered, and others.) Unlike Vietnam, it is hard to argue that some racial groups are suffering casualties disproportionately.

Another difference between the Vietnam and Iraq war deaths is that soldiers who lost their lives in Iraq and Afghanistan were, on average, four years older than those killed in Vietnam (aged twenty-six vs. twenty-two).[27] This removes another staple of the Vietnam era: soldiers dying before they could vote.

## No enemy leaders

There is no Iraqi Ho Chi Minh, the popular leader of North Vietnam. "America just saw Ho Chi Minh as a Communist," said retired Maj. Gen. Chuck Horner, who served two tours of duty in Vietnam and commanded the U.S. Air Force during the Gulf War, "but to many of his countrymen he was a patriot, and there was something quite noble in his message of unification. In contrast, the only people who want to return Saddam to power are the hard-core Ba'athists, and they are a small minority."[28]

Nor is Iraq likely to produce a charismatic resistance leader. Saddam Hussein is now in U.S. custody and will be put on trial for his crimes against the Iraqi people. Al-Zarqawi, a Jordanian terrorist, could never plausibly pose as an Iraqi nationalist leader. Muqtada al-Sadr, the Shi'ite cleric who mobilized his militia against U.S. forces, has been decisively defeated.

Indeed, the strangest aspect of the insurgency is its lack of visible leaders. Leaders can be visible, but disguised, as in other armed revolts against central authority. In the Philippines, the insurgents have had various masked leaders, like the amusingly named "Commander Robot." In Mexico, the terrorists in Chiapas were said to be led by "Sub-Commandante Marcos." Iraq's anti-democratic terrorists do not even cite a shadowy commander with a nom de guerre.

## The Vietnamese were far tougher adversaries

Whereas the Communists stormed U.S. bases in South Vietnam, the Iraqi insurgents almost exclusively favor "soft" targets such as clinics, schools, and police stations. Such tactics may terrorize, but they are unlikely to lead to the decisive defeat of American and allied forces.

## The misery index is far lower in Iraq than it was in Vietnam

In Vietnam, America's high-altitude bombardment and noxious clouds of Agent Orange and napalm despoiled the jungles and left much of the landscape unfit for human habitation. Who can forget the famous photo of the naked girl fleeing her burning village? Refugees were a major miserable dimension of the war, forcing tens of thousands of ill-clad Vietnamese to squat in squalor in southern cities.

In Iraq, the much-feared refugee crisis never materialized. While citizens are still shockingly poor for an oil-rich nation, any visitor to Iraq, especially in its southern reaches, will see many telltale home improvements: satellite dishes from Dubai, new electric generators from Japan, new pots from Malaysia. Here and there an air conditioner pokes out of a window of a home that did not even have electricity before the war.

Far from being miserable refugees, many Iraqis have materially better lives today than they did before the war. Enterprising Iraqis took advantage of the U.S. military's free-trade policies to import used cars from Syria, Jordan, and Kuwait. Many Iraqis now own automobiles for the first time in their lives. Indeed, the number of cars on the roads is three times higher than prewar levels—leading to long gas lines at Iraq's filling stations.

While tariffs are now 5 percent, that still represents a huge reduction from the Saddam era, when import taxes were 75 percent on air conditioners and 30 percent on televisions.[29] As a result, prices for consumer goods have plummeted while profits to small businesses have soared. The economy is booming, between the bomb blasts.

Fawzy al-Hashimi owns an appliance store in Baghdad with some $2 million worth of television sets, air conditioners, and refrigerators packed into his tiny storefront. He told the *Financial Times* that his small business's total revenues have climbed 300 percent since Iraq's liberation in 2003.[30] Sales are soaring. So is the Baghdad Stock Exchange. The managing director of Dar al-Salaam Insurance Company reports that his firm's portfolio of shares on the exchange have grown to 3 billion Iraqi dinars (worth roughly $2 billion) from a mere 200 million dinars in 2003.[31] "I believe this will be temporary, the looting and the terrorism. If this belief is not correct, Iraq will be ruined," he told the *Financial Times*. "We were buying and selling and there were bombs around, shooting and fighting but nobody got scared, they just continued buying and selling. You do not do this unless there is faith" in the future.[32]

It doesn't seem like these Iraqis, and others that I have met, think of their country as a lost cause like Vietnam. It might well have a different ending, if the cautious optimism of the Iraqis is justified.

Yet too many in the media are so mesmerized by the Vietnam movie playing in their heads that they can't view today's feature. They can keep looking for a quagmire in the desert.

# THE U.S. MILITARY KILLED 100,000 CIVILIANS IN IRAQ

*"The invasion of Iraq in March 2003 by Coalition forces has led to the death of at least 100,000 civilians, reveals the first scientific study to examine the issue."*

—*New Scientist* MAGAZINE

THE CLAIM THAT "100,000 CIVILIANS were killed in Iraq" derives from a study done by an international research team led by Les Roberts of Johns Hopkins University's Bloomberg School of Public Health, which included researchers from Columbia University and Al-Mustansiriya University in Iraq. The research was done in Iraq in September 2004 and was published in the online edition of the *Lancet* on October 29, so that it would appear days before the November 2004 presidential election.

The published version[1] appeared three weeks later, after George W. Bush won 60,667,812 votes.

There is little doubt that this study was rushed into print to influence the 2004 presidential election. Roberts, the study author, told the *Chronicle of Higher Education* that he hoped that the study would provoke "moral outrage."[2] Roberts's motivation was even clearer when he spoke to a Scottish newspaper: "I was opposed to the war and still think it was a bad idea," he told the *Glasgow Herald*, "but I hope the science has transcended our objectives. As an American, I am really, really sorry to be reporting this."[3]

And the editor of the *Lancet*, a well-respected British medical journal, clearly shared Roberts's political outlook. "The invasion of Iraq, the displacement of a cruel dictator, and the attempt to impose a liberal democracy by force have, by themselves, been insufficient to bring peace and security to the civilian population. Democratic imperialism has led to more deaths, not fewer," said Richard Horton.[4]

The American public did not seem to share Roberts's "moral outrage" or Horton's concerns about "democratic imperialism." George W. Bush won 286 electoral votes, carried 31 states and won 51 percent of the popular vote—the first time since 1988 that a presidential contender won more than half of the popular vote.[5]

Later, Roberts claimed he had to rush the piece into print to protect the lives of Iraqi members of the survey team.[6] Sure.

Still, politically motivated researchers can sometimes be right. The question is: how credible is Roberts's research? At first glance, fairly credible. The scientific study was purportedly based on a series of random samples gathered directly in Iraq and published in a major peer-reviewed medical journal. But a closer look reveals so many confounding variables as to render the results provably false.

Roberts et al. conducted interviews at thirty sites, allegedly randomly selected, and interviewed thirty-three people in each place. The survey teams did not ask for death certificates, trusting Iraqis to tell them who had died. "In the Iraqi culture," they wrote "it was unlikely to fabricate deaths."

"Such faith in the honesty of Iraqis is truly touching," journalist Michael Fumento writes. Fumento has visited Iraq and nearly died there.[7] "But these are the people who gave us 'Baghdad Bob' and are regularly quoted as saying that once again a U.S. air strike killed only innocents. It's as if America had developed a chip for its weapons that zeroes in strictly on women, children, and old men."

Besides, people traumatized by war and terrorism have reason to exaggerate.

There is a cultural disconnect between Western researchers and Iraqi respondents, as Stephen Apfelroth of the Albert Einstein College of Medicine notes. The survey team asked how many deaths per "household" were known to Iraqis. Americans think of a household as a nuclear family. Arabs think of a household as including the extended family, which can easily number in the hundreds. As a result, one hears about the deaths of distant in-laws and third cousins, even though many of these "relatives" might live far from the surveyed area. "Such a phenomenon is much more likely when considering violent deaths," Apfelroth writes.[8]

Roberts et al. claim that their survey used random samples. But as Slate.com's Fred Kaplan points out, the survey sites were not selected by chance. At times, the group couldn't find enough people to interview, so they expanded the area they studied. Sometimes they couldn't get access to a survey area because it was closed by checkpoints or war, so they went to another location that was convenient. "Again, at that point, the survey was no longer random, and so the results are suspect," Kaplan writes.[9]

The Roberts study claimed a 99.5 percent response rate, meaning that virtually everyone contacted instantaneously agreed to participate in the survey. Veteran statisticians find this response rate surprisingly high. "The claimed 99.5 percent response rate makes it seem highly suspect that the thirty closest doorways were actually those rigorously selected," Apfelroth writes.[10] Far from being random surveys, it appears that Roberts's team gravitated to the most vocal Iraqis.

Another bias is something statisticians call "cluster sampling." As Fumento explains, researchers usually try to avoid hot spots that skew the findings—"like determining how much of a nation's population wears dentures by surveying only nursing homes." But two-thirds of the deaths reported in the Roberts study were located in one cluster in Fallujah. Fumento contends, "That's it, game over, report worthless."[11]

Fallujah, the scene of heavy fighting for more than two years, is simply not representative of Iraq as a whole. Fourteen of Iraq's eighteen provinces have seen virtually no war-related violence at all.

Roberts and his co-authors conclude that "there were 98,000 extra deaths (95% CI 8,000–194,000) during the postwar period." This means that, as Fred Kaplan writes, "that the authors are 95 percent confident that the war-caused deaths totaled some number between 8,000 and 194,000." Kaplan calls this "an absurdly vast range."[12] The 98,000 estimate

was an attempt to split the difference between the two ends of the estimate; the 100,000 death toll is simply "rounding."

At this point, any fair-minded observer would have to conclude that
the Roberts study is pure "political science." All traditional statistical
controls—random site selection, interviews with randomly selected individuals, controls for cluster bias, and so on—were cast aside to serve an
admitted political agenda to spur "moral outrage" and defeat Bush.

A more responsible attempt to count civilian deaths in Iraq can be
viewed at www.Iraqbodycount.net.[13] Compiled by Hamit Dardagan and
John Sloboda, the site counts civilian casualties, but rather than trusting
Iraqis they meet in the street, Dardagan and Sloboda only count deaths
if they appear in at least two online media sources. Their principal
sources seem to appear in independent wire services and Iraqi newspapers. Efforts are made to avoid double counting. Their count, however,
also includes civilians killed as a result of "inadequate health care or sanitation," such as a failed water treatment plant. This is still a significant
cause of death. Many streets in Iraq are wet with open sewage, and, as in
many developing countries, poor health care and sanitation are significant causes of death and disease. Indeed, poverty may well kill more Iraqi
civilians than the war.

As of June 13, 2005, Iraqbodycount.net had estimated between
22,248 and 25,229 civilian casualties. So 25,000 should be considered as
an upper boundary estimate of civilian deaths. And these estimates
include almost all deaths since the war—including the ones that occurred
eight months after the Roberts survey team visited Iraq.

No one has precise civilian casualty figures, but clearly the best estimate is closer to 25,000—far below the 100,000 claimed by mythmakers.
One unnecessary death is a tragedy; 100,000 phony deaths is a travesty.

# WOLFOWITZ TOLD CONGRESS THAT OIL WOULD PAY FOR THE IRAQ WAR

*"I get so tired of hearing chants of 'no war for oil.' If we have to go to war—and I still hope we don't have to go to war—this will not be a war for oil. If we wanted Iraq's oil we could have had it years ago by dropping all the sanctions on Iraq."*

—PAUL WOLFOWITZ, FEBRUARY 2003[1]

**IN THE EARLY DAYS** of the Iraq War, Deputy Secretary of Defense Paul Wolfowitz walked into a congressional committee room and touched off an Internet rumor that refuses to die.

Wolfowitz appeared before the House Appropriations Committee's defense subcommittee on March 27, 2003. He was there to plead for an additional $12 billion in military spending for Iraq—less than three weeks into the war. Some of that $12 billion was supposed to be used to rebuild Mesopotamia's shattered infrastructure. Congress feared an open-ended financial commitment. Congressman Roger Wicker, a Mississippi Republican and Air Force reservist, asked if $12 billion was all that was needed for both U.S. military operations and rebuilding efforts in Iraq.

Wolfowitz spoke at length, saying:

The principle we'd like to see applied here...is to get the Iraqi people on their feet and functioning as quickly as possible. Don't create one of these dependent relationships that we have in a number of places where a doctor in Kosovo can make more money as a driver for the United Nations than practicing medicine.

And, number three, there's a lot of money to pay for this. It doesn't have to be U.S. money. And it starts with the assets of the Iraqi people. They will now own these assets instead of a dictator that owns then, and they should spend them for their own welfare. So this is not the total of what's needed, but it is an estimate of what our contribution needs to be for the rest of the fiscal year—most of it for our military contribution.

Congressman Wicker then asked how much more would be needed over and above the $12 billion the administration was requesting. "What do you think the entire package is going to be? Do you have an answer?" Wolfowitz replied:

I mean—we really don't. And the real number would be not what's going to get you through the rest of the fiscal year, but what is it going to be over two or three years. And my—a rough recollection—well, I'm—the oil revenues of that country could bring between fifty and one hundred billion dollars over the course of the next two or three years. Now there are a lot of claims on that money, but that's—we're not dealing with Afghanistan; that's a permanent ward of the international community. We are dealing with a country that can really finance its own reconstruction and relatively soon.[2]

This exchange quickly became summarized as "Wolfowitz said oil would pay for the war" or somewhat more honestly, "Wolfowitz said oil would pay for Iraqi reconstruction."

When Wolfowitz was being confirmed as president of the World Bank, the *Washington Post* reported that World Bank staffers e-mailed each other video clips of the *Daily Show* in which host Jon Stewart recounted the myth about oil paying for the Iraq war, adding: "fucked that one up, too."[3]

Read the exchange between Wolfowitz and Congressman Wicker again and it becomes clear that critics are either taking one line out of context ("We are dealing with a country that really can finance its own reconstruction and relatively soon") or not reading the exchange very closely.

Wolfowitz is clearly contending that Iraq will not need an open spigot of development aid in the future years while acknowledging that the budget demands of the U.S. military will continue to be large.

The context of this lengthy exchange should not be ignored. The Deputy Secretary of Defense is before the committee to justify a $12 billion supplemental budget item to fund the war in Iraq. If he really said that oil revenues would pay for the war, there would be no reason to ask for funds and compelling reasons for Congress to tell him to get lost.

Wolfowitz is contending that Iraq is not about to become another Afghanistan, "a permanent ward of the international community," because Iraq has assets that can be used "relatively soon" to rebuild its shattered economy. "Relatively soon" means over the next few years. He seemed to be trying to reassure Congress that rebuilding Iraq will not turn into an endless rattling of the tin cup for more aid to re-wire Iraq's failing electrical grid, fill its potholed roads, and so on.

As for the continued need for military funding, Wolfowitz pointedly refuses to say that another $12 billion is all that it will take to fund military operations for the rest of 2003, let alone in the future.

As for oil revenue, Wolfowitz ventured a very loose revenue estimate—"fifty to one hundred billion dollars over the course of two to three years"—and pointed out that "there are a lot of claims on that money."

For what it's worth, some of Iraq's oil revenue has been used by the various interim Iraqi governments to rebuild some of that nation's decrepit infrastructure.

Whatever the merits of the Iraq war, Wolfowitz—the bête noire of the antiwar crowd—never said oil would pay for it. He contended that it could help in the nation's reconstruction and development—and so far he has been right.

# THERE IS NO EVIDENCE THAT IRAQ HAD WEAPONS OF MASS DESTRUCTION

*"There were no weapons of mass destruction."*

—HOWARD DEAN, APRIL 4, 2004[1]

*"It's not a lie when you are ordered to lie."*

—DR. RIHAB TAHA, A SENIOR IRAQI BIOLOGICAL WEAPONS OFFICIAL[2]

THE STRENGTH OF THE PREWAR intelligence on weapons of mass destruction was exaggerated. But so is the postwar case against that same intelligence.

Indeed, some are now saying that there was "no evidence" that Iraq was developing weapons of mass destruction (WMD) at all. That formulation is provably false. Indeed, we know that WMD component parts were found after the war—not "stockpiles," but enough to be worrying:

> ➤ In a secret operation on June 23, 2004, U.S. forces seized 1.77 metric tons of enriched uranium—the kind used to make fuel for atomic bombs—in a nuclear facility in Iraq, according to BBC News.[3] The BBC has been consistently critical of Bush and the Iraq war. U.S. Department of Energy experts also removed 1,000 radioactive materials in "powdered form, which is easily dispersed," said Bryan Wilkes, an Energy Department spokesman. The material would have been

ideal for a radioactive dirty bomb. Then energy secretary Spencer Abraham hailed the operation as "a major achievement."[4]

➢ Polish general Marek Dukaczewski, Poland's military intelligence chief, revealed that troops in the Polish-patrolled sector of Iraq had received tips from Iraqis that chemical weapons were sold to terrorists on the black market. The weapons had been buried to avoid detection, the general told the BBC.[5] Polish military officials bought seventeen chemical-weapons warheads from Iraqis for $5,000 each to keep them from Iraq's so-called insurgents.[6] "An attack with such weapons would be hard to imagine," the general said. "All of our activity was accelerated at appropriating these warheads."[7] Tests confirmed that some of the warheads contained cyclosarin, a nerve agent five times more powerful than sarin. These chemical weapons were supposed to have been completely destroyed during the 1991–1998 UN inspector regime. Clearly, some WMD survived.

➢ U.S. soldiers stormed into a warehouse in Mosul, Iraq, on August 8, 2005, and were surprised to find 1,500 gallons of chemical agents. It was the largest chemical weapons lab found in Iraq.[8] The intelligence community remains divided over the origin of those chemical weapons (either from inside Iraq or outside) and whether they were made during Saddam's regime or after.

➢ When a roadside bomb exploded near a U.S. convoy on May 17, 2004, it was found to contain the nerve agent sarin.[9] Army Brigadier General Mark Kimmitt told reporters that an "improvised explosive" was rigged to a 155 mm artillery shell that contained sarin. The shell was a "binary chemical projectile," in which the two ingredients that produce sarin are separated by a propeller blade that spins while the shell is in flight, mixing the deadly gas to full potency. Since the chemical weapons shell was used as a bomb, and not fired from the barrel of an artillery piece, the internal rotor did not spin and the deadly agent was not widely dispersed. As a result, Kimmitt explained, only traces of sarin were produced and released. The soldiers were briefly hospitalized and decontaminated. Again, all such chemical weapons warheads were supposed to be destroyed in 1991—yet Saddam's WMD still threaten the lives of American troops to this day.

➢ The Iraq Survey Group, led by David Kay and charged with finding WMD after the war, discovered a projectile loaded with mustard gas attached to a roadside bomb in May 2004. Fortunately, the mustard gas was "stored improperly" and was "ineffective." The mustard-gas shell is believed to be part of the eighty tons of such gas still unaccounted for.[10]

Also worth remembering are the elements of the prewar consensus that have not been refuted. Consider the evidence from experts who are decidedly not neo-conservatives, nor, in many cases, even friendly to the Bush administration.

### Amatzia Baram

A political scientist at the University of Haifa, Israel, Baram convincingly demonstrated that Saddam Hussein was interested in acquiring nuclear weapons as early as 1971. In 2001, he reported that "Saddam has not yet given up his strategic goal of becoming a pan-Arab hero, if not the leader of the Arab world. He still appears to believe that a nuclear capability is necessary to acquire such status."[11]

### The Central Intelligence Agency

Long before George W. Bush was president, the CIA believed that Iraq sought WMD, including nuclear arms. "Iraq will intensify its efforts to acquire nuclear weapons and other advanced military technology to deter Iranian aggression. Its successful use of chemical weapons, missiles, and high-performance Western and Soviet aircraft has whetted its appetite for advanced technology."[12] That report was published in 1988.

### Hans Blix

The Swedish-born diplomat was executive chairman of the UN Monitoring, Verification, and Inspection Commission (UNMOVIC). His job was to supervise the UN weapons inspectors in Iraq. Blix was a staunch opponent of the war. In a speech to the UN Security Council on January 27, 2003, Blix said his agency's reports "do not contend that weapons of mass destruction remain in Iraq, but nor do they exclude that possibility.

They point to lack of evidence and inconsistencies, which raise question marks, which must be straightened out if weapons dossiers are to be closed and confidence is to arise."

If one keeps reading Blix's reports, darker realities emerge. The inspectors could not account for Iraq's 6,500 chemical weapons (which were missing) and couldn't prove that Iraq had destroyed the anthrax it admitted it had produced. In short, according to Blix, some WMD were most likely still in Iraq's arsenal. Blix said that inspectors had found evidence that Iraq had been producing VX nerve gas as well as a "mustard gas predecessor," thiodiglycol.

Blix also testified that inspectors found some evidence that Iraq had been preparing to produce missiles that were specifically banned.[13]

## Richard Butler

The former UN chief weapons inspector's book is subtitled "Iraq, Weapons of Mass Destruction, and the Crisis of Global Security."[14] Butler affirms that UN inspectors found evidence that Iraq was making VX nerve gas in 1998.[15] Iraq at first denied that it had made VX nerve gas, then claimed it had made only 200 liters, and then claimed that it had made 3,900 liters but failed to "weaponize" it.[16]

Then there was Iraq's illegal insistence on declaring many suspect sites off-limits, which clearly frustrated Butler. "The known Iraqi policy of undermining UNSCOM's disarmament mission by dividing Iraq's illegal weapons into two portions—that which would be concealed, perhaps literally underground, and that which would be revealed and then, presumably, removed."[17]

Iraq, Butler concludes, has an "aggressive concealment program" for WMD.[18] In December 1998, Butler writes with some indignation, UN weapons inspector Roger Hill was shown "empty buildings, obviously sanitized for his benefit, while the Iraqi authorities stood about laughing and saying, 'What did you expect? That we would show you anything serious?'"[19]

That same month, when UN weapons inspector Dr. Richard Spertzel "became exasperated by Iraqi evasions and misrepresentations, he confronted Dr. Rihab Taha, the woman the Iraqis identified as the head of the biological weapons program, and asked her directly, 'You know that we know you are lying. So why do you do it?'

"She straightened herself up and replied, 'Dr. Spertzel, it's not a lie when you are ordered to lie.'"[20]

If Iraq had no weapons of mass destruction, what was Dr. Taha ordered to lie about?

## Congressional Research Service

Analyst Kenneth Katzman is widely respected for his experience. In a 2002 report, he summarized what United Nations inspectors had found. Between 1991 and 1994, the inspectors had "uncovered and dismantled a previously undeclared network of about forty nuclear research facilities, including three clandestine enrichment programs. International Atomic Energy Agency inspectors discovered three tons of uranium remained in Iraq. UNSCOM in 1998 discovered that in 1996 Iraq had been producing fresh bombs laden with mustard gas. Four tons of growth media for biological agents remained unaccounted for."[21]

## Anthony R. Cordesman

Cordesman holds the Arleigh A. Burke Chair in Strategy at the Center for Strategic and International Studies. I attended a number of military briefings with him in Iraq. Officers respected him for his carefully calibrated criticisms of ongoing operations. He is also an opponent of the Iraq war. Cordesman writes, "The United States and Britain went to war in Iraq without the level of evidence needed to provide a clear strategic rationale for the war and without the ability to fully understand the threat that Iraqi weapons of mass destruction posed to U.S., British, and Australian forces. This uncertainty is not a definitive argument against carrying out a war that responded to grave potential threats. It *is* a definitive warning that this intelligence and targeting are not yet adequate to support grand strategy, strategy, and tactical operations against proliferating powers or to make accurate assessments about the need to preempt."[22] This is enough to warm the heart of any antiwar activist.

Then, Cordesman goes on to say that Iraq and other proliferators "have learned to cover and conceal, to deceive, and to create smaller and better disseminated activities." He adds that Iraq was a "proven proliferator" known to deceive and lie about WMD.[23]

## Charles Duelfer

Duelfer served as deputy executive chairman of the UN Special Commission on Iraq (UNSCOM). Set up after the Gulf War in 1991, this body was charged with eliminating Iraq's WMD. Duelfer testified in October 2004 that there was a less than 5 percent chance that Iraq had WMD before the 2003 Iraq war. But he conceded that Saddam "committed the brightest minds and much of the national treasure to developing weapons of mass destruction. Moreover, Saddam saw this investment as having paid vital dividends." He added that "given the nature of Iraqi governance, one should not look for much of an audit trail on WMD. Even Saddam's most senior ministers did not want to be in a position to tell him bad news or make recommendations from which he would recoil."

Duelfer said that "Saddam did not abandon his nuclear ambitions. He made clear his view that nuclear weapons were the right of any country that could build them."

Duelfer's theory is that Saddam Hussein tried to bluff the world on his WMD capability—to make Iraq look more powerful—but that he intended to jump-start his WMD programs as soon as sanctions were lifted.

Given Saddam's intentions, Duelfer did not rule out that Saddam might have had WMD and could not say whether such weapons might have been smuggled to Syria just before the 2003 war.[24]

## Rolf Ekeus

Ekeus is a former UNSCOM chairman and chairman of the board of the Stockholm International Peace Research Institute. In a June 2003 *Washington Post* op-ed, he argued that "the real chemical weapons threat in Iraq" was that highly trained Iraqi chemical warfare specialists would sign up with al Qaeda.

Ekeus concludes that letting Saddam "remain in power with his chemical and biological weapons capability—would have been to tolerate a continuing destabilizing arms race in the [Persian] Gulf, including future nuclearization of the region, threats to the world's energy supplies, leakage of WMD technology and expertise to terrorist networks, systematic sabotage of efforts to create and sustain a process of peace between the Israelis and the Palestinians and the continued terrorizing of the Iraqi people."[25]

## David Kay

Kay ran the Iraq Survey Group, a 1,400-man team charged with scouring Iraq for stockpiles of WMD. He did not find any. Yet he told a joint session of the Senate and House Intelligence Committees in October 2003 that the Iraq Survey Group had "discovered dozens of WMD-related program activities and significant amounts of equipment that Iraq had concealed from the United Nations during the inspections that began in late 2002, including chemical, biological, and nuclear experiments." Kay testified that Iraq had tried to obtain missiles from North Korea on several occasions.

He also said that his work was hampered by "six principal factors," of which the first two were that "from birth, all of Iraq's WMD activities were highly compartmentalized within a regime that ruled and kept its secrets through fear and terror and with deception and denial built into each program," and "deliberate dispersal and destruction of material and documentation related to weapons programs began pre-conflict and ran trans-to-post conflict."[26] What was being dispersed and hidden if there was "no evidence" that Iraq had WMD?

## Yossef Bodansky

The director of the U.S. House of Representatives Task Force on Terrorism and Unconventional Warfare, Bodansky noted in a 1998 congressional report that "Iraq does have a small but very lethal operational arsenal of WMD and platforms capable of delivering them throughout the Middle East and even beyond."[27] He also observed that Saddam Hussein

staged a massive military parade in January 2002, showcasing weapons
that have disappeared since the liberation of Baghdad.

## Kenneth Pollack

Pollack was the Clinton administration's chief Iraq expert and is now a
fellow at the Brookings Institution. At the end of the Clinton administration, he wrote a memo in which he argued that "because of the nature
of containment, the next administration would be left with two choices:
to adopt an aggressive policy of regime change to try to get rid of Saddam quickly or undertake a major revamping of the sanctions to try to
choke off the smuggling and prevent Saddam from reconstituting his military, particularly his hidden WMD programs."[28]

Pollock's views on Iraqi WMD best summarize the prewar view in the
American intelligence community.

> ➤ "The U.S. intelligence community believes that Iraq retains a small,
> covert al-Hussein force, probably on the order of twelve to forty mis-
> siles."[29]

> ➤ "Saddam has no particular need to have huge stockpiles of [chemical
> warfare] rounds but can start up production several months before an
> expected conflict and make all the [chemical weapons] he needs."[30]

> ➤ "There is a consensus that Saddam has resumed his work on nuclear
> weapons."[31]

> ➤ Due to sanctions, "Saddam has given up anywhere from $130 billion to
> $180 billion worth of oil revenues to hang on to his WMD programs."[32]

> ➤ "If Saddam is able to acquire nuclear weapons, everything else will
> become meaningless. Between his own behavior and the statements
> of Iraqi defectors, it is clear that Saddam sees nuclear weapons as
> being in a category by themselves and if he has a nuclear weapon the
> world will treat him differently."[33]

> ➤ "From experience gained at the end of Desert Storm more than ten
> years ago, it was clear to us and should have been clear to our critics
> that finding WMD in the aftermath of a conflict wouldn't be easy.
> We judged that Iraq probably possessed one hundred to five
> hundred metric tons of CW [chemical weapons] munitions fill. One
> hundred metric tons would fit in the backyard swimming pool; five

hundred could be hidden in a small warehouse. We made no assessment of the size of Iraq's biological weapons holdings but a biological weapon can be carried in a small container. (And of course, we judged that Saddam did not have a nuclear weapon.) When the Iraq Survey Group (ISG), led by David Kay, issued its interim report in October acknowledging that it had not found chemical or biological weapons, the inspectors had then visited only ten of the 130 major ammunition depots in Iraq; these ammunition dumps are huge, sometimes five miles by five miles on a side. Two depots alone are roughly the size of Manhattan. It is worth recalling that after Desert Storm, U.S. forces unknowingly destroyed over 1,000 rounds of chemical-filled munitions at a facility called Al Kamissiyah. Baghdad sometimes had special markings for chemical and biological munitions and sometimes did not. In short, much remains to be done in the hunt for Iraq's WMD."

> "We do not know whether the ISG ultimately will be able to find physical evidence of Iraq's chemical and biological weapons or confirm the status of its WMD programs and its nuclear ambitions. The purposeful, apparently regime-directed, destruction of evidence pertaining to WMD from one end of Iraq to the other, which began even before the Coalition occupied Baghdad, and has continued since then, already has affected the ISG's work. Moreover, Iraqis who have been willing to talk to U.S. intelligence officers are in great danger. Many have been threatened; some have been killed. The denial and deception efforts directed by the extraordinarily brutal, but very competent Iraqi intelligence services, which matured through ten years of inspections by various UN agencies, remain extraordinarily lethal. Finding weapons in a country that is larger than the state of California would be a daunting task even under far more hospitable circumstances. But now that we have our own eyes on the ground, David Kay and the ISG must be allowed to complete their work and other collection efforts we have under way also must be allowed to run their course. And even then, it will be necessary to integrate all the new information with intelligence and analyses produced over the past fifteen years before we can determine the status of Iraq's WMD efforts prior to the war."

➤ "Allegations about the quality of the U.S. intelligence performance
and the need to confront these charges have forced senior intelligence officials throughout U.S. intelligence to spend much of their
time looking backward. I worry about the opportunity costs of this
sort of preoccupation, but I also worry that analysts laboring under a
barrage of allegations will become more and more disinclined to
make judgments that go beyond ironclad evidence—a scarce com-
modity in our business. If this is allowed to happen, the nation will be
poorly served by its intelligence community and ultimately much less
secure. Fundamentally, the intelligence community increasingly will
be in danger of not connecting the dots until the dots have become a
straight line."

➤ "We must keep in mind that the search for WMD cannot and should
not be about the reputation of U.S. intelligence or even just about
finding weapons. At its core, men and women from across the intelligence community continue to focus on this issue because understanding the extent of Iraq's WMD efforts and finding and securing
weapons and all the key elements that make up Baghdad's WMD
programs—before they fall into the wrong hands—is vital to our
national security. 'If we eventually are proven wrong—that is, there
were no weapons of mass destruction and the WMD programs were
dormant or abandoned—the American people will be told the truth;
we would have it no other way,' says Stuart A. Cohen, a former CIA
intelligence professional and vice chairman of the National Intelligence Council."[34]

Nearly every critic of the war in Iraq who was involved with either UN
or U.S. efforts to find WMD has refused to say that there is no evidence
that Iraq had them. There may be little evidence and myriads of dark
suspicions, but this is not the same thing as "no evidence."

Why? Because there is overwhelming evidence that Iraq's more than
decade-long interference with UN weapons inspections was driven by a
desire to conceal existing WMD programs. Antiwar activists have plenty
of legitimate arguments to make—there is no need to overstate their case.

# THERE IS NO CONNECTION BETWEEN IRAQ AND AL QAEDA

*"The administration sold the connection [between Iraq and al Qaeda] to scare the pants off the American people and justify the war. There's no connection, and that's been confirmed by some of bin Laden's terrorist followers.... What you've seen here is the manipulation of intelligence for political ends."*

—FORMER SENATOR MAX CLELAND[1]

IN THE EARLY DAYS of the Iraq War, American soldiers stormed an Iraqi military base near Nasiriyah and could not believe their eyes.

Is that? Could it be? They were agape at a large, full-color mural found on a wall in the central hall. It featured a city skyline, with two towers. One was aflame, the other was threatened by a plane diving down for the kill.[2]

Like a mosaic left behind by a vanished civilization, the mural meant different things to different people. Some thought it vindicated the war effort by connecting Iraq to al Qaeda. Others, skeptical of both the war and the connection, pointed out that there was no evidence that mural was made before the September 11 attacks, and celebrating al Qaeda's deadliest attack did not mean Iraq was behind it.

The debate was part of the larger struggle for American opinion. As large units of the Iraqi army melted away into the sun-baked landscape, the antiwar movement grew bigger and bolder. It challenged each of the three main justifications for war: that Iraq was somehow linked to al Qaeda; that the Iraqi regime had weapons of mass destruction that it might share with al Qaeda; and that Saddam Hussein was a uniquely out-sized evil who persecuted his people and threatened his neighbors (some of which were U.S. bases).

While there are many valid questions about the extent of the rela-tionship between Iraq and al Qaeda, many activists and pundits have said there is no connection at all. Are they overstating their case?

Before exploring the myriad links between Iraq and al Qaeda, let us consider sources. To be persuasive, the best sources have to be authori-tative and impartial—and preferably independent of the White House. So the main sources for this chapter are the official reports of the 9-11 Commission, bipartisan reports of U.S. congressional committees, and news stories written by staff members of overseas center-left dailies, mostly the *Guardian* and the *Observer* (London) as well as established American publications, such as the *New Yorker*, and respected Arabic-language newspapers, including *Al-Hayat*.

The main administration sources relied on this chapter are Colin Powell, who was the most independent member of the Bush cabinet and was certainly not a cheerleader for war in Iraq, and former CIA director George Tenet, who was first appointed by President Clinton.

Of course, there are many aspects of this chapter that will provoke partisans of both the red and blue varieties. Die-hard opponents of Pres-ident Bush will be disappointed to see that there are indeed many proven links between the Iraqi dictator and the world's most infamous terrorist. All I can say is that the evidence is clear and uncontested. That is not to say that Iraq controlled al Qaeda, was behind the September 11 attacks, or that the war was (or was not) justified. The available evidence only shows considerable contact (or connections) between Iraq and al Qaeda, no less and no more.

Some conservatives will find fault with certain omissions, or they will contend that certain telling connections are missing. The simple prob-lem is that some of the "smoking guns" are more surmise than settled fact, such as the alleged meetings in Prague of September 11 ringleader Mohammed Atta and Iraqi diplomat Ahmed Khalil Ibrahim Samir al-Ani at Iraq's Czech embassy between March 1999 and April 22, 2001;[3] an alleged 1998 Iraq–al Qaeda plot to bomb the Czech headquarters of Radio Liberty; and alleged Iraq–al Qaeda cooperation at the al-Shifa pharmaceutical plant (the so-called "aspirin factory" in Sudan that was attacked by cruise missiles in the Clinton years), and so on.

These "connections" are omitted because they cannot be conclusively proven. While Czech intelligence stands by its story, 9-11 Commission spokesman Al Felzenberg and staff director Philip Zelikow told me that the FBI had shared with them a non-public timeline of Atta's movements that proved he could not have been in Prague on the dates in question. Would they publish this timeline? I asked. (This was several months before the Commission's final report appeared in bookstores.) "No one would be interested except for a few specialists like you," Zelikow confidently told me, adding that much of it was simply the time, date, and place that his ATM card was used. I suggested that those records and that timeline might not be conclusive; after all, he could have given his bank card to someone else. Zelikow dismissed this possibility. That is why the Prague meeting is not considered hard fact by the Commission, and, absent other compelling evidence, is considered unproven by me.

As for the 1998 bomb plot, it appears to have been a purely Iraqi operation and never moved beyond the planning stages. It tells us nothing about the relationship between Iraq and al Qaeda.

And while the "aspirin factory" was indeed making drugs for Iraq under a UN license, there is no conclusive evidence that it was making poison gases. I visited the ruins of the factory in 2002 and saw the twisted machinery. There was no piping or other equipment for moving pressured gases. And, as far as I am aware, no one has proven an al Qaeda relationship to that factory. When the factory owner threatened to sue for compensation in U.S. courts, the Clinton administration declined to present evidence of an al Qaeda link and settled the case. If the evidence were strong, surely the government would have fought, not settled.

There are, however, four kinds of undisputed connections between Iraq and al Qaeda: meetings, money, training, and personnel. Let us consider each in turn.

# MYTH #12: MEETINGS

> Photographs taken by Malaysian intelligence in January 2000 place Ahmed Hikmat Shakir, an Iraqi intelligence operative, at key planning meetings with al Qaeda members for the bombing of the USS *Cole* and the September 11 attacks.

> In 1992, according to Iraqi intelligence documents obtained after the war, bin Laden met with Iraqi intelligence officials in Syria.[4]

> Sudanese intelligence officials told me that their agents had observed meetings between Iraqi intelligence agents and bin Laden starting in 1994, when bin Laden lived in Khartoum.

> Michael Scheuer, the former head of the bin Laden unit at the CIA and a sharp critic of the Bush administration, writes in his 2002 book *Through Our Enemies' Eyes* that bin Laden "made a connection with Iraq's intelligence service through its Khartoum station."[5]

> Examining the bin Laden-Iraq-Sudan nexus in the early 1990s, *Weekly Standard* writer Stephen Hayes reports: "In Sudan, bin Laden decided to acquire and, when possible, use chemical, biological, radiological, and nuclear (CBRN) weapons against Islam's enemies. Bin Laden's first moves in this direction were made in cooperation with NIF [Sudan's National Islamic Front], Iraq's intelligence service, and Iraqi CBRN scientists and technicians. He made contact with Baghdad with its intelligence officers in Sudan and by a [Hassan al-] Turabi-brokered June 1994 visit by Iraq's then intelligence chief Faruq al-Hijazi; according to Milan's *Corriere della Sera*, Saddam, in 1994, made al-Hijazi responsible for "nurturing Iraq's ties to [Islamic] fundamentalist warriors. Turabi had plans to formulate a 'common strategy' with bin Laden and Iraq for subverting pro-U.S. Arab regimes, but the meeting was a get-acquainted session where al-Hijazi and bin Laden developed a good rapport that would flourish in the late 1990s."[6]

> Bin Laden met at least eight times with officers of Iraq's Special Security Organization, a secret police agency run by Saddam's son Qusay, according to intelligence made public by Secretary of State Colin Powell, speaking before the United Nations Security Council on February 6, 2003.[7]

- Bin Laden met the director of the Iraqi mukhabarat, Iraq's external intelligence service, in Khartoum in 1996, according to Powell.

- An al Qaeda operative now held by the United States confessed that in the mid-1990s, bin Laden had forged an agreement with Saddam's men to cease all terrorist activities against the Iraqi dictator, Powell said.[8]

- Saddam's relationship to bin Laden was documented while the arch-terrorist was based in Sudan from 1991 to 1996. Patrick Fitzgerald, an U.S. attorney in the Clinton Justice Department, prepared an indictment of bin Laden. "Al Qaeda reached an understanding with the government of Iraq that al Qaeda would not work against that government and that on particular projects, specifically including weapons development, al Qaeda would work cooperatively with the government of Iraq."[9] This is substantially what Powell would tell the United Nations years later, on the eve of the war.

- In 1999, the *Guardian*, Britain's leading left-liberal newspaper, reported that Faruq al-Hijazi, a senior officer in Iraq's mukhabarat, had journeyed deep into the icy mountains near Khandahar, Afghanistan, in December 1998 to meet with al Qaeda officers. Al-Hijazi is "thought to have offered bin Laden asylum in Iraq," the *Guardian* reported.

- "In 2000, Saudi Arabia went on kingdom-wide alert after learning that Iraq had agreed to help al Qaeda attack U.S. and British interests on the peninsula."[10]

- Stephen Hayes writes about another Iraq–al Qaeda connection, based on captured Iraqi documents: "In 1998, according to documents unearthed in Iraq's intelligence headquarters in April 2003, al Qaeda sent a 'trusted confidante' to Baghdad for sixteen days of meetings beginning March 5. Iraqi intelligence paid for his stay in Room 414 of the Mansur al-Melia hotel and expressed hope that the envoy would serve as the liaison between Iraqi intelligence and bin Laden. The DIA [the Pentagon's Defense Intelligence Agency] has assessed those documents as authentic."[11]

- In October 2000, another Iraqi intelligence operative, Salah Suleiman, was arrested near the Afghan border by Pakistani authorities, according to *Jane's Foreign Report*, a respected international newsletter. *Jane's* reported that Suleiman was shuttling between Iraqi intelligence and Ayman al-Zawahiri, al Qaeda's second in command.

Why are all of these meetings significant? The *Observer* (London) reports that FBI investigators cite a captured al Qaeda field manual in Afghanistan, which "emphasizes the value of conducting discussions about pending terrorist attacks face to face, rather than by electronic means."

- As recently as 2001, Iraq's embassy in Pakistan was used as a "liaison" between the Iraqi dictator and al Qaeda, Colin Powell told the United Nations.
- Qassem Hussein Muhammed, a twenty-year veteran of Iraqi intelligence, was interviewed by *New Yorker* veteran reporter Jeffrey Goldberg in 2002—almost a year before the Iraq War.[12] Muhammed said that he was one of seventeen bodyguards assigned to protect al-Zawahiri a 1992 trip to Iraq. Al-Zawahiri, according to Muhammed, stayed at the al-Rashid Hotel in Baghdad. Muhammed claimed that he was on the security detail that took al-Zawahiri to one of Saddam's opulent palaces for a meeting with the dictator.[13]
- Both ABC News's *Nightline* and PBS's *Wide Angle* interviewed a "twenty-year veteran of Iraqi intelligence" who told the same story. He was not named by *Wide Angle*. *Nightline* identified him by his nom de guerre, Abu Aman Amaleeki. "In 1992, elements of al Qaeda came to Baghdad and met with Saddam Hussein," Amaleeki said, "And among them was Ayman al-Zawahiri." Amaleeki added, "I was present when Ayman al-Zawahiri visited Baghdad."[14]
- Another visit by al-Zawahiri, in September 1999, was confirmed by former Iraqi premier Iyad Allawi in a wide-ranging interview with a reporter from the pan-Arab daily *Al-Hayat*. Allawi said the Iraqi secret service had documents detailing the relationship between Saddam Hussein and al Qaeda.[15]
- Allawi said that al-Zawahiri was invited to attend the ninth Popular Islamic Conference by Izzat Ibrahim al-Douri, Saddam's own second

in command.[16] The Iraqi government, he said, has the invitation and other documents.

➤ Yusuf Galán, (also known as Luis Galán Gonzales) is a Spanish convert to Islam. He has been linked to al Qaeda by Spanish investigative judge Baltasar Garzón and has been charged by a Spanish court with being "directly involved with the preparation and planning" of the September 11 attacks. In the course of their investigation, Spanish police searched Galán's home and found an array of documents related to al Qaeda—including an invitation to a party at the Iraq embassy in Madrid. Galán worked for a former roommate of Mohammed Atta, who led the September 11 attacks. The invitation used his "al Qaeda nom de guerre," London's *Independent* reports.

# MYTH #13: MONEY

➤ Documents found among the debris of the Iraqi intelligence center show that Baghdad funded the Allied Democratic Forces, a Ugandan terror group led by an Islamist cleric linked to bin Laden. According to London's *Daily Telegraph*, the organization offered to recruit young people "to train for the jihad" at a "headquarters for international holy warrior network" to be established in Baghdad.

➤ The Arabic-language daily *Al-Hayat* reported on May 23, 2005, quoting Colin Powell: "A detained al Qaeda member tells us that Saddam was more willing to assist al Qaeda after the 1998 bombings of our embassies in Kenya and Tanzania. Saddam was also impressed by al Qaeda's attacks on the USS *Cole* in Yemen in October 2000."[17]

➤ Mullah Melan Krekar ran a terror group (Ansar al-Islam) linked to both bin Laden and Saddam Hussein. Krekar admitted to a Kurdish newspaper that he met bin Laden and other senior al Qaeda officials in Afghanistan. His acknowledged meetings with bin Laden go back to 1988. When he organized Ansar al-Islam in 2001 to conduct suicide attacks on Americans, "three bin Laden operatives showed up with a gift of $300,000 'to undertake jihad,'" *Newsday* reported. Krekar is now in custody in the Netherlands. His group operated in a portion of northern Iraq loyal to Saddam Hussein—and attacked independent

Kurdish groups hostile to Saddam. A spokesman for the Patriotic
Union of Kurdistan told a United Press International correspondent
that Krekar's group was funded by "Saddam Hussein's regime in
Baghdad."

➢ *Le Monde*, the Paris-based center-left daily, reported on July 9, 2005,
that Ansar al-Islam "was founded in 2001 with the joint help of Saddam Hussein—who intended to use it against moderate Kurds—and
al Qaeda, which hoped to find in Kurdistan a new location that would
receive its members."[18]

➢ Stephen Hayes cites two phone calls intercepted by American intelligence, long before the Iraq War, linking Iraq and al Qaeda to Ansar
al-Islam. "Two intercepts in 2002—one in May, the other in
October—illuminated the Iraqi regime's role in Ansar al-Islam. The
first revealed that an Iraqi intelligence officer praised the work of the
terrorist group and passed $100,000 to its leaders. The second,
described in a report from the National Security Agency, reported that
the Iraqi regime and al Qaeda reached an agreement whereby the
regime would provide safe haven in northern Iraq to al Qaeda terrorists fleeing Afghanistan. Also, the regime agreed to fund and to arm
the incoming jihadists."[19]

➢ A captured Ansar al-Islam terrorist, Rebwar Mohammed Abdul,
revealed to the *Los Angeles Times*, "I never talked to [Abu] Wael [an
Iraqi intelligence officer] but I saw him three times in meetings with
Mullah Krekar [the head of Ansar al-Islam]. The mullah told us that
Wael was a friend of his for twenty-three years and that they had met
in Baghdad while Wael was an intelligence officer."[20]

➢ The *New Yorker*'s Jeffrey Goldberg interviewed several prisoners
held by the Patriotic Union of Kurdistan, one of the Kurdish factions
fighting Ansar al-Islam. The prisoners related an intricate web of
coordination between an al Qaeda splinter group and Saddam's
intelligence service, the mukhabarat. Goldberg writes: "The allegations include charges that Ansar al-Islam has received funds directly
from al Qaeda; that the intelligence service of Saddam Hussein has
joint control, with al Qaeda operatives, over Ansar al-Islam; that
Saddam Hussein hosted a senior leader of al Qaeda in Baghdad in
1992 [al-Zawahiri]; that a number of al Qaeda members fleeing

Afghanistan have been secretly brought into territory controlled by
Ansar al-Islam; and that Iraqi intelligence agents smuggled conventional weapons, and possibly even chemical and biological weapons,
into Afghanistan."[21]

> In a follow-up report, Stephen Hayes writes in the *Weekly Standard*:
"In 1992 the Iraqi intelligence services compiled a list of its assets. On
page 14 of the document, marked 'Top Secret' and dated March 28,
1992, is the name of Osama bin Laden, who is reported to have a
'good relationship' with the Iraqi intelligence section in Syria. The
[U.S.] Defense Intelligence Agency has possession of the document
and has assessed that it is accurate."[22]

> After October 2001, hundreds of al Qaeda fighters are believed to
have holed up in Ansar al-Islam's strongholds inside northern Iraq.

> David L. Boren was chairman of the Senate Intelligence Committee
when he was interviewed by the *Washington Post* on January 19, 1991.
The Democratic senator said he recently received a two-hour briefing from senior intelligence officials.[23] "Saddam has put in place a network involving some of the most sophisticated terrorist organizations
in the world," Boren told the *Post*, adding that the effort was "pretty
highly controlled, pretty highly disciplined."[24]

# MYTH #14: TRAINING

> An Iraqi defector to Turkey, known by his cover name as "Abu
Mohammed," told Gwynne Roberts of the *Sunday Times* of London
that he saw bin Laden's fighters in camps in Iraq in 1997. At the time,
Mohammed was a colonel in the fedayeen, a brutal strike force that
reported directly to Saddam Hussein. Mohammed described an
encounter at the Salman Pak training facility southeast of Baghdad.
At that vast compound run by Iraqi intelligence, Muslim militants
trained to hijack planes with knives—practicing on a full-size Boeing
707. Colonel Mohammed recalls his first visit to Salman Pak this way:
"We were met by Colonel Jamil Kamil, the camp manager, and Major
Ali Hawas. I noticed that a lot of people were queuing for food. [The
major] said to me: 'You'll have nothing to do with these people. They
are Osama bin Laden's group and the PKK [a Muslim terror group

known for atrocities in Turkey] and Mojahedin-e Khalq [a terror group active in Pakistan].'"

➤ After the end of major combat operations in Iraq, Ravi Nessam, an Associated Press reporter, noted that satellite photos of "Salman Pak, about 15 miles southeast of Baghdad ... show an urban assault training site, a three-car train for railway-attack instruction, and a commercial airliner sitting all by itself in the middle of the desert."[25]

➤ Nessam continued: "Speaking at an April 6, 2003, press conference, General [Vincent] Brooks said: 'The nature of the work being done by some of those people that we captured, their influences to the type of training that they received, all of these things give us the impression that there was terrorist training that was conducted at Salman Pak.'"[26]

➤ Nationally syndicated columnist Deroy Murdock sifted through the publicly available information about al Qaeda operatives training in Salman Pak, and reported on "Sabah Khodada, a former Iraqi army captain who once worked at Salman Pak. On October 14, 2001, Khodada granted an interview to the PBS television program *Frontline* stating, 'This camp is specialized in exporting terrorism to the whole world.'[27]

"He added: 'Training includes hijacking and kidnapping of airplanes, trains, public buses, and planting explosives in cities ... how to prepare for suicidal operations.'

"He continued: 'We saw people getting trained to hijack airplanes. ... They are even trained how to use utensils for food, like forks and knives provided in the plane'" to hijack the aircraft.[28]

➤ In the spring of 1998, the Iraqi regime promised to provide "weapons development" assistance to al Qaeda. "The following year, according to 9-11 Commission Staff Statement 15, bin Laden took the Iraqis up on their pledge. [Iraqi intelligence officer Farouk al-] Hijazi told his interrogators in May 2003 that bin Laden had specifically requested [from Iraq] Chinese-manufactured anti-ship limpet mines as well as training camps in Iraq."[29]

➤ Mohammad Atef, the head of al Qaeda's military wing until he was killed by the U.S. in Afghanistan in November 2001, told a senior al Qaeda member now in U.S. custody that the terror network needed labs outside of Afghanistan to learn how to make chemical weapons.

Secretary of State Colin Powell asked: "Where did they go, where did they look? They went to Iraq."[30]

➤ The Iraqis had the Third World's largest poison-gas operations prior to the 1991 Gulf War and had perfected the technique of making hydrogen-cyanide gas. The Nazis used to call that gas Zyklon-B. In the hands of al Qaeda, this would be a fearsome weapon in an enclosed space—like a suburban mall or a subway station.

➤ Summing up his agency's view, then CIA director George Tenet told the Senate Intelligence Committee in February 2003: "Iraq has in the past provided training in document forgery and bomb making to al Qaeda. It also provided training in poisons and gases to two al Qaeda associates; one of these [al Qaeda] associates characterized the relationship as 'successful.' Mr. Chairman, this information is based on a solid foundation of intelligence. It comes to us from credible and reliable sources. Much of it is corroborated by multiple sources."

## MYTH #15: PERSONNEL

➤ Ramzi Yousef, the mastermind of the 1993 World Trade Center bombing, entered the U.S. on a phony Iraqi passport.[31]

➤ Abdul Rahman Yasin was the only member of the al Qaeda cell that detonated the February 26, 1993, World Trade Center bomb to remain at large in the Clinton years. He fled to Iraq. U.S. forces recently discovered a cache of documents in Tikrit, Saddam's hometown, that show that Iraq gave Yasin both a house and a monthly salary. This confirmed American television reports from the Clinton era.

➤ ABC News correspondent Sheila MacVicar reported on July 27, 1994: "Last week, [television program] *Day One* confirmed [Yasin] is in Baghdad ... Just a few days ago, he was seen at [his father's] house by ABC News. Neighbors told us Yasin comes and goes freely."[32]

➤ Six months before the September 11 attacks, which were plotted, in part, in Germany, German federal police arrested two Iraqi men suspected of spying.[33] "They are suspected of carrying out missions for an Iraqi intelligence service in a number of German towns since the beginning of 2001," said a spokeswoman for state prosecutor Kay Nehm in Karlsruhe.[34]

➤ On March 16, 2001, a Paris-based Arabic-language newspaper reported fresh details on the arrests. The Middle East Intelligence Bulletin translated the report from *al-Watan al-Arabi*: Al-Watan al-Arabi (Paris) reports that two Iraqis were arrested in Germany, charged with spying for Baghdad. The arrests came in the wake of reports that Iraq was reorganizing the external branches of its intelligence service and that it had drawn up a plan to strike at U.S. interests around the world through a network of alliances with extremist fundamentalist parties. The most serious report contained information that Iraq and Osama bin Laden were working together. German authorities, acting on CIA recommendations, had been focused on monitoring the activities of Islamic groups linked to bin Laden. They discovered the two Iraqi agents by chance and uncovered what they considered to be serious indications of cooperation between Iraq and bin Laden. The matter was considered so important that a special team of CIA and FBI agents was sent to Germany to interrogate the two Iraqi spies.[35]

➤ In 1998, Abbas al-Janabi, a longtime aide to Saddam's son Uday, defected to the West. At the time, he repeatedly told reporters that there was a direct connection between Iraq and al Qaeda.

➤ The Senate Intelligence Committee report notes that [Abu] Zubaydah was the "senior al Qaeda coordinator responsible for training and recruiting." Zubaydah, who is in custody, is often cited by skeptics of the Iraq–al Qaeda connection because he told interrogators that he said it was "unlikely" that bin Laden would establish a formal alliance with Iraq for fear of losing his independence. But the skeptics often ignore other aspects of Zubaydah's debriefing. Stephen Hayes notes, "Again, according to the Senate Intelligence Committee report, Zubaydah 'indicated that he had heard that an important al Qaeda associate, Abu Musab al-Zarqawi, and others had good relationships with Iraqi intelligence."[36]

➤ In 2001, an al Qaeda member "bragged that the situation in Iraq was 'good,'" according to intelligence made public by then secretary of state Colin Powell. Powell added that in 2001 Saudi Arabian border guards arrested two al Qaeda members entering the oil-rich kingdom from Iraq. They were linked to al Qaeda associates in Baghdad, and one of them had received training in Afghanistan on how to use cyanide.[37]

➤ Following the defeat of the Taliban, almost two dozen bin Laden associates "converged on Baghdad and established a base of operations there," Powell told the United Nations in February 2003. From their Baghdad base, Powell said, they supervised the movement of men, materiel, and money for al Qaeda's global network.

➤ Abu Musab al-Zarqawi oversaw an al Qaeda training camp in Afghanistan, Powell told the United Nations. His specialty was poisons. Wounded in fighting with U.S. forces, he sought medical treatment in Baghdad in May 2002.[38] Official records discovered in Baghdad revealed that al-Zarqawi received medical treatment at the Olympic hospital run by Uday Hussein, Saddam's son.

➤ When al-Zarqawi recovered, he restarted a training camp in northern Iraq. In October 2002, almost a year before the Iraq War, al-Zarqawi's Iraq cell was tied to the murder of Lawrence Foley, an official of the U.S. Agency for International Development, in Amman, Jordan. The captured assassin confessed that he received orders and funds from al-Zarqawi's cell in Iraq. The assassin's accomplice escaped to Iraq. "After the attack, an associate of the assassin left Jordan to go to Iraq to obtain weapons and explosives for further operations."[39]

➤ Powell told the United Nations: "The al-Zarqawi network helped establish another poison and explosive training center camp, and this camp is located in northeastern Iraq."[40] According to Powell, "Those helping to run this camp are al-Zarqawi lieutenants operating in northern Kurdish areas outside Saddam Hussein's controlled Iraq, but Baghdad has an agent in the most senior levels of the radical organization Ansar al-Islam, who controls this corner of Iraq. In 2000, this agent offered al Qaeda safe haven in the region."[41]

➤ Iraq was clearly harboring al-Zarqawi before the Iraq War and twice refused to turn him over to the United States, Powell told the UN: "We asked a friendly security service to approach Baghdad about extraditing al-Zarqawi and providing information about him and his close associates. This service contacted Iraqi officials twice, and we passed details that should have made it easy to find al-Zarqawi. The network remains in Baghdad; al-Zarqawi still remains at large to come and go."[42]

➤ Abu Abdullah al-Iraqi was sent to Iraq by bin Laden to purchase poison gases several times between 1997 and 2000. He called his relationship with Saddam's regime "successful," Powell told the United Nations. [43]

➤ Mohamed Mansour Shahab, a smuggler hired by Iraq to transport weapons to bin Laden in Afghanistan, was arrested by anti-Saddam Kurdish forces in May 2000.

➤ Deroy Murdoch, writing for the Hoover Institution, reported on "Hisham al-Hussein, the former second secretary at Iraq's embassy in Manila. The Philippine government expelled him on February 13, 2003, just five weeks before the start of Operation Iraqi Freedom. Cell phone records indicate he had spoken with Abu Madja and Hamsiraji Sali, two leaders of Abu Sayyaf, al Qaeda's de facto franchise for the Philippines. The timing was particularly suspicious, as he had been in contact with the Abu Sayyaf terrorists just before and after they conducted an attack in Zamboanga City.[44]

➤ "Abu Sayyaf's nail-filled bomb exploded on October 2, 2002, injuring twenty-three individuals and killing two Filipinos and one American. That American was U.S. Special Forces Sergeant First Class Mark Wayne Jackson, age forty."[45]

➤ Vice President Dick Cheney sat down with Tim Russert, host of NBC's *Meet the Press*, in 2004. Here is how Cheney summarized the evidence:

> **Russert:** But is there a connection [between Iraq and al Qaeda]?
>
> **Cheney:** We don't know. You and I talked about this two years ago. I can remember you asking me this question just a few days after the original attack. At the time I said no, we didn't have any evidence of that. Subsequent to that, we've learned a couple of things. We learned more and more that there was a relationship between Iraq and al Qaeda that stretched back through most of the decade of the '90s, that it involved training, for example on BW [biological weapons] and CW [chemical weapons], that al

Qaeda sent personnel to Baghdad to get trained on the systems that are involved, the Iraqis providing bomb-making expertise and advice to the al Qaeda organization.[46]

> CIA director George Tenet and Secretary of State Colin Powell testified that the trail of meetings between Iraq and al Qaeda stretch back to the early 1990s. Tenet wrote the Senate Intelligence Committee on October 7, 2002, that the CIA and other American intelligence services had amassed "solid reporting" of contacts between Iraq and al Qaeda going back a decade.[47]

> Speaking to the United Nations, Powell said that the U.S. had documented "decades-long experience with respect to ties between Iraq and al Qaeda."[48] These ties went back "to the early and mid-1990s when bin Laden was based in Sudan . . . [and] Saddam and bin Laden reached an understanding that al Qaeda would no longer support activities against Baghdad."[49] At a hearing of the Senate Foreign Relations Committee on September 26, 2002, Powell testified: "There is evidence of linkage between al Qaeda and Iraq. There is not linkage to 9-11 that we are aware of, but I can't dismiss that possibility."

To those who contend that Saddam Hussein was a secular strongman with no connection to radical Islamic terror organizations, remember that the record of his cooperation with other Islamist terrorist organizations is clear. Hamas opened an office in Baghdad in 1999, and Iraq hosted conferences attended by Palestine Islamic Jihad.

Or consider the chart on the following page. Deroy Murdock, a member of the Council on Foreign Relations, developed it for a presentation to the Hoover Institution at Stanford University.

As Murdock notes, many of the terror attacks Iraq paid for killed Americans. One was "Abigail Litle, the daughter of a Baptist minister, just fourteen years old when she was killed on an Israeli bus on March 5, 2003."[53]

Saddam Hussein sent $25,000 "bonus checks" to the families of PLO suicide bombers. "These bonus checks were handed out at ceremonies where banners proclaimed the friendship of the PLO's Yasser Arafat and Saddam Hussein."[54]

**Terrorist Organizations Given Funds, Shelter, and/or Training by Saddam Hussein[50]**

| Organization | Total Killed | Total Wounded | Americans Killed[51] | Americans Wounded |
|---|---|---|---|---|
| Abu Nidal Organization | 407 | 788 | 10 | 58 |
| Ansar al-Islam[52] | 114 | 16 | 1 | 0 |
| Arab Liberation Front | 4 | 6 | 0 | 0 |
| Hamas | 224 | 1,445 | 17 | 30 |
| Kurdistan Workers Party (KWP) | 44 | 327 | 0 | 2 |
| Mojahedin-e Khalq (MEK) | 17 | 43 | 7 | 1 |
| Palestine Liberation Front | 1 | 42 | 1 | 0 |
| **Total** | **811** | **2,667** | **36** | **91** |

Iraq also provided diplomatic help to Islamic extremists. Abu Abbas, former secretary general of the Palestinian Liberation Front, hijacked the Italian cruise ship *Achille Lauro* on October 7, 1985. Murdock details what happened next. "At one point, they segregated the Jewish passengers on board. One of them was a sixty-nine-year-old New York retiree named Leon Klinghoffer. He happened to be confined to a wheelchair. Without mercy, Abu Abbas's men shot Klinghoffer, then rolled him, wheelchair and all, into the Mediterranean."[55]

Abu Abbas escaped aboard an Egypt Air jet. "However, four U.S. fighter planes forced the airliner to land at a NATO base in Sicily. Italian officials took the hijackers into custody. But Abbas possessed the ultimate get-out-of-jail card: an Iraqi diplomatic passport."[56]

Bettino Craxi, then Italy's prime minister, explained to a UPI correspondent on October 14, 1985: "Abu Abbas was the holder of an Iraqi diplomatic passport.... The plane was on an official mission, considered covered by diplomatic immunity and extra-territorial status in the air and on the ground." So Abbas escaped justice. He ended up in Baghdad in 1994, living in a villa supplied by the Iraqi dictator. American soldiers captured Abbas in 2003 in Iraq. If Saddam was a devoutly secular strongman hated by radical Islamists, why did he provide Abbas with an Iraqi passport and support him in splendor in Iraq?

Saddam also sheltered other Islamic terrorists. The infamous Abu Nidal lived in Iraq from 1999 to 2002, when the terrorist leader "accidentally" shot himself in the head four times. The Associated Press reported on August 21, 2002, that Nidal's Beirut office said he entered Iraq "with the full knowledge and preparations of the Iraqi authorities."[57]

Some skeptics still dismiss the emerging evidence of a long-standing link between Iraq and al Qaeda by contending that Saddam and bin Laden did not like each other.

But self-interest can trump personal chemistry. There are many "Hitler-Stalin" partnerships between international terrorists and Muslim dictators. Saddam and bin Laden had common enemies, common purposes, and interlocking needs. They shared a powerful hate for America and the Saudi royal family. They both saw the Gulf War as a turning point. Saddam suffered a crushing defeat that he had repeatedly vowed to avenge. Bin Laden regards the U.S. as guilty of war crimes against Iraqis and believes that non-Muslims shouldn't have military bases on the holy sands of Arabia. Al Qaeda's avowed goal since 1990 has been the removal of American forces from Saudi Arabia, where they stood in harm's way solely to contain Iraq.

The most compelling reason for bin Laden to have worked with Saddam is money. Al Qaeda operatives have testified in federal courts that the terror network was always desperate for cash. Senior employees fought bitterly about the $100 difference in pay between Egyptians and Saudis (the Egyptians made more). One al Qaeda member who was connected to the 1998 embassy bombings told a U.S. federal court how bitter he was that bin Laden could not pay for his pregnant wife to see a doctor.

Saddam adopted an increasingly Islamist pose after the 1991 Gulf War. At a Popular Islamic Conference in Iraq, one of Saddam's top aides, Izzat Ibrahim al-Douri, said: "We are blessed in this country for having the Islamic holy warrior Saddam Hussein as a leader, who is guiding the country in a religious holy war against the infidels and nonbelievers."[58]

Starting in 1990, Saddam held terror conferences under the guise of "Islamic" conferences, gathering an array of Islamist terrorist cadres. "Beginning in June 1990, Saddam inaugurated a series of 'Popular

Islamic Conferences' in Baghdad. One such conference ended on January 13, 1991, four days before the Gulf War. With hundreds of thousands of American soldiers on Iraq's borders, the clerics ended the conference with a call for 'holy war' if the coalition attacked. Six days later, the general secretariat of the conference issued a statement calling jihad the duty of all Muslims."[60]

Stephen Hayes adds: "The Islamic conferences were not just another of Saddam's attempts to ingratiate himself with the fundamentalists. According to several U.S. officials, the summits were crawling with Iraqi intelligence agents recruiting these radicals to help fight a terror war against the West."[59]

* * *

No connection? Well, al Qaeda and the Iraqis certainly had a lot of meetings, money changed hands, some terrorist training seems to have occurred in Iraq, a lot of personnel—including Abu Musab al-Zarqawi—moved freely through the Iraqi police state. In other words, there *are* connections.

None of this means that Iraq ran al Qaeda or had foreknowledge of its most gruesome attacks. It certainly does not mean Iraq was behind the September 11 attacks or even knew about them in advance.

For there to be "no connection," between Iraq and al Qaeda, it would mean no meetings, no money, no training, and no movement of personnel. On the strength of much weaker evidence, Saudi Arabia is "connected" to al Qaeda. Why is Iraq the one nation given the benefit of the doubt?

# TERRORISM IS CAUSED BY POVERTY

*"We fight against poverty because hope is an answer to terror."*

—PRESIDENT GEORGE W. BUSH[1]

**NEARLY EVERYONE** from the president[2] to former vice president Al Gore to former White House economic adviser Laura Tyson[3] to the dean of Harvard's Kennedy School of Government seems to think poverty is a major cause, if not *the* cause, of terrorism.[4]

Everyone, that is, except the scholars who actually study terrorists.

At first, it seems quite plausible that terrorists are economically deprived persons, driven by desperation. After all, the instinct goes, a person with a good education, a decent salary, and a loving family has a lot to live for. Terrorists, who often say that they are impatient to die, must have none of these advantages.

Except that most of them do.

Perhaps the most authoritative study of terrorist demographics was recently published by Marc Sageman, who teaches at the University of Pennsylvania.[5]

Sageman is not your typical Ivy League expert. He was a CIA case officer working with the anti-Soviet Afghan rebels in Islamabad, Pakistan, from 1987 to 1989. For the past decade, he has practiced forensic psychiatry, which means that he devotes many hours to "interviewing, analyzing, and writing and testifying about murderers."[6]

Then came September 11. "After leaving the CIA, I was happy in my naïve belief that I had left all that behind me. But after 9-11, like everyone, I wanted to do something."[7]

What he decided to do was compile one of the largest databases of terrorists in the world outside of government hands. He collected 400 biographies of (mostly al Qaeda) terrorists from publicly available records, assembling the data in a sophisticated matrix. Fusing his skills as a CIA officer with those of forensic psychiatry and social science, Sageman was looking for patterns that would become visible only after surveying hundreds of cases.

The results surprised him. While he had learned a lot about common killers over the years, some of it firsthand, he realized that "nothing in my experience with solitary murderers, even mass murderers, helps me understand the collective murder-suicides of September 11, 2001."[8] The thought patterns of murderers and political killers, Sageman came to understand, are just too different.

Sageman's database reveals patterns that confound most of the conventional wisdom about terrorists.

> Most people think that terrorism comes from broken families, ignorance,
> immaturity, lack of occupational responsibilities, weak minds susceptible
> to brainwashing—the sociopath, the criminals, the religious fanatic, or,
> in this country, some believe they're just plain evil.[9]
>
> Taking these perceived root causes in turn, three-quarters of my sample came from the upper middle class. The vast majority—90 percent—came from caring, intact families. Sixty-three percent had gone to college, as compared with the 5 to 6 percent that's usual for the Third World. These are the best and brightest of their societies in many ways.[10]

These people are not poor, nor are they deprived of opportunities. "[A]bout three-fourths of global Salafi Mujahedin [the radical Islamic movement of which al Qaeda is part] was solidly upper- or middle-class," Sageman writes, "refuting the argument that terrorism arises from poverty."[11]

What about the roughly one-quarter of terrorists from poor backgrounds? All of them are either Arab emigrants from Morocco or Algeria or French Catholics who converted to Islam, often in French prisons.[12] Most are beneficiaries of a generous European welfare state, receiving free or low-cost housing, free education (through graduate school), free medical care, and a small stipend for daily expenses. By the standards of the Third World, these people are not poor. What these poorer terrorists have in common with their well-heeled comrades is a sense of social exclusion or alienation, a point we will return to.

Sageman's study challenges other notions about terrorists. He finds that, on the whole, al Qaeda recruits are not immature or easily impressionable youngsters. They join the bin Laden network at the average age of twenty-six, according to Sageman's research.

Nor have they been denied opportunities for advancement. Many are professionals, mostly with backgrounds in science or engineering, or skilled semi-professionals, such as police officers or mechanics. There is a pattern to their educational choices, however. Very few of the terrorists in Sageman's sample studied the liberal arts or, interestingly, religion. Indeed, most were not very religious before joining the terror organization.

Seventy-three percent of Sageman's sample were married men. Most of the rest were teenagers or students. Again, this does not support the idea of destitution and desperation as a driving force for terrorism; employed, educated men in the Arab world are more likely to find wives than jobless and uneducated ones.

Bringing the picture into focus, we see educated people from intact families, who went on form families of their own, who live productive lives in a profession or skilled semi-profession. Just looking at the demographic details, we see the pattern of social and economic striving that is the basis for any successful society. Sageman observes: "An argument can be made that, far from being a product of falling expectations, the jihad was more a result of rising expectations among its members."[13]

If the catalyst was not poverty or the loss of opportunities, what transformed these men from pillars of their societies to enemies of it and ours? Were they crazy? Sageman doesn't think so.

> As a psychiatrist, originally I was looking for any characteristics common to these men. But only four of the 400 had any hint of a disorder. This is below the worldwide base-rate for thought disorders. So they are as healthy as the general population.[14]

Sageman doesn't seem surprised by the lack of mental disorders.

> While terrorism is a profoundly anti-social activity, from the terrorists' point of view, it is also a highly social one. It is carried out by groups— groups that don't tolerate sociopaths like Unabomber Ted Kaczynski.[15]

Sageman's research, which we will return to, is backed by the findings of other scholars. The demographics of Palestinian terrorists have been extensively examined and all the research fits the same pattern: the terrorists, especially suicide bombers, tend to be drawn from the middle class or better and have a much higher level of education than their countrymen. Consider two recent studies of the demographics of Palestinian terrorists.

While working for a United Nations relief agency, Nasra Hassan spent three years, from 1996 to 1999, interviewing Palestinian terrorists in the Gaza Strip. Hassan noted: "None of them were uneducated, desperately poor, simple-minded, or depressed. Many were middle-class, and, unless they were fugitives, held paying jobs. . . . Two were the sons of millionaires."[16]

Claude Berrebi, a Princeton University economist, created a database of 285 suicide bombers' biographies, drawing on material published in the Arabic-language magazines of Hamas, Palestinian Islamic Jihad, and the Palestinian National Authority from 1987 to 2002.[17] Suicide bombers tend to come from better-off families than average, Berrebi found. Less than 15 percent of suicide bombers were from poor families, while 30 percent of Palestinians of comparable age (ages sixteen to fifty in both samples) were poor.[18]

Nor were they uneducated. Some 60 percent of suicide attackers have attended or completed college, compared to less than 20 percent of the Palestinian population.[19]

Foreign anti-democratic terrorists in Iraq hail from the same backgrounds as other radical Islamic killers. Israeli researcher Reuven Paz conducted a study of 154 Arab terrorists killed in Iraq in 2004 and found that "many of the bombers were married and well educated" and from well-off Saudi families.[20] Reuven's research was based on web postings by radical Islamic groups, notices not meant for the outside world but the friends and family of deceased terrorists. "Many are students or from wealthy families," Reuven noted, "the same sociological characteristics as the September 11 hijackers."[21]

Consider two examples. One was a medical student named Ahmed Said Ghandi; he died in a suicide bombing that killed twenty-two people. Another was "the reigning kung fu champion of Jordan."[22] Doctors and Olympic-class athletes do not hail from the bottom of any society. Something else, not poverty, was driving these people to kill.

Other studies confirm the same pattern. The evidence, according to an academic peer-reviewed study written by Princeton economist Alan B. Krueger and Charles University (Prague) associate professor Jitka Maleckova, "suggests little direct connection between poverty or education and participation in terrorism. Indeed, the available evidence indicates that compared with the relevant population, members of Hezbollah's militant wing of Palestinian suicide bombers are at least as likely to come from economically advantaged families and have a relatively high level of education" as not.[23]

Interestingly, surveys of terrorists from the 1960s and 1970s reveal the same pattern: that terrorism is primarily a middle-class occupation. Krueger and Maleckova cite a set of data compiled by Charles Russell and Bowman Miller, tracking 350 terrorists in Latin America, Europe, and Asia (including the Middle East) from 1966 to 1976—major terrorism's first decade.[24] Their conclusion: More than two-thirds of arrested terrorists "came from the middle or upper classes in their respective nations or areas. . . . The vast majority of these individuals involved in terrorist activities as cadres or leaders are quite well educated. In fact, approximately two-thirds of these identified terrorists are persons with some university training, university graduates, or post-graduate students."[25]

Every study that I have been able to find examining a large sample of terrorists and drawing statically valid results comes to the conclusion that terrorists are not uniformly poor, uneducated, or desperate individuals. In fact, these studies come to the opposite conclusion. More often than not, terrorists come from the moneyed, educated elites of their societies.

Perhaps terrorists (who are not poor) are motivated by concern about the perceived poverty of their fellow countrymen? This is possible, but seems unlikely. If the poverty of their people were an important issue, then economic deprivation would be regularly cited in terrorist manifestos or audiotapes. Yet when one reads the long lists of "injustices" suffered by the people the terror group claims to represent, poverty rarely, if ever, is mentioned. Terrorists tracts, especially those distributed by al Qaeda and its various affiliates and front groups, rarely mention economic concerns at all.

If sympathy with the poor was a major motivation for terrorists, the poorest countries would produce the most terrorists. Despite the odd al Qaeda figure from Tanzania or the Koromos Islands, most hail from oil-rich lands or Western Europe. Nor do the world's poorest nations suffer more terrorism than richer countries. While violence and civil war are common in the planet's most destitute countries, terrorism in Burma, Chad, and so on is all but unheard of. And when the terrorists do attack in poor nations, the target is almost invariably a U.S. embassy or another building affiliated with a foreign power, and the attackers usually come from richer countries.

Finally, a terrorist attack, as well as the resulting clampdown by the police and military, tends to be economically harmful: businesses relocate, investors retreat, roadblocks and other measures restrict the movements of workers and customers. Consider the economy of the West Bank, which has been devastated by bombings as well as by Israeli roadblocks. The target government (Israel) has suffered little, while the local Palestinians have been made jobless by the thousands. If a terrorist's goal was economic development, each car-bomb blast would move him further from that goal.

Consider the targets of terrorists. New clinics, schools, and bridges designed to improve the local economy are frequent scenes of bombings. If improving the economic lot of their nation's poor was a goal, they would not select targets certain to damage the economy. They would bomb symbols of government power, not banks, restaurants, and roads. If terrorists were focused on alleviating the misery of their fellow countrymen, why would they specially target aid workers who are trying to deliver free medical care or provide clean water?

The reason is simple and carries us far from the idea that poverty provokes terror. The terror network gets no political benefit, no credit, for these good works. They are, in fact, put at a disadvantage—others are building a base of support in the community while they are not. That is why aid workers are treated as political enemies and killed or kidnapped. From a terrorist's perspective, they *are* political enemies—rivals as much as any government or other terrorist bands. This suggests that terrorists are more concerned with winning political points than righting economic wrongs.

Terrorism is a continuation of politics by deadly means; its goals are inherently political and not economic. The chief aim of most significant terrorist campaigns—from the Tamil Tigers in Sri Lanka to al Qaeda—is to force a government to yield sovereign control over some slice of territory to the terror group. The Tamil Tigers want their state. Al Qaeda wants, among other things, the closure of U.S. bases in Saudi Arabia with the aim of taking control of the oil kingdom. These are simply not economic goals, but political ones.

So why do people from middle-class families and good educations—the majority of recruits—join terror networks? This is a deep and complicated question. There are three interrelated causes that seem to be supported by available statistics: alienation, personal bonds with terrorists, and group dynamics.

## Alienation
Returning to Sageman's sample of al Qaeda and other terrorists, we discover that "80 percent were in some way totally excluded from the society they lived in."[2b] They were foreign students who did not fit in or

immigrants who did not assimilate. Seventy percent of the terrorists in Sageman's sample joined a terror group while living outside their homeland.

My own research into the September 11 attacks supports Sageman's view. The Hamburg cell, which planned and carried out the attacks, was born when a group of Muslim immigrants at a German technical school came together. All seemed alienated and friendless until they united. Mohamed Atta, the September 11 ringleader, was originally staying with a German host family. That family, interviewed by a colleague of mine at the *Sunday Times* (of London), were German liberals who believed that cultural exchange could bridge the divide between the West and Middle East. To their horror, they watched Atta become more and more alienated. He would cover his eyes whenever a commercial featuring a bikini-clad model appeared on television; he grew increasingly hostile to Western music and insisted on cooking his native cuisine. Overwhelmed by Western society, he was friendless and alone, according to the German family. Eventually, he moved out and spent as much time as possible with fellow Muslim immigrants. He met other students like himself and, tragically for more than 3,000 innocents, an al Qaeda recruiter, who led him to the jihad.

## Personal bonds

Eighty-eight percent of terrorists in the Sageman study were related by blood, marriage, or friendship to other terrorists.[27] Sixty percent of them worshipped at one of ten mosques worldwide or attended one of two schools in Indonesia (both of which are now closed).[28] "So you're talking about a very select, small group of people," Sageman concludes. "This is not as widespread as people think."

Sageman sees a "common trajectory" for the terrorists in his study. Alienated and far from home, they sought out people like themselves and simply made the wrong friends, who were connected to the global jihad.

> When they became homesick, they did what anyone would and tried to congregate with people like themselves, whom they would find at mosques. So they drifted towards the mosque, not because they were

religious, but because they were seeking friends. They moved in together, in apartments, in order to share the rent and also to eat together—they were mostly *halal*, those who observed the Muslim dietary laws, similar in some respects to the kosher laws of Judaism. Some argue that such laws help to bind a group together since observing them is something very difficult and more easily done in a group. A micro-culture develops that strengthens and absorbs the participants as a unit.

## Group dynamics

Once a network of friendships forms into a cell, certain group dynamics take over. It becomes hard to back out. Like Communist traitors in the UK and the U.S., the cell members feel that they cannot betray their friends. As Sageman writes:

> These cliques, often in the vicinity of mosques that had a militant script advocating violence to overthrow the corrupt regimes, transformed alienated young Muslims into terrorists. It's all really group dynamics. You cannot understand the 9-11 type of terrorism from individual characteristics. The suicide bombers in Spain are another perfect example. Seven terrorists sharing an apartment and one saying "Tonight we're all going to go, guys." You can't betray your friends, and so you go along. Individually, they probably would not have done it.[29]

In time, the group gives an empty life purpose and the secrecy involved imbues it with a sense of importance and drama. Nasra Hassan interviewed a Hamas leader, who explained how the organization uses indoctrination to keep cell members motivated, explaining that "we focus his attention on paradise, on being in the presence of Allah, on meeting the Prophet Mohammed."[30]

The group usually records videotapes, in which a cell member declares allegiance to the cause and his willingness to die for it. The videos serve as a kind of blackmail, an implied threat to shame the individual if he backs out. Ariel Merari, a psychologist at Tel Aviv University, calls it a "brotherhood mentality," used by groups as diverse as the September 11 attackers, Japanese kamikaze pilots, and Irish hunger-strikers,

to ensure that the desire to remain an honored member of the brotherhood overcomes an individual's natural desire for self-preservation. History shows that it works.

Journalist Michael Bond surveyed the research by psychologists and
other experts on the demographics of terrorism for *New Scientist* magazine. He found that the average terrorists are "no less rational or sane, no
worse educated, no poorer and no more religious than anyone else."[31]

People become terrorists for many reasons. But poverty isn't one of
them.

# SUITCASE NUKES ARE A REAL THREAT

*"It is the duty of Muslims to prepare as much force*
*as possible to terrorize the enemies of God."*

—OSAMA BIN LADEN, MAY 1998[1]

*"Bin Laden's final act could be a nuclear attack on America."*

—GRAHAM ALLISON, WASHINGTON POST[2]

*"One hundred suitcase-size nuclear bombs were lost by Russia."*

—GERALD CELENTE, "PROFESSIONAL FUTURIST," BOSTON GLOBE[3]

LIKE EVERYONE ELSE rushing off the Washington subway one rush-hour morning, Ibrahim carried a small leather briefcase. No one paid him or his case much mind, except for the intern in the new Brooks Brothers suit who pushed past him on the escalator and banged his shin. "What do you have in there? Rocks?"

Ibrahim's training had taught him to ignore all provocations. *You will see*, he thought.

The escalator carried him up and out into the strong September sunlight. It was, as countless commentators would later say, a perfect day.

As he walked from the Capitol South metro stop, he saw the Republican National Committee headquarters to his right. Two congressional office buildings loomed in front of him. Between the five-story structures, the U.S. Capitol dome winked in the sun. It was walled off in a mini-Green Zone of jersey barriers and armed police. He wouldn't trouble them. He was close enough.

He put the heavy case down on the sidewalk and pressed a sequence of buttons on what looked like standard attaché-case locks.

It would be just a matter of seconds. When he thought he had waited long enough, he shouted in Arabic: "God is great!" He was too soon. Some passersby stared at him.

Two-tenths of a second later, a nuclear explosion erased the entire scene.

Birds were incinerated mid-flight. Nearly 100,000 people—lawmakers, judges, tourists—became super-heated dust. Only raindrop-sized dollops of metal—their dental fillings—remained as proof of their existence.

In tenths of a second—less time than the blink of a human eye—the ten-kiloton blast wave pushed down the Capitol (toppling the Indian statute known as *Freedom* at the dome's top), punched through the pillars of the U.S. Supreme Court, smashed down the three palatial Library of Congress buildings, and flattened the House and Senate office buildings.

The blast wave raced outward, decapitating the Washington Monument, incinerating the Smithsonian and its treasures, and reducing to rubble the White House and every office tower north to Dupont Circle and south to the Anacostia River. The secondary, or overpressure, wave jumped over the Potomac, spreading unstoppable fires to the Pentagon and Arlington, Virginia. Planes bound for Reagan and Dulles airports tumbled from the sky.

Tens of thousands were killed instantly. By nightfall, another 250,000 people were dying in overcrowded hospitals and impromptu emergency rooms set up in high school gymnasiums. Radiation poisoning would kill tens of thousands more in the decades to come.

America's political, diplomatic, and military leadership was simply wiped away. As the highest-ranking survivor, the postmaster general took charge. He moved the capital to Cheyenne, Wyoming.

• • •

That is the nightmare—or one version, anyway—of the nuclear suitcase.

In the aftermath of the September 11 attacks, this nuclear nightmare did not seem so fanciful.

A month after September 11, senior Bush administration officials were told that an al Qaeda terrorist cell had control of a ten-kiloton atomic bomb from Russia and was plotting to detonate it in New York City. CIA director George Tenet told President Bush that the source, code-named "Dragonfire," had said the nuclear device was already on American soil.[4] After anxious weeks of investigation, including surreptitious tests for radioactive material in New York and other major cities, Dragonfire's report was found to be false.[5] New York's mayor and police chief would not learn of the threat for another year.[6]

The specter of the nuclear suitcase bomb is particularly potent because it fuses two kinds of terror: the horrible images of Hiroshima and the suicide bomber, the unseen shark amid the swimmers. The fear of a suitcase nuke, like the bomb itself, packs a powerful punch in a small package. It also has a sense of inevitability. A December 2001 article in the *Boston Globe* speculated that terrorists would explode suitcase nukes in Chicago, Sydney, and Jerusalem . . . in 2004.[7]

Every version of the nuclear suitcase bomb scare relies on one or more strands of evidence, two from different Russians and one from a former assistant secretary of defense.

The scare started, in its current form, with Russian general Alexander Lebed, who told a U.S. congressional delegation visiting Moscow in 1997—and, later that year, CBS's series *60 Minutes*—that a number of Soviet-era nuclear suitcase bombs were missing.

It was amplified when Stanislav Lunev, the highest-ranking Soviet military intelligence officer ever to defect to the United States, told a congressional panel that same year that Soviet special forces might have smuggled a number of portable nuclear bombs onto the U.S. mainland to be detonated if the Cold War ever got hot.

The scare grew when Graham Allison, a Harvard professor who served as an assistant secretary of defense under President Clinton, wrote a book called *Nuclear Terrorism: The Ultimate Preventable Catastrophe*. In that slim volume, Allison worries about stolen warheads, self-made bombs, and suitcase nukes. Published in 2004, the work has been widely cited by the press and across the blogosphere.

Let's walk back the cat, as they say in intelligence circles. The foundation of all main nuclear suitcase stories is a string of interviews given by General Lebed in 1997.

Lebed told a visiting congressional delegation in June 1997 that the Kremlin was concerned that its arsenal of one hundred suitcase-sized nuclear bombs would find their way to Chechen rebels or other Islamic terrorists. He said that he had tried to account for all one hundred but could find only forty-eight. That meant fifty-two were missing. He said the bombs would fit "in a 60-by-40-by-20 centimeter case" and would be "an ideal weapon for nuclear terror. The warhead is activated by one person and easy to transport."[8] It would later emerge that none of these statements were true.

Later that year, the Russian general sat down with Steve Kroft, an anchor for *60 Minutes*. The exchange could hardly have been more alarming.

**Kroft:** Are you confident that all of these weapons are secure and accounted for?

**General Alexander Lebed:** (through a translator) Not at all. Not at all.

**Kroft:** How easy would it be to steal one?

**Lebed:** It's suitcase-sized.

**Kroft:** You could put it in a suitcase and carry it off?

**Lebed:** It is made in the form of a suitcase. It is a suitcase, actually. You can carry it. You can put it into another suitcase if you want to.

**Kroft:** But it's already in a suitcase.

**Lebed:** Yes.

**Kroft:** I could walk down the streets of Moscow or Washington or New York, and people would think I'm carrying a suitcase?

**Lebed:** Yes, indeed.

**Kroft:** How easy is it to detonate?

**Lebed:** It would take twenty, thirty minutes to prepare.

**Kroft:** But you don't need secret codes from the Kremlin or anything like that.

**Lebed:** No.

**Kroft:** You are saying that there are a significant number that are missing and unaccounted for?

**Lebed:** Yes, there is. More than one hundred.

**Kroft:** Where are they?

**Lebed:** Somewhere in Georgia, somewhere in Ukraine, somewhere in the Baltic countries. Perhaps some of them are even outside those countries. One person is capable of actuating this nuclear weapon—one person.

**Kroft:** So you're saying these weapons are no longer under the control of the Russian military.

**Lebed:** I'm saying that more than one hundred weapons out of the supposed number of 250 are not under the control of the armed forces of Russia. I don't know their location. I don't know whether they have been destroyed or whether they are stored or whether they've been sold or stolen. I don't know.[9]

Nearly everything Lebed told visiting congressmen and *60 Minutes* was later contradicted, sometimes by Lebed himself. In subsequent news accounts, he said forty-one bombs were missing, at other times he pegged the number at fifty-two or sixty-two, eighty-four or even one hundred. When asked about this disparity, he told the *Washington Post* that he "did not have time to find out how many such weapons there were."[10] If this sounds breezy or cavalier, that is because it is.

Indeed, General Lebed never seemed to have made a serious investigation at all. A Russian official later pointed out that Lebed never visited the facility that houses all of Russia's nuclear weapons or met with its staff.[11] And Lebed—who died in a plane crash in 2002—had a history of telling tall tales.

As for the small size of the weapons and the notion that they can be detonated by one person, those claims also been authoritatively dismissed. The only U.S. government official to publicly admit seeing a suitcase-sized nuclear device is Rose Gottemoeller. As a Defense Department official, she visited Russia and the Ukraine to monitor compliance with disarmament treaties in the early 1990s. The Soviet-era weapon "actually required three footlockers and a team of several people to detonate," she said. "It was not something you could toss in your shoulder bag and carry on a plane or bus" [12]

Lebed's onetime deputy, Vladimir Denisov, said he headed a special investigation in July 1996—almost a year before Lebed made his charges—and found that no army field units had portable nuclear weapons of any kind. All portable nuclear devices—which are much bigger than a suitcase—were stored at a central facility under heavy guard.[13]

Lieutenant General Igor Valynkin, chief of the Russian Defense Ministry's 12th Main Directorate, which oversees all nuclear weapons, denied that any weapons were missing. "Nuclear suitcases . . . were never produced and are not produced," he said. While he acknowledged that they were technically possible to make, he said the weapon would have "a life span of only several months" and would therefore be too costly to maintain. Valynkin is referring to the fact that radioactive weapons require a lot of shielding. To fit the radioactive material and the appropriate shielding into a suitcase would mean that a very small amount of material would have to be used. Radioactive material decays at a steady, certain rate, expressed as "half-life," or the length of time it takes for half of the material to decay into harmless elements. The half-life of the most likely materials in the infinitesimal weights necessary to fit in a suitcase is a few months. So as a matter of physics and engineering, the nuclear suitcase is an impractical weapon. It would have to be rebuilt with new radioactive elements every few months.

Valynkin's answer was later expanded by Viktor Yesin, the former chief of staff of Russia's Strategic Missile Forces. Yesin was asked by Alexander Golts, a reporter at the Russian newspaper *Ezhenedelny Zhurnal*: "The nuclear suitcases—are they myth or reality?"

Let's start by noting that "nuclear suitcase" is a term coined by journalists. Journalistic parlance, if you wish. The matter concerns special compact nuclear devices of knapsack type. Igor Valynkin, commander of the 12th Main Directorate of the Defense Ministry responsible for nuclear ordnance storage, was absolutely honest when he was saying in an interview with *Nezavisimaya Gazeta* in 1997 that "there have never been any nuclear suitcases, grips, handbags, or other carryalls." As for special compact nuclear devices, the Americans were the first to assemble them. They were called Special Atomic Demolition Munitions (SADM). As of 1964, the U.S. Army and Marine Corps had two models of SADM at their disposal— M-129 and M-159. Each SADM measured 87 x 65 x 67 centimeters [34 x 26 x 26 inches]. A container with the backpack weighed 70 kilograms [154 lbs.]. There were about 300 SADMs in all. The foreign media reported that all these devices were dismantled and disposed of within the framework of the unilateral disarmament initiatives declared by the first President Bush in late 1991 and early 1992. The Soviet Union initiated production of special compact nuclear devices in 1967. These munitions were called special mines. There were fewer models of them in the Soviet Union than in the United States. All of these munitions were to be dismantled before 2000 in accordance with the Russian and American commitments concerning reduction of tactical nuclear weapons dated 1001. [When the Soviet Union collapsed, Yeltsin reiterated the commitment in January 1992.] Foreign Minister Igor Ivanov said at the conference on the Nuclear Weapons Nonproliferation Treaty in April 2000 that Russia had practically completed dismantling "nuclear mines." It means that Russia kept the promise Yeltsin once made to the international community.[14]

Yesin added that all "portable" nuclear weapons were strictly controlled by the KGB in the Soviet era and were held in a single facility on Russian soil, where they were regularly counted before they were dismantled. The special mines that the press calls "nuclear suitcases" are no more. American officials, including Gottemoeller, insist that there is no evidence that any are missing, stolen, or sold. American experts charged with monitoring the destruction of these weapons have repeatedly testified to Congress that no special mines are unaccounted for.

What about the Russian army units trained to use the special mines? Is it possible that a few such weapons remain in their hands? According to Yesin, "they always used simulators and dummy weapons. Needless to say, the latter looked like the real thing—the same size and weight, the same control panel. Instead of nuclear materials, however, they contained sand."[15]

Despite Lebed's many changing accounts, his reputation for exaggeration, and the denial of nearly every Russian official with knowledge of Russian nuclear weapons, his tale lives on in breathless newspaper articles and web posts. Perhaps the most amusing was an article in the *Sunday Express* (London) claiming that al Qaeda bought twenty "nuclear suitcases for 25 million pounds" (roughly $45 million) from "Boris" and "Alexy."[16] What, not Natasha?

Still, Graham Allison puts his faith in Lebed's story. How does Allison account for the high-level rebuttals? He makes two brief arguments. "Moscow's assurance that 'all nuclear weapons are accounted for' is wishful thinking, since at least four nuclear submarines with nuclear warheads sank and were never recovered by the Soviet Union."[17] (One was recovered by the U.S. in 1974.) This is true, but beside the point; the subs were carrying nuclear missiles, not nuclear suitcases.

Allison's more pointed rebuttal is:

The Russian government reacted to Lebed's claim in classic Soviet style, combing wholesale denial with efforts to discredit the messenger. In the days and months that followed, official government spokesmen claimed that (1) no such weapons ever existed; (2) any weapons of this sort had been destroyed; (3) all Russian weapons were secure and properly accounted for; and (4) it was inconceivable that the Russian government could lose a nuclear weapon. Assertions to the contrary, or even questions about the matter, were dismissed as anti-Russian propaganda or efforts at personal aggrandizement.[18]

Allison is unfairly summarizing the official Russian view. There is no contradiction between points (1) and (2) because (1) refers to suitcase nukes, a journalist term for a weapon that never existed. The portable nuclear devices—the special mines that filled three footlockers and weighed hundreds of pounds—were destroyed as required by U.S.–Russia treaties. We don't have to take Russia's word for this; the disposal and destruction of these weapons were supervised by expert American officials like Gottemoeller. So point (2) checks out. As for points (3) and (4), Russia's claims have been independently verified by U.S. officials. If Allison has specific evidence of misplaced nuclear suitcases, he doesn't provide it in either the hardcover or paperback editions of his book or in his speeches to the Council on Foreign Relations or elsewhere.

What about the testimony of Soviet defector Colonel Stanislav Lunev? Certainly his tale is cloaked in high drama. Lunev entered the congressional hearing room in a black ski mask and testified behind a tall screen. He described a portable nuclear device that was "the size of a golf club bag"[19] and testified that "one of my main directives was to find drop sites for mass destruction weapons" that would be smuggled into the U.S. using drug routes and detonated by special teams. Lunev did not testify that he saw those weapons, only that, as a TASS reporter working in Washington, D.C. (his cover as a military intelligence officer), his job was to scout for "drop sites."

I tracked Lunev down in suburban Maryland, where he is battling lymphatic cancer. Over the phone, he sounds like a bear of a man, with a charming Russian accent. He calls me "Riche," as in "Riche, you must switch off all recording devices." When I say I have no such devices, only a bad line, he agrees to call back. When he does, I ask him if he has ever seen a portable nuclear device.

"No," he says.

Then he asks if I have ever heard of Albuquerque, New Mexico. There is a museum there, he explains, that displays America's portable nuclear device, the SADM. "The Soviet model probably looks similar," he says, adding that he is not an expert in such things.

Finally, there is Graham Allison's book. It is a serious and valuable work, with many practical suggestions for arresting the spread of nuclear technology. Still, Allison's concerns about a nuclear suitcase-sized device rest on three shaky pillars: that Lebed was right about the missing suitcase nukes, that Stanislev Lunev's account is persuasive, and that Russian nuclear security is lax.

As we have seen, General Lebed's changing story is highly question-able and the nuclear mines have long since been dismantled. Allison him-self concedes that nuclear suitcases might not be operative. Speaking at a Council on Foreign Relations conference in September 2004, Allison said that the weapons General Lebed referred to are now at least seven years old and that "many of these would be beyond warranty," requiring extensive refurbishing to function at full power.[20]

Allison does not refer to Lunev by name, possibly because he does not know it. Lunev is not named in his congressional testimony and discov-ering his identity requires a bit of sleuthing. Allison does not cite Lunev's book or even acknowledge talking to him. (Lunev, a friendly and direct fellow, has never heard of Allison.)

As for Allison's contention that the Russians do not keep their nuclear weapons as secure as we do, he is quite right. But the Russians probably do well enough. Allison cites a number of cases in which nuclear material— though not bombs—was stolen from Russian reactors. Yet in each of the cases he cites, the thieves were caught before they could transfer the material. And the small amounts stolen could not have been, even if com-bined, converted into a single bomb. And there is no evidence that any of the Soviet Union's "special mines" have gone missing.

• • •

No one seriously doubts Osama bin Laden's intense desire for nuclear weapons, suitcase-sized or otherwise.

Michael Scheuer, the former head of the CIA's bin Laden station (and an outspoken critic of the Bush administration's conduct of the War on Terror), said that the CIA was aware of "the careful, professional manner in which al Qaeda was seeking to acquire nuclear weapons" since 1996.[21]

There is a plethora of human and documentary intelligence to support Scheuer's conclusion. Perhaps the most chilling is a fatwa that bin Laden asked for and received from Shaykh Naṣir bin Hamid al-Fahd in May 2003. It was called "A treatise on the legal status of using Weapons of Mass Destruction against infidels." The Saudi cleric concludes: "If a bomb that killed ten million of them and burned as much of their land as they have burned Muslims' land were dropped on them, it would be permissible."[22]

Fatwas are not enough. There are only three ways for al Qaeda to realize its atomic dreams: buy nuclear weapons, steal them, or make them. Each approach is virtually impossible.

Buying the bomb has not worked out well for al Qaeda. The terror organization has tried and, according to detainees, been scammed repeatedly.

In Sudan's decrepit capital of Khartoum, an al Qaeda operative paid $1.5 million for a three-foot-long metal canister with South African markings. Allegedly it was uranium from South Africa's recently decommissioned nuclear program. According to Jamal al-Fadl, an al Qaeda leader later detained by U.S. forces, bin Laden ordered that it be tested in a safe house in Cyprus. It was indeed radioactive, but not of sufficient quality to be weapons-grade.[23]

One American intelligence analyst said that he believed the material was taken from the innards of an x-ray machine. It is not clear what it actually was, but the canister was ultimately discarded by al Qaeda.

Al Qaeda's next attempt to buy bomb-making material involved Mamduh Mahmud Salim, a nuclear engineer. He was captured in Germany in 1998, before he could obtain any nuclear material.

In a third case, al Qaeda paid the Islamic Army of Uzbekistan for some radioactive material. It turned out that the uranium al Qaeda received was not sufficiently enriched to create an atomic blast, though it could be used in a "dirty bomb."[24]

For what it is worth, there are actually no documented cases of the Russian mafia or Russian officials selling nuclear weapons or material. Given that Russian gangsters have sold everything from small arms to aircraft carriers, this might seem surprising. Michael Crowley and Eric Adams, writing in *Popular Science* magazine, theorize that it might be that Russian security forces are less tempted by money than is commonly assumed or that Russian mobsters find other illicit material more profitable than nuclear material.[25] Whatever the reason, there is simply no known case of the Russian mob selling nuclear devices or parts to anyone, let alone to al Qaeda.

What about theft? Stealing a bomb—or its component parts—is far more difficult than it sounds. The United Nations International Atomic Energy Agency maintains a detailed database of thefts of highly enriched uranium, the kind needed to make an atomic bomb. There have been ten known cases of highly enriched uranium theft between 1994 and 2004. Each amounted to "a few grams or less."[26] The total loss is less than eight grams, and even these eight grams, which have differing levels of purity, could not be productively combined. To put these quantities in perspective, it takes some 15,900 grams to make a highly enriched uranium bomb.

Stealing highly enriched uranium is extremely difficult. Every nation with an active nuclear weapons program guards access to its breeder reactors and enrichment plants. Employee backgrounds are scrutinized and workers are under near-constant surveillance. Transporting radioactive material invites detection and is a constant danger to those moving it without shielding. If it were shielded, the immense weight of the small container would be a giveaway to authorities.

Could terrorists storm a reactor and steal the radioactive material? Not likely. An investigation by *Forbes* magazine reveals the difficulties:

> Assuming attackers could shoot their way past the beefed-up phalanx of armed guards, traffic barriers, and guard towers that now surround every nuclear plant, they'd still have to fight their way into the reactor building through multiple levels of remote-activated blast doors—where access requires the right key card and palm print—to get to the spent-fuel pond, says Michael Wallace, president of Constellation Energy's generation group, which operates five nuclear reactors. The pond where highly radioactive used fuel rods sit in 14-foot-long stainless steel assemblies cooling under 40 feet of water. Terrorists couldn't just grab this stuff and run because, unshielded, it gives off a lethal dose of radiation in less than a minute. To avoid exposure, terrorists would have to force workers to use a giant crane inside the reactor to load the assemblies into huge transfer casks, then open the mammoth doors of the reactor building and use another crane to lift the cask onto a waiting truck—all the while being shot at by the National Guard. [27]
>
> It may be easier to steal radioactive material outside the U.S.—but not much.

What about hijacking a plane and crash-diving it into a nuclear reactor? It would make a spectacular movie scene, but as *Forbes* explains, it would not cause much harm to those outside the plane.

Assume that terrorists could get past tightened airport security and fight off passengers to get through new, improved cockpit doors and take control of a plane. Even then they'd have to crash the jet directly into a reactor to have any chance of breaking containment. In 2002 the Electric Power Research Institute performed a $1 million computer simulation to assess such a risk. Conclusion: A direct hit from a 450,000-pound Boeing 767 flying low to the ground at 350 mph would ruin a plant's ability to make electricity but not break the reactor's cement shield. Reason: A reactor, smaller in profile than the Pentagon or World Trade Center, would not absorb the full force of the plane's impact. And, for all the force behind it, a plane, built of aluminum and titanium, has far less mass than the 20-foot-thick steel-and-concrete sarcophagus enclosing a nuclear reactor. It would be like dropping a watermelon on a fire hydrant from 100 feet.[28]

Another problem with theft is fencing the goods. Most uranium thieves have been caught when they tried to sell the small amounts of radioactive material they have stolen.[29]

And the difficulties of theft do not end once al Qaeda gets its prize.

Even if al Qaeda terrorists managed to steal a nuclear device or bought one from those standby villains of choice, Russian mobsters, they would still have to figure out how to break the codes and overturn the failsafes. All Russian and American devices have temperature and pressure sensors to defeat unauthorized use. Since intercontinental missiles are designed to pass through the upper atmosphere before descending to their targets, the terrorists would have to find a laboratory facility that could mimic the environment of the outer stratosphere. Good luck. Council on Foreign Relations fellow Charles Ferguson told the *Washington Post* that "you don't just get it [a nuclear weapon] off the shelf, enter a code, and have it go off."[30]

So could al Qaeda make its own bomb? It appears that the terror network has tried and failed.

In August 2001, bin Laden was envisioning attacks bigger than what happened on September 11. Almost a month before the attacks on New York and Washington, bin Laden and his deputy, Ayman al-Zawahiri, met with Sultan Bashiruddin Mahmood and Abdul Majeed, two officials once part of Pakistan's nuclear program. Mahmood had supervised the plant that enriched uranium for Pakistan's first bomb and later managed efforts to produce weapons-grade plutonium. Both scientists were arrested on October 23, 2001. They remain under house arrest in Pakistan.

At their meeting with bin Laden, they discussed plans to mine uranium from plentiful deposits in Afghanistan and talked about the technology needed to turn the uranium into bomb fuel.[31] It was these scientists who informed bin Laden that the uranium from Uzbekistan was too impure to be useful for bomb making.

Al Qaeda will keep trying, no doubt. But there is no evidence that they are near succeeding. A wide array of documents and computer hard drives found in al Qaeda safe houses reveals a serious effort to build weapons of mass destruction. The U.S. military also obtained a document with the sinister title of "Superbomb."[32]

In addition, CNN discovered a cache of documents at an al Qaeda safe house that outlined the terror network's WMD plans. David Albright, a physicist and president of the Institute for Science and International Security, was retained by CNN to evaluate the al Qaeda documents. In "Al Qaeda's Nuclear Program: Through the Window of Seized Documents," a research paper for a think tank linked to the University of California at Berkeley, Albright concluded: "Whatever al Qaeda had accomplished towards nuclear weapon capabilities, its effort in Afghanistan was 'nipped in the bud' with the fall of the Taliban government. The international community is fortunate that the war in Afghanistan set back al Qaeda's effort to obtain nuclear weapons."[33]

For now, suitcase-sized nuclear bombs remain in the realm of James Bond movies. Given the limitations of physics and engineering, no nation seems to have invested the time and money to make them. Both U.S. and the USSR built nuclear mines (as well as artillery shells), which were small but hardly portable—and all were dismantled by treaty by 2000. Alexander Lebed's claims and those of defector Stanislev Lunev were not based on direct observation. The one U.S. official who saw a small nuclear device said it was the size of three footlockers—hardly a suitcase. For now, the desire to obliterate cities is portable—inside the heads of believers—while, thankfully, the nuclear devices to bring that about are not.

# OLIVER NORTH WARNED US ABOUT AL QAEDA IN THE 1980s

*"It's scary when you think fifteen years ago the government
was aware of Osama bin Laden and his potential threat
to the security of the world."*

—UNNAMED E-MAIL WRITER, 2001

COLONEL OLIVER NORTH is the host of FOX News Channel's series *War Stories* and was a key figure in the Reagan administration's "Iran-Contra" affair. Yet to some of his many fans, he is much more: a prophet who warned America about the evil designs of Osama bin Laden back in the 1980s.

In the weeks after the September 11 attacks, a widely circulated e-mail allegedly documenting North's clairvoyance spammed much of the known universe. This account still turns up in the queries of talk-radio callers (where I first heard it) and on some political websites. It is provably false.

Under the headline "Oliver Twisted," Snopes.com collected a representative sample of this e-mail:

I was at a UNC lecture the other day where they played a video of Oliver North during the Iran-Contra deals during the Reagan administration. I was only 14 back then but was surprised by this particular clip. There was

Ollie in front of God and Country getting the third degree. But what he said stunned me. He was being drilled by some senator I didn't recognize who asked him:

"Did you not recently spend close to $60,000 for a home security system?"

Oliver replied, "Yes I did sir."

The senator continued, trying to get a laugh out of the audience, "Isn't this just a little excessive?"

"No sir," continued Oliver.

"No. And why not?"

"Because the life of my family and I were threatened."

"Threatened? By who."

"By a terrorist, sir."

"Terrorist? What terrorist could possibly scare you that much?"

"His name is Osama bin Laden."

At this point the senator tried to repeat the name, but couldn't pronounce it, which most people back then probably couldn't. A couple of people laughed at the attempt. Then the senator continued.

"Why are you so afraid of this man?"

"Because sir, he is the most evil person alive that I know of."

"And what do you recommend we do about him?"

"If it were me I would recommend an assassin team be formed to eliminate him and his men from the face of the earth."

The senator disagreed with this approach and that was all they showed of the clip.

It's scary when you think 15 years ago the government was aware of Osama bin Laden and his potential threat to the security of the world. I guess like all great tyrants they start small but if left untended spread like the virus they truly are.[1]

To some, this e-mail was plausible. After all, they remember North testifying in his U.S. Marine Corps uniform. They remember that he was harshly questioned by someone and they hazily recall something about North spending a lot of money on a home security system.

But these small truths are merely camouflage for a far bigger untruth. Without any further examination, the e-mail itself contains a number of tell-tale elements that should have tipped off any observant person. The writer claims that North's congressional hearings occurred when he was fourteen; that would make him twenty-eight in 2001. That is a little old for a college student. Next, the writer twice alludes to an unnamed senator playing to the audience. Anyone with a passing acquaintance with C-SPAN knows that senators rarely play to the audience—they play to the cameras and each other.

Other versions of this add another conspiratorial detail: that unnamed senator was . . . Al Gore.

The typos and poor language suggests someone who is careless with details—and yet there are many precise details here. Also, any laughing audience members would most likely be escorted out by the sergeant-at-arms.

A little investigation and this myth dissolves like early morning fog. North himself sent out a point-by-point rebuttal.

FROM THE DESK OF LTCOL OLIVER L. NORTH (USMC) RET.

NOVEMBER 28, 2001

OVER THE COURSE OF THE LAST SEVERAL WEEKS, I HAVE RECEIVED SEVERAL THOUSAND E-MAILS FROM EVERY STATE IN THE U.S. AND 13 FOREIGN COUNTRIES IN WHICH THE ORIGINATOR PURPORTS TO HAVE RECENTLY VIEWED A VIDEOTAPE OF MY SWORN TESTIMONY BEFORE A CONGRESSIONAL COMMITTEE IN 1987.

A COPY OF ONE OF THOSE E-MAILS IS ATTACHED BELOW. AS YOU WILL NOTE, THE ORIGINATOR ATTRIBUTES TO ME CERTAIN STATEMENTS REGARDING USAMA BIN LADEN AND OTHER MATTERS THAT ARE SIMPLY INACCURATE. THOUGH I WOULD LIKE TO CLAIM THE GIFT OF PROPHESY, I DON'T HAVE IT.

I DON'T KNOW WHO SAW WHAT VIDEO "AT UNC." (OR ANY-WHERE ELSE) BUT, FOR THE RECORD, HERE'S WHAT I DO KNOW:

1. IT WAS THE COMMITTEE COUNSEL, JOHN NIELDS, NOT A SENATOR WHO WAS DOING THE QUESTIONING.

2. THE SECURITY SYSTEM, INSTALLED AT MY HOME, JUST BEFORE I MADE A VERY SECRET TRIP TO TEHRAN, COST, ACCORDING TO THE COMMITTEE, $16K, NOT $60K.

3. THE TERRORIST WHO THREATENED TO KILL ME IN 1986, JUST BEFORE THAT SECRET TRIP TO TEHRAN, WAS NOT USAMA BIN LADEN, IT WAS ABU NIDAL (WHO WORKS FOR THE LIBYANS—NOT THE TALIBAN AND NOT IN AFGHANISTAN).

4. I NEVER SAID I WAS AFRAID OF ANYBODY. I DID SAY THAT I WOULD BE GLAD TO MEET ABU NIDAL ON EQUAL TERMS ANYWHERE IN THE WORLD BUT THAT I WAS UNWILLING TO HAVE HIM OR HIS OPERATIVES MEET MY WIFE AND CHILDREN ON HIS TERMS.

5. I DID SAY THAT THE TERRORISTS INTERCEPTED BY THE FBI ON THE WAY TO MY HOUSE IN FEB. 87 TO KILL MY WIFE, CHILDREN AND ME WERE LIBYANS, DISPATCHED FROM THE PEOPLE'S COMMITTEE FOR LIBYAN STUDENTS IN MCLEAN, VIRGINIA.

6. AND I DID SAY THAT THE FEDERAL GOVERNMENT HAD MOVED MY FAMILY OUT OF OUR HOME TO A MILITARY BASE (CAMP LEJEUNE, NC) UNTIL THEY COULD DISPATCH MORE THAN 30 AGENTS TO PROTECT MY FAMILY FROM THOSE TERRORISTS (BECAUSE A LIBERAL FEDERAL JUDGE HAD ALLOWED THE LIBYAN ASSASSINS TO POST BOND AND THEY FLED).

7. AND, FYI: THOSE FEDERAL AGENTS REMAINED AT OUR HOME UNTIL I RETIRED FROM THE MARINES AND WAS NO LONGER A "GOVERNMENT OFFICIAL." BY THEN, THE UNITED STATES GOVERNMENT HAD SPENT MORE THAN $2M PROTECTING THE NORTH FAMILY. THE TERRORISTS SENT TO KILL US WERE NEVER RE-APPREHENDED.

SEMPER FIDELIS,

OLIVER L. NORTH

North is many things to many people, but, as he admits, he is no Nostradamus.

# PRESIDENT BUSH SAID IRAQ WAS AN "IMMINENT THREAT" TO AMERICA

*"Some ask how urgent this danger is to America and the world. The danger is already significant, and it only grows worse with time. If we know Saddam Hussein has dangerous weapons today—and we do— does it make any sense for the world to wait to confront him as he grows even stronger and develops even more dangerous weapons?"*

—PRESIDENT GEORGE W. BUSH, 2002[1]

ENTER ANY TELEVISION GREEN ROOM, press club bar, or political blog and chances are you will meet someone who will insist that President Bush called Iraq an "imminent threat," as a justification for war.

The trouble is, there is no evidence that President Bush ever said Iraq was an "imminent threat," or anything similar. Indeed, he famously said otherwise.

Before the Iraq war, the president spoke to Congress and the world in the 2003 State of the Union address:

Some have said we must not act until the threat is imminent. Since when have terrorists and tyrants announced their intentions, politely putting us on notice before they strike? If this threat is permitted to fully and suddenly emerge, all actions, all words, and all recriminations would come too late. Trusting in the sanity and restraint of Saddam Hussein is not a strategy, and it is not an option.[4]

Read that again. Bush is saying that Iraq is not an imminent threat and therefore America should go to war before it is too late to prevent Saddam Hussein from giving catastrophic weapons to terrorists. After September 11, the president argues, we cannot wait for threats like Iraq to become "imminent." This is the root of Bush's controversial doctrine of "preemptive war." Whatever the merits of that doctrine, it is focused on threats that have not fully emerged, unlike say, North Korea. If Bush had said Iraq was an "imminent threat," he would be contradicting both his words in the State of the Union and his notion of preemptive war.

And, after an exhaustive Lexis-Nexis search, I could not find a single case of President Bush or his cabinet officials using the phrase "imminent threat" with respect to Iraq. There are dozens of instances in which the president or senior administration officials said that Iraq was a threat, but never an imminent one.

Spinsanity.org writer Ben Fritz has largely come to the same conclusion: there is no evidence that George Bush ever called Iraq an "imminent threat."[5]

> In recent weeks, a debate has raged over the phrase "imminent threat." Many liberal critics have asserted that a central claim in President Bush's case for war in Iraq was that Iraq posed an "imminent threat." They argue that it's now clear that no such threat existed, and thus the President's argument has been revealed as deceptive or illegitimate. Conservatives retort that Bush never actually used the phrase and in fact specifically used language indicating that the threat was not imminent on several occasions.
>
> As a factual matter, conservatives are largely correct and liberal critics and journalists are guilty of cheap shots or lazy reporting.[6]

Joshua Micah Marshall, whose liberal-leaning blog was at the forefront of this debate, argues that the 2002 National Security Strategy of the United States, an official government document, "essentially argues that the concept of 'imminent threat' must be reinterpreted to apply to countries like Iraq." Marshall must have a very fuzzy computer screen. Here is what the 2002 National Security Strategy actually says:

For centuries, international law recognized that nations need not suffer an attack before they can lawfully take action to defend themselves against forces that present an imminent danger of attack. Legal scholars and international jurists often conditioned the legitimacy of preemption on the existence of an imminent threat—most often a visible mobilization of armies, navies, and air forces preparing to attack.

We must adapt the concept of imminent threat to the capabilities and objectives of today's adversaries. Rogue states and terrorists do not seek to attack us by conventional means. They know such attacks would fail. Instead, they rely on acts of terror, and, potentially, the use of weapons of mass destruction—weapons that can be easily concealed, delivered covertly, and used without warning.[7]

The passage begins by reiterating the consensus view about international law and the doctrine of "imminent threat" and then begins to lay the groundwork for an alternative, broader understanding of threats in the post–September 11 world to include terrorists and rogue states. Iraq is not mentioned, let alone categorized as a threat of any kind.

The Center for American Progress, a Washington think tank run by former Clinton administration staffers, contends that the Bush administration called Iraq an "imminent threat" by not correcting reporters when they used the term.

Both examples cited by the Clintonian think tank involve reporters trying to put words into the mouth of White House press secretary Ari Fleischer. One example is enough to show the pattern. On October 16, 2002, a reporter said: "Ari, the president has been saying that the threat from Iraq is imminent, that we have to act now to disarm the country of its weapons of mass destruction, and it has to allow the UN inspectors in, unfettered, no conditions, so forth."

Fleischer replied, simply, "Yes."[8]

It seems that the only people who called Iraq an "imminent threat" were reporters.

As *National Review* columnist Jonah Goldberg notes: "Teams of rhetoric inspectors have been pouring over Bush's comments, utterances, speeches, and gesticulations for about as long as we've been looking for

WMD in Iraq and, to date, nobody has found a shred of proof that the president—or anyone else in his cabinet—ever once said Iraq or Saddam Hussein posed an 'imminent' threat to the United States."[9]

Still, this media myth has a life of its own. Just recently, the *New York Times* thundered: "Nothing found so far backs up administration claims that Mr. Hussein posed an imminent threat to the world."[10]

The idea that Bush called Iraq an "imminent threat" may be a criticism that jumped the Atlantic. British prime minister Tony Blair, a key Bush ally, certainly sold the Iraq war by claiming that Iraq could strike British forces on the Mediterranean island of Cyprus or that WMD could be deployed "in forty-five minutes," as one intelligence source memorably put it.

Whatever the merits of Blair's claims, it is clear that Bush made a different case—one that did not rely on the idea that Iraq was an imminent threat.

The longer this myth marches on, the more it becomes an imminent threat to the credibility of those who repeat it.

# HALLIBURTON MADE A FORTUNE IN IRAQ

*"But no matter how well we position ourselves in the market, I am struck by the extent to which the success or failure of a project is as much of a political decision as it is an engineering decision. Many times the engineering and technical aspects of a project can be relatively easy, but the project may be thwarted by unresolved political issues."*

—VICE PRESIDENT DICK CHENEY, IN *THE LEGEND OF HALLIBURTON*[1]

**THANKS TO THE IRAQ WAR,** military contractors are flying high. And, some, like Icarus, get burned.

Is Halliburton one of those? Some antiwar activists scoff even at the question. They have little doubt that Halliburton made massive profits on the Iraq War and that its former chief executive, Vice President Dick Cheney, greased the skids.

This line of antiwar thought is not new. In the 1960s, critics of the Vietnam War alleged that the military-industrial complex made millions from the war and that President Lyndon Johnson was rewarded when fighter jets were built in his home state of Texas.

So is Halliburton a war profiteer?

At first glance, it would seem that a firm cannot be a war profiteer if it had next to no profits. Halliburton earned $85 million from $3.6 billion in Iraqi contracts, a profit margin of roughly 2.4 percent, in 2003.[2] In the second quarter of 2004, Halliburton reported that it earned 1.4 percent profits on $1.7 billion worth of work in Iraq.[3] These are pitifully small rates of return.

Would you stick with a mutual fund that invested for less than a 2 percent return? Neither would Halliburton.

As a result of poor performance, Halliburton wants to sell the division that runs Iraqi operations, Kellogg, Brown & Root (KBR). It "has become an albatross for them," according to Jason E. Putnam of Victory Capital Management, which owns some two million shares of Halliburton.[4]

Could Halliburton be burying its Iraq profits elsewhere in its vast conglomerate? Not likely. The parent company itself is not very profitable: Mergent (formerly Moody's) reports that the company *lost* $979 million on total world-wide sales of $20.4 billion in 2004.[5]

Consider Halliburton's stock price. When current CEO David J. Lesar took over from Dick Cheney in August 2000, the company's shares were trading at $54. They sank to a record low of $8.70 in 2001. As of August 9, 2005, they trade at $58. If Halliburton had been raking in record profits in the war years (from 2003 to the present), its stock price would have climbed, not flatlined.

But these small, essential facts have not stopped critics from fulminating about secret deals, no-bid contracts, and yes, fat profits extracted from taxpayers.

Of course, corporate income statements are always a minefield of footnotes, lawyerly evasions, and results from myriad unrelated divisions. In this case, it appears that Halliburton was brought low by trial lawyers, not by Iraqi terrorists.

In 1998, while Dick Cheney was Halliburton's CEO, Halliburton acquired Dresser Industries, its former rival in the oil-services business. A Dresser subsidiary, Harbison-Walker Refractories (which Dresser had sold in 1992), had made insulating bricks and coatings with asbestos decades before asbestos was banned. But the courts found Halliburton liable anyway.

Halliburton finally settled its asbestos cases in December 2004, at a cost of $5.1 billion.[6]

The bottom line? Because of that payout, Halliburton has earned virtually no net profits for the last five years.

Is it possible that the Iraq operations made mountains of money, but simply not enough to compensate for the Everest of litigation costs? Independent journalists who have extensively investigated Halliburton's operations reluctantly conclude that Iraq has not been a geyser of money for the troubled industrial giant.

"The truth is that the conspiracy theories about the vice president's involvement in Halliburton's Iraq contracts are either unproven or flat-out wrong," writes *Fortune*'s Peter Elkind. "And while the company's Middle East operation is the subject of scathing audits and investigations, it's hardly raking in scandalous profits. Indeed, Kellogg, Brown & Root, the part of Halliburton's business that America seemed to hate because it was raking in far too much, is the part of the business Wall Street hates because it is making far too little."[7]

In early 2001, before September 11, Halliburton won the Defense Department's "super contract," which covers food, maintenance, construction, and other services worldwide.[8] In hopes of getting more government business, Halliburton "bid a price that was shockingly low. In addition to being reimbursed for what it spent, Halliburton would get a base fee of 1 percent and a maximum performance award of just 2 percent," noted Elkind.

After September 11, that already awarded "super contract" meant that Halliburton received an avalanche of unexpected business—at very low profit margins. Elkind found one anonymous source on the contract who said, "LOGCAP [the 'super contract'] could be the first cost-plus contract in history that's lost money."[9]

How is this possible? "Cost plus" does not cover every cost. Certain unforeseen costs (such as additional security) are not covered. When those unreimbursable costs exceed 3 percent—the maximum profit plus bonuses Halliburton can legally extract—the cost-plus contract becomes a money loser. And in Iraq, there are loads of unforeseen, unreimbursable expenses. Convoys are attacked, supplies are destroyed in mortar strikes, insurance rates surge, local contractors demand higher than anticipated "hazardous duty" wages, and so on.

The *Financial Times* reported in 2004 that Halliburton was strained by borrowing to pay the unexpectedly large expenses for the vast number of contractors needed to service the contract. The company had thought about getting out of LOGCAP and concluded it couldn't legally do it.[10]

Halliburton gets about two-thirds of its business in Iraq (which is about $12 billion) from LOGCAP and the remaining one-third from a contract called Restoring Iraqi Oil (RIO). The RIO contract was controversial because it was a sole-source contract awarded secretly before the war's onset. Whistleblowers, particularly Corps of Engineers auditor Bunnatine Greenhouse, have come forward to accuse KBR of all sorts of abuses. So far, the company has not been successfully prosecuted for these alleged abuses.

Why the secret no-bid contract? Because, as Halliburton CEO David Lesar pointed out, Halliburton was the only contractor the Defense Department "had determined was in a position to provide the services within the required time frame given classified prewar planning requirements."[11] This was confirmed by Congress's General Accounting Office.

In other words, no one else could do the job, so competitive bidding would not have accomplished much and prewar planning had to be kept secret in order to maintain the tactical advantage of surprise. And, yes, foreign governments read *Federal News* and other specialty publications to keep up to date on military contracts and to predict what the U.S. military is planning.

Wasn't Halliburton punished for bad service? While there was a blizzard of articles reporting that Halliburton was *threatened* with financial penalties, there is precious little evidence that those threats ever materialized. As far as I can tell, the only punishment imposed by the Pentagon on Halliburton was by the U.S. Army, which withheld $55.1 million in a food service billing dispute in April 2005—and then one month later awarded Halliburton $72 million in bonuses.[12]

The confusion of threatened penalties and actual ones corrupted the analysis in a MoveOn.org ad, which claimed that "the Pentagon caught Halliburton overcharging $61 million for gasoline." In fact, the Defense Contract Audit Agency found "potential overcharges of up to $61 million for gasoline." So $61 million was the upper limit on the estimated overbilling. And it was Halliburton's own auditors who caught the two Middle Eastern subcontractors overcharging for gasoline and turned them in. Halliburton offered to return $6.3 million to the Pentagon.

Dan Briody is the author of *The Halliburton Agenda: The Politics of Oil and Money*, the ur-text of the anti-Halliburton crowd. But Briody, an award-winning business journalist whose articles have graced *Forbes*, *Wired*, and the *Industry Standard*, presents a more careful indictment than many of his more partisan summarizers. He dismisses the "Cheney helped Halliburton win untold riches at taxpayer expense in Iraq" meme, writing, "Whether Dick Cheney had a hand in doling out contracts to his former company is unimportant, not to mention unprovable. Everyone in the industry and the military, with few exceptions, agrees that Halliburton was the right company for the job in Iraq because of its experience and the speed with which it was able to operate."[13]

Briody continues: "There was no question they were doing a quality job. Every military officer, past or present, I spoke with was more than satisfied with [Halliburton subsidiary] Kellogg, Brown & Root's performance. They made life better at the camps, and that made the troops happier. And as many commanding officers told me, a happy army is a motivated army."[14]

Briody, however, rightly criticizes Halliburton for something else. To understand Briody's criticism of Halliburton, one has to go back to 1992, when the Pentagon decided to expand the Logistics Civil Augmentation Program—LOGCAP.[15]

What the U.S. Army decided to do (conspiracy theorists take note!) while Dick Cheney was Secretary of Defense was consider combining all of its overseas contracts into one "super contract." This way, the Pentagon would only have "one necktie to pull" if they needed results rapidly. The Defense Department put out a request for proposals to research this concept. By all accounts, it was a competitive, lawful bid process.

The research contract was won by Kellogg, Brown & Root, which had been a Halliburton subsidiary since 1962. KBR recommended that the "super contract" be designed as a cost-plus arrangement, or what the Pentagon calls a "cost-reimbursement, indefinite-delivery/indefinite-quantity contract."[16] Implicit in this scheme is what economists cheerfully call a "moral hazard." Briody points out: "The structure of the contract encourages the contractor to spend excessive amounts of money.

When your profit is a percentage of the cost, the more you spend, the more you make."[17]

Actually, the truth is more complicated. As Stan Crock of *Business Week Online* points out:

> If the alternative is fixed-price contracts, under which the contractor has to eat cost overruns or squeeze profits by keeping expenses down, that won't work.... That's not what Iraq is like. Contractors would have to build in profit margins of 200 percent or even more because of the uncertainty over whether convoys would be blown up or facilities bombed—and the same products would have to be shipped or the same work done time and again. Imagine the howls in the halls of Congress when such practices come to light. The best solution probably is cost-plus contracts, with a heavy dose of oversight by the folks with green eye-shades at the Pentagon, by the denizens of Capitol Hill, and by the media—exactly what's happening now.[18]

What happens next is where Briody calls foul.

In 1992, the Army tendered its LOGCAP contract, and Halliburton won it. "And the lucky recipient of the first five-year LOGCAP contract was the very same company hired to draw up the plan in the first place: Kellogg, Brown & Root."[19] While this kind of cozy arrangement is typical in government contracting, it doesn't make it right or legal.

Briody interviewed a law professor who specializes in government contracts, who confirmed, "The idea behind the conflict of interest rules, as stated by the Code of Federal Regulations, is to prevent the existence of conflicting roles that might bias a contractor's judgment and prevent unfair competitive advantage."[20] Yet that is apparently what happened.

The contract came up for renewal in 1997, and Halliburton lost to DynCorp. In 2001, Halliburton's KBR division won it back. Unlike previous contracts, this one ran for ten years. Then came the September 11 attacks.

Briody, one of Halliburton's most persistent critics, sees little wrong in this arrangement: "LOGCAP became part of the popular vocabulary after Halliburton was awarded several contracts in Iraq, which some lawmakers saw as blatant favoritism to the company once headed by Cheney, who was CEO from 1995 to 2000. Many of these arguments were undercut by the fact that the task orders awarded to Halliburton, with the exception of Operation Restore Iraqi Oil, in Iraq fell under the existing LOGCAP contract, competitively bid back in 2001. This was, of course, true."[21]

Briody's main claim against Halliburton is that it won a defense contract in 1992 that it should not have. This is a long way from war profiteering and, anyway, the crime, if that is what it was, occurred in 1992—eleven years before the Iraq War. It might be government graft, but it is not war profiteering.

Halliburton has been a bad bet for investors—and for conspiracy theorists. Its Iraq operations have been barely profitable and the company has performed poorly. There is no evidence that Vice President Cheney had a hand in awarding the Iraq contracts, and they were awarded in 2001, long before the Iraq War in 2003 (except for the RIO contract, which was secretly but legitimately let in the months before the war). Even Halliburton's most devoted critic concedes as much. As they say in Texas, that dog won't hunt.

# RACIAL PROFILING OF TERRORISTS WORKS

*"Time to get real: Only Muslims commit Islamic terrorism. By definition. Ask Osama bin Laden, who called on Muslims, and Muslims only, to kill Americans wherever they can find us. Yet the New York Police Department has promised that its new policy of subway bag checks will be scrupulously random. This senseless sacrifice to political correctness will waste precious police resources with little improvement in public safety."*

—HEATHER MAC DONALD[1]

**AS A CONTRIBUTOR** to the Manhattan Institute's *City Journal* magazine, Heather Mac Donald devotes a lot of ink to calling for racial profiling of terrorists. In her view, political correctness requires random searches when past experience shows that it is Arab males commit most terror strikes.

She is not alone. Michael A. Smerconish, a *Philadelphia Daily News* columnist and radio talk-show host, recently wrote a book titled *Flying Blind: How Political Correctness Continues to Compromise Airline Safety Post 9-11.*

Mac Donald and Smerconish are making a strictly practical argument. If you strip away moral concerns and constitutional niceties, they say, it makes sense to search the kind of people who are most likely to be terrorists. It might not be pretty, they argue, but it would work.

Actually, it wouldn't. There are four overwhelming reasons why racial profiling would fail: Intent is not a physical characteristic; the category of

"Arab male" is too broad to be useful and too narrow to include all known al Qaeda suspects; profiling ignores the most likely al Qaeda counter-measure: recruiting non-Arab, non-male terrorists; and it would quickly become unenforceable.

## WHAT DOES A TERRORIST LOOK LIKE?

"We're fighting a war against young Arab male extremists, and yet our government continues to enforce politically correct 'random screening' of airline passengers," Smerconish writes, "instead of targeting those who look like terrorists."[2]

But who looks like a terrorist? Identifying deadly intent is an immensely complicated task.

The Transportation Security Administration (TSA) made a stab at divining deadly intent when it launched Screening of Passengers by Observation Techniques (SPOT) in 2004. "Passengers who flag concerns by exhibiting unusual or anxious behavior will be pointed out to local police, who will then conduct face-to-face interviews to determine whether any threat exists."[3] The September 11 hijackers did not display any unusual or anxious behavior; they had the kind of confidence that extremism imparts. The TSA's SPOT policy would catch only amateurs or the anxious businessman who desperately wants to catch the last flight out to see his son's Little League debut.

Whatever its shortcomings, SPOT at least targets intent, which is the relevant factor, not race. Like racial profiling, however, it drags in too many potential suspects, swamping security officers and clogging the system, making it more likely that a weary screener will wave a terrorist through.

## CATEGORICAL ERRORS

An effective screening system would separate the vast majority of ordinary travelers from potential terrorists—without missing a single suicide killer. That is an extremely difficult task, but not, as we will see, an impossible one.

Although Heather Mac Donald seems to recognize the difficulties of basing judgments on personal appearance, she quickly brushes them aside.

> There are, however, no ambiguous physical markers for being a Muslim. So rational Islamic-terror investigators must use a surrogate: apparent national origin. Al Qaeda and other Islamic-terror groups have drawn the vast majority of their members from what [syndicated columnist Charles] Krauthammer calls the "Islamic belt"—the Middle East, Pakistan, and North Africa, where white skin is not indigenous. Does that mean that Islamic-terror investigators are biased against people with darker skin? Of course not. Nor does it mean that antiterror agents should treat every Middle Easterner as a suspect. But they should be allowed to factor in apparent Muslim identity in evaluating whether certain behavior is suspicious. A string of eight Saudi males seeking to purchase large quantities of fertilizer at a garden supply store outside of Las Vegas should raise more questions than if eight Mormon missionaries were to do so.[4]

As a logistical matter, searching all people who appear to be Muslim will prove to be a daunting task. The U.S. census and the U.S. Immigration and Naturalization Service, by law, do not track citizens by religion, so there is no central database of Muslim Americans. Some 1.8 million Americans of Arab descent are either U.S. citizens or legal residents. Only 24 percent of Arab Americans are Muslim, according to the Arab American Institute.[5] More than one-quarter of people describing themselves "of Arab ancestry" in the 2000 census were from Lebanon,[6] and it is a good bet that a disproportionate number of Lebanese Americans are Christian.

Most American Muslims hail from outside the Arab world; indeed, many are homegrown. Only 25 percent of mosque-goers are of Arab extraction, according to U.S. State Department studies. By contrast, 33 percent are South Asian (from Pakistan, India, Bangladesh, or Afghanistan) and 30 percent are African American.[7]

As for searching Arab males, good luck. The Arab American population is 57 percent male, compared to the national average of 49 percent male. And more males of Arab ancestry were aged twenty to forty-nine (31 percent) than the American average (22 percent).[8] So concentrating on Arab males or young Arabs is not much help if one is trying to narrow the field.

Almost half of the Arab Americans counted in 2000 were native U.S. citizens;[9] they were either born in America or born to American parents abroad. The misconception that most Arabs in the United States are aliens with limited English is provably false, as census reports show. Three-quarters of people with Arab ancestry spoke only English at home or spoke English "very well."[10]

So searching all Arab males, or in Mac Donald's phrase, all those from the "Islamic belt," would fail to achieve the whole point of profiling, which is to narrow the number of people to be searched, to winnow the law-abiding from the plane bombers. While Mac Donald and Smerconish's approach would exclude tens of millions of Americans, it would still snare millions in its dragnet. Virtually all of those would be American citizens with no links to terrorism. Racial profiling would not end pointless searches; it would end them only for some white Americans.

## NEW RECRUITS

If American authorities started detaining Arab men, wouldn't al Qaeda simply recruit others who don't fit the profile? Mac Donald dismisses this argument. "It is unlikely that al Qaeda and other Muslim terror groups have recruited large numbers of Anglo-Europeans to their cause; the vast majority of would-be killers remain al Qaeda's core constituency: disaffected Middle Easterners, South Asians, and North Africans."[11]

Michael Smerconish told syndicated columnist Daniel Pipes that his book-length argument someday might become outdated, "but that day is not today."[12]

Actually, that day is today. Famed French counter-terrorism judge Jean-Louis Bruguiere noted in 2003 that "al Qaeda has stepped up its European recruiting efforts and was on the lookout for women and light-skinned converts in particular."[13]

I met with a senior Philippine intelligence official in Manila in March 2004. He said he was nervous about the increasing recruitment of Filipina women into al Qaeda. Some were the wives of Arab immigrants; others had worked in hotels or hospitals in the Arab world. "It is a big problem for us," the official said.

Does that mean "Maria," a light-skinned Manila-born woman with Roman Catholic parents, could be working with al Qaeda?

The official didn't know about any particular woman named "Maria" who was linked to al Qaeda, but he said women with Christian names are interestingly common among Muslim converts. Some of them are married to men linked to Islamic terror groups, including the al Qaeda affiliate Abu Sayyaf.

These women would slip right by the racial profiles recommended by Mac Donald and Smerconish. They are light-skinned, female, have Christian names, and come from a non-Muslim region of a predominantly Catholic country that has been a long-standing ally of the United States.

This is far from a hypothetical threat. "Project Bojinka" was a wide-ranging plot to kill Pope John Paul II and explode a number of U.S. planes in mid-air. It began in Manila in 1994 and was headed by the mastermind of the 1993 World Trade Center bombing, Ramzi Yousef. Three Filipina women helped the al Qaeda terrorists by opening bank accounts and leasing apartments in their names, not those of the terrorists. Other women seem to have been used to scout locations. If the U.S. began racially profiling all air and rail passengers, is there any doubt that Filipinas could be pressed into service?

Another potential source of recruits would be American-born converts recruited from the nation's prisons. They could be of any color and simply lie about their new faith. In the Algerian civil war in the 1950s, the French gendarmerie soon learned that some of their most devoted Muslim enemies were converts who had found their calling in French jails. There is no reason why history could not repeat itself.

Or consider the July 7, 2005, bombings in central London. None of the four bombers were Arab and almost all had been born in Britain.

Racial profiling targeting Arab males would not have derailed the plot that took the lives of fifty-five Britons.

## CAN IT BE ENFORCED?

This is a question that doesn't seem to interest Mac Donald or Smerconish much. They seem to presume that all laws and regulations will be enforced. But there is always a degree of interpretation. Perhaps Mac Donald and Smerconish have not seen the Somali women in Islamic headscarves screening passengers at Reagan National Airport in Washington, D.C.

Given that 30 percent of all regular attendees in the nation's some 1,200 mosques are African American, a screening policy focused on all "Muslims" would quickly be deemed racist. Lawsuits would follow and the policy would be struck down.

Mac Donald is right that al Qaeda has not recruited "large numbers of Anglo-Europeans," according to the best evidence available. Of course, it takes only a few "Anglo-Europeans" to wreak enormous harm.

We know that at least four people—one American and three Australians—have joined al Qaeda and have become involved in terror operations against the U.S. or its allies. Let's examine the men who Mac Donald and Smerconish would whisk past airport screeners.

### John Walker Lindh

The infamous "American Taliban" commonly regarded as hailing from Marin County, California, Lindh spent his early years in Takoma Park, Maryland, another liberal enclave.

He converted to Islam at the age of sixteen. He traveled to Yemen to learn what he considered pure, Koranic Arabic. He moved on to Pakistan before arriving in Afghanistan. He was recruited by the Harakut-ul-Mujahideen, which intended to train him to kill Indians in Kashmir.

But Lindh was unhappy with Harakut-ul-Mujahideen's lack of martial vigor—a *New Yorker* writer described it as a "fat camp for Arabs"—and gravitated to the Taliban. Since he spoke Arabic—rather than the native languages of the Taliban—he was sent to the al-Farooq camp, an al Qaeda facility in Afghanistan. He saw bin Laden as many as five times and had a small group audience with the arch-terrorist at least twice. Bin Laden even thanked him for coming.

Lindh's case shows how easy it is to penetrate al Qaeda and to train with the world's most notorious terrorist band—and how even white Americans can be seduced into its ranks.

Paul Bremer told the *San Francisco Chronicle* that Lindh was a "California bubblehead."[14] But only a bigger bubblehead would design American security to avoid searching people like Lindh.

## David Hicks

The second-to-last time David Hicks's family heard his voice, he was on the line from Khandahar. As they talked, his stepmother, Beverley Hicks, jotted a note: "David calls from Afghanistan, says he's with the Taliban."[15]

His father, Terry Hicks, took the phone.

"I said, 'I suppose you would have heard what happened in America with the aeroplanes flying into buildings?'" It was September 25, 2001.

David Hicks said, "No," and added, "That sounds like propaganda."[16]

His last call to his family was on November 3. He was in Khandahar, selected for a "martyr mission" by the head of al Qaeda's military wing, Mohammed Atef. He was told to guard a Taliban tank at the Kandahar airport.[17]

Roughly a month later, he was captured in the city of Kunduz[18] by the Northern Alliance and ultimately was sent under American guard to Camp X-Ray, Cuba, in January 2002. In mid-air, he wriggled out of his bonds and threatened to kill the troops on board. He was duct-taped into his seat.

Speaking generally of the prisoners held in U.S. custody in Cuba, Air Force general Richard Myers said: "These are people that would chew through hydraulic lines in the back of a C-17 to bring it down."[19]

In Guantanamo Bay, Hicks vowed: "Before I leave here, I am going to kill an American."[20]

Prosecutors charge that Hicks, like Lindh, was trained at the al-Farooq camp in 2001.

They say that Hicks not only met bin Laden, but also complained about the lack of terrorist training manuals in English. He was put to work as a translator.

Australia, unlike the United States, did not prohibit its citizens from serving as mercenaries until 2002. According to the *Sydney Daily Telegraph*, the Australian Security Intelligence Organisation says that at least ten Australians trained in Afghanistan, but remain free because their activities were not illegal at the time.[21]

## Jack Roche

With two failed marriages and a drinking problem, Roche discovered radical Islam in an Australian mosque. At first he was a member of an Indonesian Muslim terror group. He was later recruited by regional al Qaeda chief Hambali to go to Afghanistan in 2000. According to the *Australian*, his only exchange with bin Laden was when the arch-terrorist told him not to go into the married men's section of the al-Farooq training camp. He did, however, meet with September 11 mastermind Khalid Sheikh Mohammed. Roche was given $8,000 and told to lay the groundwork for a plot to kill spectators at the Sydney Olympics, a scheme that was personally cancelled by Abu Bakar Bashir, a key terrorist leader.

Roche blew the $8,000 on high living and tried to tell his story to Australian intelligence. They refused to listen. He then began surveillance of the Israeli embassy in Canberra. He also plotted to assassinate an Australian Jewish businessman named Joe Gutnick.

Roche was discovered by Australian police after the Bali bombings (planned by Roche's contact Hambali) and is currently serving a nine-year sentence.[22] He is exactly the kind of "Anglo-European" that Mac Donald and Smerconish want to speed past the airport screeners.

## "Jihad" Jack Thomas

Arrested in November 2004, Thomas attended the al-Farooq training camp in 2001 and was instructed by Khalid Sheikh Mohammed and Abu Bakar Bashir. He's charged with possessing terrorist money and with having a false passport. According to the *Australian*, John Walker Lindh gave Thomas's name to interrogators. As he has yet to stand trial, details of Thomas's purported crimes are sketchy.[23]

These are only a few of the terrorists who would have escaped Mac Donald and Smerconish's dragnet. If the United States used racial profiling at airports, these potential hijackers would have gone straight onto their planes.

None of this is to say that America's current screening process is ideal. Many of the screening procedures are outdated or pointless. If a little old lady with a walker is going to face down 300 passengers and take over a 747, I would like to see it. Likewise, there is no point in asking whether a traveler has packed his bags himself (the bags will be scanned anyway) or screening for "nervous" passengers (as if harassed business fliers, harried parents, and those who fear flying in any event might not be nervous at the airport).

Currently, buying a one-way ticket or paying cash for one or buying a ticket on the same day as departure are all "red flags" that require searches. This, at best, betrays an outdated sense of terrorist tactics. All of the September 11 hijackers bought round-trip tickets, used SunTrust debit cards to pay online, and made their purchases before the day of travel.

If profiling for race or sex (what Mac Donald and Smerconish recommend) and nervousness (what TSA does) doesn't work, what does?

Here we enter what is surely controversial territory. Yet there is one form of profiling that has a record of success. It is known to the Germans as *rasterfahndung*, which roughly means "category search" or "grid search."

It was first used by West Germany in the 1970s to detect Communist terrorists who had assumed false identities. Using computers, investigators simultaneously combed the databases of banks, utilities, universities, and government agencies for suspects who met a list of criteria. In the 1970s, the technique "successfully tracked down two members of the Red Army Faction [a violent terror sect] by searching utility company records for people who paid their electric bills in cash."[24]

Following the September 11 attacks, German interior minister Otto Schily brought back computer-aided profiling. So far, results have been mixed. Critics charge that the technique has targeted too many suspects (more than 10,000 in one German state alone)[25] and violated the privacy rights of people who have not even been suspected of committing any crime. Schily points to the large number of investigations opened and has refused to back down.

Building on the German experience, it is possible to imagine a more effective, less invasive method of screening people. Instead of asking if a person fits into one suspect category, the system would send up a red flag if he belongs in several simultaneously. Categories based on race or ethnicity need not be used. One category: using the FBI's database of more than 300,000 names of people who have either phoned a known terrorist or been called by one. Another category: has he ever shared a lease or bank account with a known terrorist? And so on. The al Qaeda membership rolls captured in Afghanistan would be used, as would the databases of Arab and European intelligence services. All money transfers, marriage records, and birth records would be included. Add enough data and you end up with a global database of everyone somehow connected to a known terrorist.

The computer could even issue a score to all passengers that would rank their links to terrorists. The many innocent zeros would pass through, as would the ones and twos (say John Walker Lindh's high school classmates). But everyone above, say, five would get a thorough examination.

Would it work? Most likely.

Yet there is little chance it would ever be enacted.

Admiral John Poindexter tried a similar approach with a program called "Total Information Awareness"—and was attacked by the press and stopped by Congress.

That is the real political correctness that endangers air safety—but you won't hear about this from Mac Donald and Smerconish.

# THE U.S. BORDER WITH MEXICO IS THE MOST LIKELY PLACE FOR AL QAEDA TERRORISTS TO SNEAK INTO THE HOMELAND

*"A top al Qaeda lieutenant has met with leaders of a violent Salvadoran criminal gang with roots in Mexico and the United States—including a stronghold in the Washington area—in an effort by the terrorist network to seek help infiltrating the U.S.–Mexico border."*

—JERRY SEPER, WASHINGTON TIMES[1]

AS UNLIKELY AS IT SOUNDS, there are no known cases of al Qaeda terrorists sneaking across the Mexican border.

While hundreds of illegals steal across America's almost 2,000-mile border with Mexico every day, so far there is not a single confirmed report that al Qaeda operatives have joined the throng. "Among the thousands of undocumented immigrants streaming into Arizona from Mexico each week," reports the *Arizona Republic*'s Dennis Wagner, "the U.S. Border Patrol has yet to discover a known terrorist. The FBI and Department of Homeland Security likewise have failed to detect a single al Qaeda operative who infiltrated the United States via our southern boundary."[2]

Wagner notes that militiamen—private citizens who voluntarily patrol the southern line in the sand—have claimed that U.S. Border Patrol agents captured illegal immigrants who were said to be terrorists. In June 2004, militia member Chris Simcox claimed that the Border

Patrol had arrested seventy-seven "Arabic-speaking males"—all of whom later turned out to be Mexicans.[3]

Wagner also interviewed Lt. Col. Norm Beasley, the Arizona Department of Public Safety's top counter-terrorism official. "I'm concerned about the Mexican border," Beasley said. "But, from a pure terrorism issue, I'm more concerned about the Canadian border."[4]

A 2004 report by Robert S. Leiken, director of the Immigration and National Security Program at the Nixon Center, examined precisely how 212 "suspected or convicted" terrorists had entered the country. Of all the ways terrorists could enter the U.S., "terrorists stealing across the Mexican border comes last, virtually nil."[5] Leiken did not cite a single case of terrorists coming from Mexico; his "virtually nil" is an excess of caution.

With so many people illegally crossing from Mexico every day, why hasn't al Qaeda walked through the open door? Leiken thinks that "Latin America in general and Mexico in particular are inhospitable to Muslim extremists in ways Canada and our sea and air borders are not." In the course of this chapter, we will discover why Canada is more hospitable to al Qaeda than Mexico is.

Leiken notes that "publicly, U.S. officials say they have found no links with Middle East terrorists" and Mexico. Leiken concedes that when he asked Homeland Security Secretary Tom Ridge whether he was more worried about Mexico or Canada, Ridge said "Mexico." But Leiken points out that "other senior DHS officials offered a different answer, suggesting that Canada was of more concern because of ease of entry and hospitable surroundings."[6]

A 2003 report on Mexican criminal organizations from the Library of Congress's Federal Research Division (a branch of the Library of Congress that does contract research for spy agencies) found that while Mexican officials were worried about al Qaeda terrorism, there was not a single case of al Qaeda activity in Mexico or of an al Qaeda operative crossing the border into the U.S. from Mexico. The Federal Research Division's report was thorough, and did find that other international criminal organizations—including Chinese triads and Japanese yakuza—were active in Mexico.[7]

What about those media reports about bin Laden operatives at the border? There are two cases of terrorists or alleged terrorists who have supposedly been seen in Mexico.

Adnan G. El Shukrijumah has a $5 million U.S. government bounty on his head, due to his documented ties to global terrorism. Federal prosecutors in northern Virginia swore out an arrest warrant for El Shukrijumah in March 2003 for his involvement in a terror plot against U.S. targets. An FBI alert described him as "armed and dangerous."[8] Believed to be a Yemeni national, he has been known to carry passports from Saudi Arabia, Trinidad, Guyana, and Canada.[9] The Saudis have publicly denied he is a citizen of the oil kingdom.[10]

*Washington Times* reporter Jerry Seper wrote that El Shukrijumah had been spotted in Honduras in July 2004, where he was allegedly attempting to make a deal with the Mara Salvatrucha, the infamous gang commonly known as MS-13.[11] The gang is notorious for its brutality and for its odd induction ritual: new members are beaten by a number of gangsters while others count to 13. The gang's tell-tale tattoo prominently includes the number 13.

Seper's story, however, does not stand up to scrutiny.

Sam Dealey, a former *Asian Wall Street Journal* editorial writer and foreign correspondent for *Time* magazine, investigated MS-13 for *Reader's Digest*. In the course of his reporting, he found that the source for the story that El Shukrijumah was in Honduras was "a patron at a seedy Honduran café" who "thought" he saw the terrorist. The patron phoned the police. When they arrived, the man the patron had seen was gone. A high-ranking Department of Homeland Security official told Dealey: "The whole thing is bullshit, based on no real intelligence, just third-party accounts from Honduras."

Ricardo Menesses, chief of the El Salvador National Civil Police, told Central American reporters that Honduran intelligence "did not confirm" that the meeting between the alleged al Qaeda operative and MS-13 even took place.[12]

A later account of El Shukrijumah, which put him in northern Mexico, was also reported by Seper. According to U.S. intelligence officials, that report is also believed to be wrong. Allegations that he was in Tampa in March 2003, apparently casing MacDill Air Force Base, have also been shown to be false.[13]

The DHS official told Dealey: "El Shukrijumah and other al Qaeda cadres are reported to have been sighted in Latin America more than the Virgin Mary."

The closest report of a Muslim alien possibly having links to MS-13 is tenuous at best. Fakrhul Islam, a Bangladeshi Muslim, was arrested by the U.S. border patrol near Brownsville, Texas. He was arrested with twelve other illegals, including Frankie Sanchez-Solorzano, who was initially believed to be an MS-13 member. Sanchez-Solorzano had no known criminal record, and his link to MS-13 was "probably just a tattoo," an FBI official told Dealey. As for Islam, he was quickly deported. If he had ties to terrorism, he would have been held for questioning.

Amer Haykel, a British citizen, was arrested in Mexico in June 2005, on suspicion that he was connected to the September 11 atrocity. He was released twenty-four hours later. Mexican Interior Ministry officials had determined that he was just a tourist. A *Houston Chronicle* report on Haykel's arrest concluded that, as of June 2005, "no terrorists are known to have been captured in Mexico."[14]

There may well be other cases of terrorists active in Mexico that law enforcement or intelligence officials do not want to disclose. But, at this time, the balance of evidence shows that no known al Qaeda terrorist has entered the United States from Mexico. That is not to say there is no danger of terrorists sneaking across the southern border. Certainly that potential exists. But, so far, it seems the threat from Mexico is purely speculation.

Less speculative, however, is the threat from the north.

Stewart Bell is a reporter for the *National Post* of Canada. For the last few years, he has invited the wrath of his fellow countrymen by meticulously documenting al Qaeda's long-term presence in Canada—and that nation's weak response to it. His book *Cold Terror: How Canada Nurtures and Exports Terrorism Around the World* is a devastating indictment of our northern neighbor:

> Canadian terrorists spill blood around the world. They are known to have taken part in the 1993 World Trade Center truck bombing in New York,

as well as suicide bombings in Israel and bombings by the Provisional Irish Republican Army; political killings in India and the murder of tourists in Egypt; a 1996 truck bombing in the heart of Colombo, Sri Lanka, that killed close to one hundred civilians; the 1995 bombing of the Egyptian embassy in Islamabad, which killed seventeen; and the Bali bombing of October 2002, which killed more than two hundred innocent people. A Canadian was part of the group blamed for the 2003 bombing of Western housing complexes in Riyadh. In 1985, Canadians were behind one of the deadliest terror attacks in history.[15]

Part of the problem, as Bell explains, is Canada's self-image:

> Canadians like to think of themselves as benevolent world citizens, peacekeepers in blue berets who bring kindness and calm to troubled lands. In many parts of the world, Canada is no longer seen that way at all. In Sri Lanka, Canada is the country that allows the Tamil Tigers, the world's leading practitioners of suicide bombings, to operate freely and raise money that bankrolls terrorism and a brutal civil war. The same is true in India, which suffered through years of Sikh terrorist violence originating in Canada. Israel has had to deal with Canadian terrorists, and so have France, Italy, Turkey, Saudi Arabia, Singapore, the Philippines, Indonesia, Egypt, and Pakistan, not to mention Canada's closest partner, the United States. "To many Americans," says a report published in May 2003 by the Washington, D.C.–based Center for Immigration Studies, "the longest undefended border in the world now looks like a 4,000-mile-long portal for terrorists."[16]

Indeed, Canada is a friendly staging area for attacks on the U.S., as Bell's extensive reporting—some of it from the Middle East and Central Asia—reveals:

> Terrorists themselves have taken note of Canada's posture. In France, I met a young Algerian who was part of a terror cell based out of Montreal. I spoke to him during breaks in his trial and he asked me detailed questions about Canada. The last thing he said to me was, "Maybe I'll see you in Canada."

Another member of his cell was named Mourad. Mourad recalled a song he had heard back in Algeria: "We are going to Canada, and even if we end up planting lettuce, we will be happy." Mourad moved to Montreal but he never planted lettuce. Instead, he took part in a terrorist bomb plot.

"There are a variety of factors which explain why Canada is vulnerable," according to [Director of the Canadian Security Intelligence Service (CSIS) Ward] Elcock. "Our borders and coastlines are long. Our society, like all developed countries, is comparatively wealthy—a source of technology, of equipment and funds. As with other democracies, our openness and respect for rights and freedoms limit the ability of the state to suppress terrorism in a ruthless, repressive fashion."[17]

As we shall see, Canada has a political climate far different from Mexico—one that actually defends accused terrorists. Consider the cases of documented al Qaeda terrorists who hailed from Canada.

Ahmed Ressam was Algerian, claimed asylum in Canada, and embarked on a life of petty crime—until he met members of al Qaeda. By his own admission, he lived on welfare and theft.

Ressam roomed at the Montreal YMCA at first, but then moved in with fellow Algerians, including Moustapha Labsi, Adel Boumezbeur, and Karim Atmani, Fateh Kamel's [an al Qaeda cell leader] deputy. He supplemented his welfare income with the proceeds from pickpocketing and passport theft. "I used to steal tourists, rob tourists," he said during court testimony in New York. "I used to go to hotels and find their suitcases and steal them when they're not paying attention ... I used to take the money, keep the money and if there are passports, I would sell them, and if there are Visa cards, I would use them up, and if there were any travelers' checks I would use them or sell them."[18]

Canada's law enforcement system was, in Ressam's case, like its preferred fishing policy: catch and release. He was arrested four times and convicted once. He was hardly a hardworking model immigrant. As Bell notes, Ressam "held one legitimate job, distributing advertising leaflets. He quit after a week."[19]

When his bogus claims of political persecution in Algeria were denied and he was ordered to leave Canada, Ressam vanished into the immigrant underground. He later broke into a nearby Roman Catholic church, pilfered a blank baptismal certificate, forged a priest's signature, and created a new identity, Benni Antoine Noris. "That, along with a photograph, was all Ressam needed to get a Canadian passport," Bell writes. "He didn't even have to take the forged certificate to the passport office himself, instead paying an acquaintance $300 to pick it up. Benni Noris, a Montreal native with a strangely Algerian accent, could now travel the world."[20] Again, Canada's lax policies made Ressam's evil ambitions possible.

With his new passport, Ressam flew to Frankfurt, Germany, in 1998 to meet al Qaeda cell members. They provided letters of introduction to al Qaeda leaders in Pakistan. Ultimately, he sat down with Abu Zubaydah, the third highest-ranking man in bin Laden's terror network.[21]

By April 1998, Ressam was training, alongside other Algerians, at al Qaeda's camp in Khalden, Afghanistan. He was taught to fire automatic weapons and make bombs.

Ressam was also trained to make chemical weapons, as Bell details. "While Ressam watched, wearing a face mask, his chief led a small dog into a box and placed a small quantity of cyanide inside. Then he added sulfuric acid. The dog was dead within five minutes. Imagine, the instructor told Ressam, what would happen if you placed this gas at the air intake of a building in America."[22]

With the equivalent of $12,000 in his hands, Ressam was sent back to Canada in February 1999. He was changing planes at Los Angeles International Airport on February 7, 1999, when inspiration struck.[23] He had found his target. Less than an hour later, he boarded his flight to Canada. He had a lot of work to do.

Eleven months later, Ressam drove a rented car off the ferry at Port Angeles, Washington. Diana Dean, a U.S. Customs official, noticed that he seemed nervous. She opened the trunk and found explosives and detonators.

Ressam soon confessed that he was plotting to blow up Los Angeles International Airport on the night of the millennium celebrations. Convicted in an April 2001 jury trial, Ressam's sentencing was delayed as U.S.

Justice Department officials pressed him for information about other al Qaeda plots. U.S. district judge John Coughenour sentenced him to a twenty-two-year prison term on July 28, 2005.[24]

Ressam could have been caught sooner if Canada had taken a tougher line on terrorism, as Bell explains: "Jean-Louis Bruguiere [a French anti-terrorist judge] sent a letter to Canadian authorities in April 1999 concerning his investigation [into Ressam], but the RCMP [Royal Canadian Mounted Police] took its time responding, and it was not until October that the paperwork was done and police finally searched Ressam's apartment."[25] By then, it was too late.

Some immigration officials, eager to expel illegal immigrants with criminal backgrounds, find that Canada's ruling center-left politicians often prevent them from doing their jobs. As Bell relates: "An immigration official told me how he works all day at trying to get terrorists out of the country, and then watches as politicians court these same violent organizations for votes. When he gets home, his wife sometimes asks him why he even bothers. 'I honestly don't know what to tell her,' he said."[26]

Canada's unwitting aid to terrorists is documented fact, not the gripe of a lone disgruntled official. Consider the cases of Canadian citizens or residents linked to al Qaeda.

Ahmed Said Khadr, also known as Abu Abd al-Rahman Al Kanadi, was the hub of the Egyptian branch of the Canadian al Qaeda network. According to a Canadian Security Intelligence Service (CSIS, Canada's CIA) report, "Khadr is a close associate of bin Laden and is reported to have had contact with bin Laden in Afghanistan."[27] There is little doubt about Khadr's connections to al Qaeda. He was seen with bin Laden at a number of weddings and religious feasts.[28] And he ran his terror operation with Canadian help. Khadr received tens of thousands of dollars from the Canadian International Development Agency, a Canadian government agency that funds schools, clinics, and other good works in the Third World. Khadr was running a phony charity that seems to have been diverting money to al Qaeda.

Khadr ran Human Concern International in Pakistan in the 1980s and 1990s. Human Concern International was clearly a scam, as one intrepid journalist discovered.

Tim Deagle was a young freelance journalist when he heard about a Hope Village. It was the winter of 1988 and he was killing time in Pakistan, waiting for the Soviets to withdraw [from Afghanistan] so he could go into Afghanistan with the mujahideen . . . He tried again and again to reach HCI by telephone but was never able to get an appointment, which he found odd because the other nonprofit groups working with Afghan refugees were desperate for media attention, so one day he arrived unannounced at the charity's office in Peshawar. It was just a room with a broken computer. A group of young men armed with AK-47s sat on the floor drinking chai.[29]

Deagle then checked out HCI's Hope Village itself.

Two hours outside Peshawar, near the border with Afghanistan, he came to the entrance. . . . It was run-down, with little in the way of humanitarian activity; Deagle saw a group of about two dozen kids weaving carpets and a lot of heavily armed young men. "All they did in Hope Village was weave carpets," he said. "It was politicized, militaristic, and it smacked of Hezb-i-Islami," the armed faction of Gulbuddin Hekmatyar, a strongly anti-Western Afghan warlord.[30]

Canadian intelligence soon concluded that Khadr was running military-style training camps with the humanitarian funds supplied by Canadian taxpayers.[31]

When twenty Pakistani troops came to Khadr's door, his wife told them to get lost. "She said that, as a Canadian, she did not believe she had to [let them in]. 'I felt so proud that I'm Canadian,' she told the *Ottawa Citizen* later. 'I told the officer I'm a Canadian citizen, and he said 'To hell with you and your Canada.'"[32]

When Khadr was arrested by Pakistani police for his ties to al Qaeda, he called the Canadian embassy. Canada's prime minister publicly demanded his release. Khadr was set free.[33]

Khadr's sons, Abdullah and Omar, followed him into the jihad business. One trained at al Qaeda's Khalden camp and the other learned about explosives at an al Qaeda facility near Khost, Afghanistan.

The Khadr clan fought alongside bin Laden until the bitter end, as Bell reports:

> On October 12 [2003], the Islamic Observation Centre in London issued a statement claiming that two Canadians were among the dead, Ahmed Khadr and a fourteen-year-old it identified as his youngest son, Abdul Karim. The statement called Khadr by his alias, Abu Abd al-Rahman Al Kanadi, and said he was a founding member of al Qaeda.[34]

Al Kanadi means "the Canadian."

Why Canada? Al Qaeda suspects in Canada can count on vocal pressure groups to press their case while vilifying the police and intelligence services. Bell cites several cases of this sad syndrome. "When a suspected al Qaeda sleeper agent was arrested in Montreal in May 2003, Islamic organizations portrayed it as an 'inquisition against Muslims.' Likewise, when the Federal Court of Canada ruled that Mahmoud Jaballah was indeed a member of the Egyptian Islamic Jihad, as CSIS said he was, that was portrayed as an example of Canada's intolerance."[35]

Perhaps the strongest case is that of Mohammed Harkat. Harkat was arrested in Ottawa by a Royal Canadian Mounted Police tactical team on December 10, 2002. Canadian intelligence discovered that he was a member of bin Laden's network and that he had trained in Afghanistan under Abu Zubaydah, who ran the al Qaeda training camps.

Bell documents Harkat's resume of terrorist ties—and the sympathetic response of some Canadians.

> Harkat is an Algerian who came to Canada in 1995 and married a French Canadian named Sophie, all the while, according to CSIS, concealing his links to terrorism. He received large amounts of cash from points overseas, worked in Pakistan for a Saudi aid organization tied to bin Laden, and was a friend of Fahad Shehri, a Saudi deported for terrorism in 1997. "Prior to arriving in Canada, the Service believes that Harkat engaged in terrorism by supporting terrorist activity," CSIS said. "The service furthermore believes that Harkat has engaged in those activities as a member of a terrorist entity known as the bin Laden network, which includes al Qaeda."

The evidence against Harkat was not to be taken lightly. Zubaydah himself had identified him to authorities after being captured in Pakistan.

A support group was soon created to lobby for Harkat's release. An Internet site was launched, featuring photos of Harkat and letters concerning his "fight for justice." Harkat was a victim of "racial profiling and scapegoating," it said. "Stop the insanity," Mrs. Harkat pleaded. She claimed that CSIS lies and breaks the law, and that her husband had done no wrong. "In my husband's eyes," she said, "I can read innocence." In March 2003, Mrs. Harkat and forty others staged a demonstration in downtown Ottawa. She waved a placard reading "Save My Husband, My Friend, My Love, My Hero."[36]

Some Canadians treat captured members of al Qaeda as heroes, while intelligence agents are called cheats or worse. No wonder terrorists view the country as a haven. "Canada," a Russian security official once told an RCMP officer in Moscow, "is the land of the trusting fools."[37]

Bell is unsparing. He believes it is Canada's political culture that makes into uniquely welcoming to al Qaeda.

The list of specific government failures is extensive, from an immigration system seemingly incapable of deporting even known terrorists, to laws that have proven ineffective at shutting down charities and ethnic associations fronting for terror. But it all stems from a political leadership unwilling to take a stand and secure Canadians and their allies from the violent whims of the world's assorted radicals, fundamentalists, and extremists.

Time and again, politicians have been tested, and they have failed. They have dined with terrorist fronts, lobbied on behalf of captured terrorists, and given extremists access to the decision-making process. Canada's official terrorism policy—in effect, denying that there is a problem—is merely a public relations strategy intended to manage Washington in order to prevent the Americans from imposing border security measures that would slow North-South trade.[38]

America does face a real threat from its borders. If history is any guide, al Qaeda will come from the north.

# EPILOGUE

*"This story is too good to check."*

—AN OLD JOURNALISTIC PUNCHLINE

**HURRICANE KATRINA** took hundreds of lives, leveled billions of dollars worth of property, and produced a score of media myths. Here are two: Because the Louisiana National Guard was deployed in Iraq, it was unable to save lives in New Orleans, while the USS *Bataan*—with its hospital beds and helicopters—was not deployed until days after the levee broke.

## Louisiana National Guard

Actually, by federal law, no more than 50 percent of any state's National Guard can be deployed outside the state, let alone outside the country. And, as a matter of fact, some 75 percent of the Louisiana National Guard was stationed at home at the time of the hurricane—and could have been immediately deployed to New Orleans by Louisiana's governor, Kathleen Blanco. By law, only a state governor can mobilize the Guard for activity inside a state. It was not the demands of the Iraq war that kept the Guard from Louisiana's flooded parishes, but the dilatory decisions of that state's governor.

## The USS *Bataan*

*New York Times* columnist Paul Krugman—who once described himself
as "a future Nobel Prize winner"—helped foster this myth. Citing the
*Chicago Tribune*, Krugman wrote that the "USS *Bataan*, equipped with
six operating rooms, hundreds of hospital beds, and the ability to produce
100,000 gallons of fresh water a day, has been sitting off the Gulf Coast
since last Monday—without patients."

Actually, the *Bataan* story was an Internet urban legend born on antiwar websites. The ship's official website tells a different story, as the
eagle-eyed folks of Powerline.com first noticed:

> If Krugman had taken the trouble, he would have found that on August
> 30, the same day on which New Orleans' levees burst, precipitating the
> crisis, men and women from the [USS] *Bataan* were already in action,
> and by the following day they were busy saving lives. . . . How about the
> unused operating rooms and empty hospital beds? It seems not to have
> occurred to Krugman that the most efficient way to get medical treat-
> ment to hurricane survivors is not to helicopter them, individually or in
> small groups, to a ship at sea. Instead, what happened was that medical
> personnel were assembled and equipped on board the *Bataan*, then
> flown to shore where they could treat the sick and wounded. . . . This all
> happened during the three days prior to the appearance of Krugman's
> column describing the "hospital beds" "without patients" aboard the
> *Bataan*.

Sometimes it seems that there must be some secret assembly line somewhere that produces media myths. Some on the right call it "liberal bias,"
while others on the left see a bias caused by corporate ownership of
media outlets.

The reality, as one might expect, is more complex. Often, as the New
Orleans examples show, assumptions are presented as facts. Since journalistic assumptions often dovetail with a liberal outlook, this tends to fuel
charges of liberal bias. But assumptions must be checked. A simple
phone call to the Louisiana National Guard or the public affairs officer
responsible for the USS *Bataan* or a Google search would have revealed

the bankruptcy of those assumptions. But writers and editors decided they were "too good to check."

The solution to such sloppy reporting is tough-minded editing. And here the left-wing critics of media bias are onto something: the corporate cultures of too many media organizations discourage criticism or confrontation. It hurts morale, encourages lawsuits, and infuriates human resource departments. And it is no fun for the editor either. (Ever notice that Lou Grant–style editors seem to have disappeared, except in movies set in the past?)

Yet pain avoidance comes at a price. All of the infamous journalistic hoaxes of the last two decades—from Janet Cooke to Stephen Glass to Jayson Blair—were perpetuated by staff writers, not freelancers or bloggers. That suggests that modern editors only know how to be tough on outsiders, not colleagues. Until this club-like mentality is cast aside, disinformation will continue.

Without skeptical editors questioning reporters about their stories, there is no such dynamic tension and judgment. A gruff and skeptical editor might have stopped *Newsweek* from reporting that U.S. Army interrogators flushed a Koran down a prison toilet. A good editor would have demanded that his reporter find the answers to certain basic questions: How does a 900-page book go down a toilet? What are the dimensions of the Korans distributed to prisoners and what is the width of the toilet pipe? How many Korans were distributed? Are any missing, according to the military? What was the name of the guard who allegedly did the deed? Was he actually stationed there at the time? Will he go on the record?

Another source of disinformation is advocacy groups of every stripe, from trial lawyers and nonprofits to public-relations outfits and die-hard partisans. These folks love to plant stories to advance their cause. Some are not above fabricating evidence (as CBS's Dan Rather learned) or leaving out relevant context. There is little use in calling on these operators to reform; they are within their rights and would not listen anyway. Reporters are smart to court them; they often have legitimate scoops. But their wares should be extensively checked for product defects—recalls (corrections) can be painful and embarrassing. The myths about Halliburton (Myth #20)

and the civilian body count in Iraq (Myth #9) were peddled by such partisans. Editors should be especially careful of stories from such brazenly self-
interested sources.

Calling on reporters and editors to do their jobs—to be skeptical and
demand evidence—may seem like common sense, but, in fairness, there
is no easy prescription for what ails the media. Editors who are hard on
reporters or contributors too often find that their careers suffer as a
result; it is they, not lazy or sloppy reporters, who are penalized. Why is
he so hard to work with? Why is she so demanding?

Clearly newsroom cultures have to change. While writers can become
stars with style or scoops, the contribution of editors is like gravity: invisible, but without it the whole enterprise flies apart. Executives must back
demanding editors and encourage laissez-faire editors to take a harder
line. That means that senior management must create incentives to
undermine the cozy culture we have now.

The government also has a role to play. A few legislative changes
would lead to a better informed press and public.

> Open up FBIS. The U.S. government maintains the Foreign Broad-
cast Information Service, which translates into English most overseas
radio and television broadcasts as well as many magazines and newspapers. It is an invaluable service that allows intelligence analysts to
track events abroad. But access to FBIS publications requires a security clearance. This is just one example of the excessive secrecy of the
spy community. The information that FBIS collects and translates is
purely public. No secret agents or spy satellites are involved. It should
be made available to the tax-paying public over the Internet.
Researchers would uncover new leads, reporters would find new
sources to contact, and the public could read about a range of stories
that the American media ignore. Of course, most of the broadcasts
and publications that FBIS translates are from outlets controlled by
foreign governments that present a party line. Surely the press and the
public know how to read between the lines. If FBIS were widely available, the public would have learned that bin Laden had denied he was
on dialysis years before the American media reported it.

> Make CRS Reports Public. The Congressional Research Service pro-
> duces a wide array of reports for members of Congress. Again, these
> are neither classified nor contain classified information. Yet they are
> not easily available to the public. A single government-run website
> with a decent search engine would provide citizens with timely and
> more-or-less impartial information used by decision makers to write
> laws and change policy.

> Release the transcripts. Following the 2000 election, the Defense
> Department began releasing its own transcripts of one-on-one inter-
> views between major reporters and senior department officials. As a
> result, the public can now read whole conversations between the
> *Washington Post*'s Bob Woodward and Defense Secretary Donald
> Rumsfeld or *Vanity Fair*'s David Rose's chat with Paul Wolfowitz. With
> these transcripts in hand, which are produced from government
> recordings and prepared by civil servants, one can see the comments
> of senior officials in context and discover news nuggets overlooked by
> reporters. Usually the transcripts are not released until after the story
> is published, so a reporter's scoop is preserved. This occasional prac-
> tice by the Defense Department should be made routine and govern-
> ment-wide. Open government is the best antidote to disinformation.

For now, the avalanche of disinformation continues.

Readers interested in having potential media myths investigated may
send suggestions to mediamyths@richardminiter.com.

Remember, they must be widely believed and provably false to qual-
ify. I will not be able to respond to every query (let alone investigate them
all), but I will examine the best entries. Who knows, there may even be
a *Disinformation II*.

# CLASSIFIED MEMORANDUM FROM RICHARD CLARKE TO CONDOLEEZZA RICE, JANUARY 25, 2001

30009

NATIONAL SECURITY COUNCIL
WASHINGTON, D.C. 20504

January 25, 2001

INFORMATION

MEMORANDUM FOR CONDOLEEZZA RICE

FROM:           RICHARD A. CLARKE

SUBJECT:        Presidential Policy Initiative/Review -- The Al-
                Qida Network

Steve asked today that we propose major Presidential policy
reviews or initiatives. We _urgently_ need such a Principals
level review on the al Qida network.

Just some Terrorist Group?

As we noted in our briefings for you, al Qida is not some
narrow, little terrorist issue that needs to be included in
broader regional policy. Rather, several of our regional
policies need to address centrally the transnational challenge
to the US and our interests posed by the al Qida network.   By
proceeding with separate policy reviews on Central Asia, the
GCC, North Africa, etc. we would deal inadequately with the need
for a comprehensive multi-regional policy on al Qida.

al Qida  is the active, organized, major force that is using a
distorted version of Islam as its vehicle to achieve two goals:

     --to drive the US out of the Muslim world, forcing the
withdrawal of our military and economic presence in countries
from Morocco to Indonesia;

     --to replace moderate, modern, Western regime in Muslim
countries with theocracies modeled along the lines of the
Taliban.

al Qida affects centrally our policies on Pakistan, Afghanistan,
Central Asia, North Africa and the GCC. Leaders in Jordan and
Saudi Arabia see al Qida as a direct threat to them.   The
strength of the network of organizations limits the scope of
support friendly Arab regimes can give to a range of US

Classified by:  Richard A. Clarke      NSC DECLASSIFICATION REVIEW [E.O. 12958]
Reason:   1.5(d)(x6)                    /X/ Exempt In part and redact as shown
Declassify On:  1/25/25                 by D.Sanborn Date 4/7/2004
Derived From:  Multiple Sources

2

policies, including Iraq policy and the Peace Process. We would make a major error if we underestimated the challenge al *Qida* poses, or over estimated the stability of the moderate, friendly regimes al *Qida* threatens.

## Pending Time Sensitive Decisions

At the close of the Clinton Administration, two decisions about al *Qida* were deferred to the Bush Administration.

     -- First, should we provide the Afghan Northern Alliance enough assistance to maintain it as a viable opposition force to the Taliban/al Qida?    If we do not, I believe that the Northern Alliance may be effectively taken out of action this Spring when fighting resumes after the winter thaw. The al Qida 55th Brigade, which has been a key fighting force for the Taliban, would then be freed to send its personnel elsewhere, where they would likely threaten US interests. For any assistance to get there in time to effect the Spring fighting, a decision is needed now.

     -- Second, should we increase assistance to Uzbekistan to allow them to deal with the al Qida/ IMU threat?

Operational detail, removed at the request of the CIA

Three other issues awaiting addressal now are:

     --First, what the new Administration says to the Taliban and Pakistan about the importance we attach to ending the al Qida sanctuary in Afghanistan. We are separately proposing early, strong messages to both.

     --Second, do we propose significant program growth in the FY02 budget for anti-al Qida operations by CIA and counter-terrorism training and assistance by State and CIA?

     --Third,   when and how does the Administration choose to respond to the attack on the USS Cole. That decision is obviously complex. We can make some decisions, such as the those above, now without yet coming to grips with the harder decision about the Cole. On the Cole, we should take advantage of the policy that we "will respond at a time, place, and manner of our own choosing" and not be forced into knee jerk responses.

Attached is the year-end 2000 strategy on al Qida developed by
the last Administration to give to you.  Also attached is the
1998 strategy.  Neither was a "covert action only" approach.
Both incorporated diplomatic, economic, military, public
diplomacy and intelligence tools.  Using the 2000 paper as
background, we could prepare a decision paper/guide for a PC
review.

I recommend that you have a Principals discussion of al Qida
soon and addresss the following issues:

    1.   Threat Magnitude:  Do the Principals agree that the al
Qida network poses a first order threat to US interests in a
number or regions, or is this analysis a "chicken little" over
reaching and can we proceed without major new initiatives and by
handling this issue in a more routine manner?

    2.   Strategy:  If it is a first order issue,  how should
the existing strategy be modified or strengthened?

Two elements of the existing strategy that have not been made to
work effectively are a) going after al Qida's money and b)
public information to counter al Qida propaganda.

    3.   FY02 Budget:  Should we continue the funding increases
into FY02 for State and CIA programs designed to implement the
al Qida strategy?

    4.   Immediate ██ Decisions:   Should we initiate ██ funding
to the Northern Alliance and to the Uzbek's?


Please let us know if you would like such a decision/discussion
paper or any modifications to the background paper.


Concurrences by:     Mary McCarthy, Dan Fried, Bruce Reidel, Don
                     Camp



Attachment
Tab A   December 2000 Paper:  Strategy for Eliminating the Threat
from the Jihadist Networks of al-Qida: Status and Prospects

Tab B   September 1998 Paper:  Pol-Mil Plan for al-Qida

# INTERCEPTS OF PHONE CONVERSATIONS BETWEEN MADRID AL QAEDA BOMBERS

# The Surveillance Tapes

Police in Milan had <u>Rabei Osman El Sayed Ahmed</u> under surveillance for several months after his phone number was found in the address book of a suspect in the March 11, 2004 Madrid train bombings. Here are excerpts from the Italian police transcripts, which came from both phone taps and microphones placed in Rabei's apartment. [Note: Recorded in May 2004, the conversations were conducted in Arabic; the Canadian Broadcast Corporation received the Italian translations and translated them into English.]

**This first excerpt**, from May 26, is a face-to-face conversation between Rabei and Yahia Ragheh, a 21-year-old Egyptian whom Rabei is grooming to become a suicide bomber. The two men listen to tapes about jihad and martyrdom. Rabei tells Yahia of a potential female suicide bomber, who had been captured, but says he has another who is ready to go. Then Rabei reveals, "The Madrid attack was my project and those who died as martyrs, they are my very dear friends."

**Rabei**: Listen, you'll see, and start studying for the jihad, for the jihad and for martyrdom.

**Yahia**: Also, is there any audio material that concerns this?

**Rabei**: There is everything, but I think that for you it is best to read, so that each page goes inside of you and lets you know its meaning. There are about 2,000 pages that can explain to you what is the meaning of the jihad, and then you can listen, look at me, I always have the martyrdom tape. I always listen to it.

**Yahia**: Do you have it here?

**Rabei**: Yes, I have it here now, "The Martyr's Strength." I also have other ones that talk about martyrdom, many more. But listen to me, you must start watching the videos, too. Watch and learn. There are about 300 tapes of mujahedeens' actions in Chechnya, in Afghanistan, in Algeria, in Kashmir and in other countries. Technically they are very interesting tapes. You learn many things there, they are special tapes.

**Yahia**: Can I listen to this one? So that I can start memorizing it?

**Rabei**: Please.

He turns on the stereo and they listen to an audiotape in which the speaker praises the jihad and martyrdom.

**Rabei:** These are very special tapes. They indicate the direction to the martyr. These will facilitate everything when you listen to them. They enter your body, but you must listen to them constantly. I listen to them constantly, even now that I am working. During breaks I use both the CD and the tapes, while for you it's better if you listen first to the tapes and then to the CD...

**Yahia:** Good.

**Rabei:** In particular, this tape has an indescribable voice. It enters your veins. This one -- in Spain, they all learned it by heart. It gives you a lot of confidence and peace. It takes your fear away...

**Yahia:** Give, give, give me one of them, so that I can learn it.

**Rabei:** Yes, but you must learn it by heart.

**Yahia:** No, no, I will learn it by heart.

...

**Rabei:** You cannot not fight in the name of God. It is a duty to do charity, both monthly and yearly. It depends on how much you earn. If you are employed you can give 50 Euros, otherwise whatever you can.

**Yahia:** Even an employed person can give yearly between 300 and 400 Euros. It depends on his honesty and his devotion to God. To sacrifice oneself in the name of God is the most beautiful thing, something you cannot describe.

**Rabei:** If one has the desire to sacrifice himself in the name of God, he must be ready. It is a shame we young people must be the first ones to sacrifice ourselves, like, for example, Muhammad, because God tests all of us and makes us tired, because he tests the faith in all of us, tests our soul. The solution is only one: be part of Al Qaeda. Here we are sleepers. It is one of our duties to go first to the jihad. Here they are torturing us and making us tired. Think, we come from our country far away to come to the non-believers' country. We made a mistake, but it's never too late, because our destination should be, for example, Chechnya, Kashmir, etc. We see death every day. Let's wish that God will give us the courage to win. The reward for those who choose death is limitless. Why one has to stay like this, then they catch you and you go to prison? Why not "tak, tak, tak" and you're a martyr, serve God.

**Yahia:** Stay always by my side. Unfortunately I was stopped from the beginning, but stay by my side and you'll see how I rise, with God's strength, and I'll go in.

**Rabei:** It takes a blow and then it's over. You see what they are doing to our brothers in Iraq; you see what they do to Arabs; you see the prisons; you see the humiliation. Isn't it better to die rather than to stay in prison there? What do the Americans believe, that they can stop us? There are other methods, they'll see. Do you remember that woman of whom I talked to you about, do you remember? That one whose name is Hotaf? I have bad news -- she was uncovered, but Islam will have the victory. I am sorry. There are other women ... she is not the first one and she won't be the last one. ... I am sorry that the tactics of the first one did not go well, that she was uncovered. Now we have Amal, she's ready. God is great. I am very sincere with you, you need to know that. Listen carefully to me, I am sincere. Know that I have many friends who died as martyrs in Afghanistan, who also died in jail. There is something that I don't hide from you -- the Madrid attack was my project and those who died as martyrs, they are my very dear friends.

**Yahia**: Ah!

**Rabei**: I am the thread of Madrid. At the time of the event I was not there, but I tell you the truth, before the operation, on the 4th, I had contacts with them. Do not open your mouth. I move alone, they work in a group.

**Yahia**: All died as martyrs?

**Rabei**: Five died as martyrs and eight were arrested. They are the best of friends. They are friends of the heart, of faithfulness. Already on the 4th I started to plan, to plan at a high level. I had wanted to plan so that it would be an unforgettable thing, including to me, because I was ready to blow up. But they stopped me, and we obey to God's will. I wanted a heavy burden but I did not find the means. This project took me a lot of studying and a lot of patience. It took me two and a half years. Do not mention anything and do not talk to Jalil, in any way, not even on the phone.

**Yahia**: Not even with the calling card?

**Rabei**: No, nothing. In any way, know that this information that I gave you, nobody in the world knows it. All my friends are dying one after the other. There are those who blew up in Afghanistan and there are many people that I know that are ready. I can tell you that there are two groups ready for martyrdom. The first group leaves the 25th, the 20th of next month for Iraq, through Syria. There are four ready for martyrdom. You cannot say anything, not even to Muhammad, even though he knows everything, and he knows those who are leaving on the 20th, but you don't know anything, okay?

**Yahia**: Okay, and Ahmed?

**Rabei**: Yes, he's there.

**Yahia**: The passports?

**Rabei**: Everything is ready, the passports are not a problem. They are already ready.

**Yahia**: Egyptian passports?

**Rabei**: Egyptian passports are not good. In Spain they were already bought for 200, 300 Euros, it depends on the color. French, Moroccan, Syrian, English and Pakistani passports, they are on the market, it is not a problem. Listen, your brother Muhammad knows everything, but I repeat myself, this is the first lesson that I give you. I've been wanting to tell you this for a long time, on the phone, nothing

**Yahia**: Even at the call centers?

**Rabei**: Nothing, nothing. When the moment arrives, you can't use anything. It's the first lesson, if you have a phone card, throw it away.

**Yahia**: Isn't my passport good for anything?

**Rabei**: No, the Egyptian passport is not good.

**Yahia**: I am ready to sacrifice myself.

**Rabei**: Brother Yahia, I praise you for your enthusiasm, but stay calm. Consider yourself as being already in paradise, just for the fact that you are already ready to sacrifice your life.

[They recite verses from the Quran.]

**Rabei**: You need to know that the jihad has several mechanisms, several components. There is knowledge, information, studying. Why don't you deal with obtaining information on the embassy and on the movements of its officers and employees? Try to meet someone from the embassy, because it's always useful to us if our brothers want to go in and out. Know that our brothers need information about the consulates in Europe. We have to talk more about this subject. Anyway, if you commit, you can't forget that you have made a commitment with God. I have met several brothers of the jihad, may God bless them, and they don't have any documents, nothing. They are ready for the jihad. They don't have any money, they have nothing. Oh my God, oh my God, know that in Holland there was a group who was ready to go, then, for different reasons, the knot was untied and now there is only one who's ready. He's agitated, he just got out of jail, but everything at its time. Know also that I met other brothers ... before they were drug dealers, criminals. I introduced them to the faith and now they are the first ones to ask me when is their moment for the jihad. Some of them went to Afghanistan and others are praying and waiting. ...

The second excerpt is from a May 28 face-to-face conversation between Rabei, Yahia and another man called Hussam. Rabei describes how when he lived in Germany, he hid his nationality, pretending to be Palestinian, and used techniques to disguise his fingerprints so the authorities couldn't keep track of him.

**Hussam**: Have you been to Germany?

**Rabei**: Yes, I lived in Germany.

**Hussam**: Is Germany nice?

**Rabei**: Yes, they are organized. If you work or study and they are not around you, they respect you. It is a population who wakes up early. They are hard workers. At eight o'clock they are already at work, do you understand, Yahia? But unfortunately half of my friends (in Germany) were arrested. If you have the documents you live well in Germany. I also had many Palestinian friends. It's easy for them to obtain the documents; they ask for political asylum, I also lived with them, in a detention center (for immigrants). The police there are very tough, especially since they've started to take fingerprints.

**Yahia**: Did they fingerprint you?

**Rabei**: Yes, once I scratched my fingers, once I used the transparent glue and still another time, when I was in the detention center and I pretended to be a Palestinian, I used a product, there is a special product that modifies fingerprints. I drove them crazy. In Germany I had to be ready because every two or three months they would fingerprint you and therefore you had to have the product with you.

They laugh.

**Rabei**: This way they can never find you. You make them confused. They are not able to know your nationality.

They laugh. ... Later, Hussam leaves and Rabei and Yahia watch a video of the decapitation of American contractor Nicholas Berg, who is believed to have been killed by Abu Musab al-Zarqawi.

**Rabei**: Come close. Watch closely with your own eyes. This is the policy we need to follow, the policy of the sword. Come and see our brother Abu Musab [al-Zarqawi].

At this point, we can hear the sound of a computer keyboard. The two men are now viewing the video of Nicholas Berg's decapitation, the American kidnapped in Iraq by Islamic militants.

**Rabei**: We need to be very firm, the decision is the decision.

We can hear the voice of the individual who reads the announcement and, immediately after that, Nicholas Berg's excruciating scream. Rabei is excited by the scene he's watching and teases the kidnapped man.

**Rabei**: This is the policy. God is great. God is great. God is great. Go to hell, God's enemy. Kill him, kill him. Yes, like that, slaughter him well, cut his head off. God is great, God is great.

**Yahia**: Isn't that a sin?

**Rabei**: Who said that? It's never a sin! It's never a sin for the cause. Everyone must end up like this. This is the truth, this is the truth. This is the final decision everyone. We wish that their parents also end up like this dog. Everyone, everyone. We only need to be sure in making the decisions. Yahia, are you scared? Are you shocked?

**Yahia**: No, no, I think it's a sin. I'm only thinking that it's a sin.

**Rabei**: When you are part of a movement, it is never a sin, because there is a cause, the Islamic cause. Everyone ends up in hell, everyone. This is the end for those who hurt Islam. Every thing that is done for Islam is a right thing. Every action is right -- the important thing is that you obtain results. ...

APPENDIX C

# "STRATEGY FOR ELIMINATING THE THREAT FROM THE JIHADIST NETWORKS OF AL QIDA: STATUS AND PROSPECTS"

# Strategy for Eliminating the Threat from the Jihadist Networks of al Qida: Status and Prospects

## 1. Summary

The al Qida terrorist organization lead by Usama bin Ladin has stitched together a network of terrorist cells and groups to wage jihad. Al Qida seeks to drive the United States out of the Arabian Peninsula and elsewhere in the Muslim world. It also seeks to overthrow moderate governments and establish theocracies similar to the Taliban regime in Afghanistan. The al Qida network is well financed, has trained tens of thousands of Jihadists, and has a cell structure in over forty nations. It also is actively seeking to develop and acquire weapons of mass destruction.

The United States' goal is to reduce the al Qida network to a point where it no longer poses a serious threat to our security or that of other governments. That goal can be achieved over a three to five year period, if adequate resources and policy attention are devoted to it.

Toward that end, the United States has developed a comprehensive and coordinated strategy that employs a variety of tools including: diplomacy, covert action, public information and media, law enforcement, intelligence collection, foreign assistance, financial regulation enforcement, and military means to affect al Qida to its core.

## 2. The Threat

Al Qida ("the base" or "the foundation") is both an independent terrorist organization and a sponsor and coordinator of a network of other semi-independent terrorist groups. The Al Qida network provides its members as well as its affiliates with a broad range of support:

--sophisticated media propaganda, through use of internet sites, videos, magazines, brochures, and speakers throughout the world

--substantial funding from its own investments and from a fund raising network throughout the world

Classified by Richard A. Clarke
Reason 1.5(d)(x6)
Declassify on: 12/29/25

2

--global recruitment and covert transportation of trainees through safe houses with false documentation

--advanced training in espionage, sabotage, weapons, and explosives at a series of al Qida camps in Afghanistan

--a multi-national pool of trained terrorists and Jihad fighters available to support Jihad in countries other than their own

--a global cell structure available to assist transport of terrorists, acquisition of materials, attack operations, and provide safe havens

The organizations substantially sponsored by the al Qida network include:

--al Ittihad in Kenya and Somalia

--Egyptian Islamic Jihad

--the Islamic Movement of Uzbekistan

--the Abu Sayyaf Group in the Philippines

--the Libyan Islamic Fighting Group

--the Abayan Islamic Army of Yemen

--the Chechnyan Mujaheedin

--the Palestinian Asbat al Ansar

--the Armed Islamic Group (GIA)

Al-Qida has recently increased its contacts with the Palestinian rejectionist gorups, including Hizbollah, Hamas and Palestine Islamic Jihad. There are substantial cells of Moroccans, Tunisians, Saudis, Pakistanis, and Algerians operating on a global basis supported by al Qida. In addition to the Arab and Central Asian nations, al Qida supports cells in the United States, Canada, Ireland, England, Israel, Italy, Turkey, Germany, Spain, Belgium, and Thailand. The cells include "sleeper agents" who marry into the local community, find local employment and

3

engage in criminal activity to raise funds (cell phone number cloning, credit card fraud, etc.) to sustain themselves and help support the international network..

al Qida developed beginning in the late 1980s as an outgrowth of the international jihad against the Soviet Union in Afghanistan. The avowed purpose of the organization is to evict the United States from the region and to replace "unholy" governments with Islamic fundamentalist regimes.

Initially, the group's chief targets were Saudi Arabia and Egypt. The group's leader and some of its central infrastructure were located in Sudan, although the training camps were in Afghanistan. Following successful diplomatic pressure on Sudan, al Qida moved its headquarters to Afghanistan in 1996. As their network grew, al Qida began to focus more attention on supporting operations in Bosnia and Central Asia (Chechnya, Dagestan, Uzbekistan, Tajikistan), while their targeting of the US, Saudi Arabia, and Egypt continued unabated.

    o  Direct Attacks on US:    In retrospect, we have discovered ties between what we now understand to be the al Qida network and a series of high profile attacks on the US in the early 1990s.   al Qida played a role in the attempted attack on US Air Force personnel in Yemen in 1992. There are indications that al Qida played a role in the World Trade Center bombing and the attack on US forces in Mogadishu, both in 1993. Sheik Rahman and the cell arrested in New York and New Jersey for planning to destroy the NY-NJ tunnels were also linked to al Qida. In fact, the Sheik's son is now a major al Qida network commander. It also appears likely that the Manila cell that was preparing bombs for six US flag 747s in 1993 was funded and trained by al Qida.

In 1998, Usama bin Ladin publicly declared war on the United States. In August, 1998 al Qida launched attacks on US embassies in Kenya and Tanzania. Attacks were also planned on US embassies in Albania and Uganda that year, but were disrupted. During 1998-99, al Qida cells were disrupted in several countries. Intelligence indicated that the al Qida network planned these attacks around the first of January, 2000, including: an al Qida network cell in Jordan where three attacks were to occur at sites where US citizens would be present; an al Qida network cell in Yemen was to attack a US Navy ship; and in December, a Canadian-based al Qida cell aligned with former GIA members was engaged in smuggling of bombs into the United States. All three sets of attacks were disrupted or failed, but the attack on a US Navy ship in Yemen was attempted again, successfully, in October, 2000.

4

o <u>Presence in the US</u>: al Qida is present in the United States. al Qida has been linked to terrorist operations in the U.S. while also conducting recruiting and fundraising activities. U.S. citizens have also been linked to al Qida.

Two al Qida members key to the planned multi-site attacks on Americans in Jordan (December 1999) were naturalized American citizens who had lived in Los Angeles and Boston. The plot to smuggle bombs from Canada to the US in 1999 revealed connections to al Qida supporters in several states. The 1993 World Trade Center and NY-NJ Tunnels conspiracies revealed an extensive terrorist presence, which we now understand was an early manifestation of al Qida in the US. A suspect in the East Africa bombings (former US Army Sergeant Ali Muhammad) has informed ███US███ that an extensive network of al Qida "sleeper" agents currently exists in the US.

o <u>Subversion of Other Governments</u>: Jihadists trained at al Qida network camps in Afghanistan are among those engaged in terrorism against several governments, notably Egypt, Algeria, Jordan, Uzbekistan, and the Philippines. The al Qida network-sponsored religious and Jihadist propaganda is spread throughout the Gulf (Kuwait, Saudi Arabia, UAE) and Arab communities in Europe. The propaganda links the US and Israel to moderate Islamic regimes, making it more difficult for some governments to cooperate openly with the US. While al Qida alone cannot overthrow a government, it can substantially assist in the creation of a climate driven by propaganda where trained indigenous oppositionists supported by al Qida will engage in violence at their behest. Up to 50,000 Jihadists from over three dozen nations have been trained in al Qida camps in Afghanistan and then returned to their home countries.

o <u>Weapons of Mass Destruction</u>: Numerous sources have reported that al Qida is attempting to develop or acquire chemical or radiological weapons. The al Qida acquisition network in Europe and the former Soviet Union have repeatedly attempted to obtain WMD components. Al Qida's Derunta camp near Jalalabad in Afghanistan has been identified as a development and testing facility for poisons and chemical weapons and poisons. [References to ███████████ nerve gases) have been founded on captured computers[Operational detail, removed at the request of the CIA

5

### 3. The US Goal:  Roll Back

The United States goal is to roll back the al Qida network to a point where it will no longer pose a serious threat to the US or its interests, as was done to previously robust terrorist groups such as the Abu Nidal Organization and the Japanese Red Army.  In order to significantly reduce the threat al Qida poses to US interests, every element of its infrastructure must be considerably weakened or eliminated, most notably:

--the significant camp and facility infrastructure for training and safehaven sanctuary in Afghanistan

--access to large amounts of money and the ability to disperse it internationally to support cells and affiliated terrorist groups.

--multiple active cells capable of launching military style, large-scale terrorist operations

--a large pool of personnel willing to risk being identified as al Qida members and willing to reside at al Qida facilities.

The United States actively seeks to reduce al Qida to such a rump group in the next three to five years through a steady and coordinated program employing all relevant means.

### 4.  Implementing the Strategy: The Record to Date

To implement this strategy, the US has used diplomacy, intelligence collection, covert action, law enforcement, foreign assistance, force protection and diplomatic security in a coordinated campaign against al Qida:

o Intelligence Collection:  Beginning in 1996, the al Qida network was singled out for special treatment within the US counter-terrorism community.  A "Virtual Station" was created by CIA, an organization modeled on a CIA overseas station dedicated to collection and operations against al Qida.  NSA and CIA made collection against the al Qida network a major requirement, with higher priority given only to support of on-going US military operations.

o Sanctuary Sudan Eliminated:  The US placed significant diplomatic pressure on Sudan, resulting in a decision by the Sudanese government to request

6

bin Ladin to abandon Khartoum and move his headquarters to the camps in Afghanistan. US diplomacy with Saudi Arabia resulted in the Kingdom depriving bin Ladin of his Saudi citizenship and taking steps to deny him access to financial assets held in his name.

o Diplomacy with Pakistan and the Taliban: Repeated diplomatic efforts with Pakistan gained some limited law enforcement and intelligence cooperation against al Qida. The Pakistani government requested that the Taliban cease to provide sanctuary to al Qida, but the Pakistanis did not condition their support of the Taliban on compliance. Similarly, frequent direct diplomatic contact with the Taliban by the US has failed to gain any cooperation on ending the al Qida presence in Afghanistan. Beginning in late 1998, the US has repeatedly told the Taliban leadership that their complicity in harboring al Qida makes them equally culpable for al Qida operations against us. While some in the Taliban leadership appear willing to cooperate with the US, the ruler (Mullah Omar) has prohibited any action against al Qida.

o Saudi Support Gained: By 1997, CIA was identifying al Qida cells in several nations and working with local security services to disrupt them. Also that year, the Saudis disrupted a plot by the al Qida cell in the Kingdom ▮▮▮
Operational detail, removed at the request of the CIA
Subsequently, the Saudis began taking the al Qida threat seriously and pressured the Taliban to check bin Ladin's activities. Saudi Arabia then joined in demanding bin Ladin's arrest by the Taliban and, when Saudi efforts failed, they severed diplomatic ties and terminated direct assistance to the Taliban.

o UN Security Council Sanctions: By 1999, the Saudis and others joined us in sponsoring limited UN sanctions on Afghanistan because of its harboring of bin Ladin. The US seized over $250,000,000 in Taliban funds. At the end of 2000, the United States and Russia co-sponsored a further round of UN sanctions that included a one sided arms embargo (only on the Taliban, not on the Northern Alliance) and expanded UN demands to include closure of the terrorist infrastructure in Afghanistan. The resolution passed 13-0-2, China and Malaysia abstaining.

o Renditions and Disruptions: With two, nearly simultaneous, suicide truck-bomb attacks, al Qida destroyed the US embassies in Kenya and Tanzania in 1998. The US stepped up the al Qida cell disruption effort. In addition to disrupting cells, the US found and brought to the US for trial al Qida operatives in Jordan, Egypt, Pakistan, Malaysia, South Africa, Kenya, Tanzania, Germany, and the

7

United Kingdom. Other al Qida operative[s] not indicted in the US were brought to
[countries]              where they were wanted by authorities.

o <u>Building Partner Capability</u>: Through the CIA's Counter-terrorism Center
(CTC) and State's Anti-Terrorism Assistance Program (ATA) the US has
enhanced the capabilities of several nations to collect intelligence on al Qida and to
disrupt their operations. [Operational detail, removed at the request of the CIA]

Counter-terrorism training and equipment have been provided to several nations'
security forces.. As a result of these partnerships, simultaneous disruptions of over
twenty al Qida cells were conducted in December, 1999 to prevent possible
Millennium celebration period attacks. The FBI has also greatly strengthened
counter-terrorism cooperation with foreign counterparts, including stationing of
FBI personnel overseas and training partner organizations at home and abroad.

o <u>Inside Afghanistan</u>: CIA developed sources inside Afghanistan who were
able to report on the activities and locations of al Qida commanders. One group
was developed as a covert action team designed to forcibly apprehend al Qida
commanders and hand them off to US arrest teams. An Intelligence Finding
authorized the use of lethal force as part of operations against the al Qida
commanders. Several efforts to apprehend or attack the al Qida leadership using
Afghan personnel were unsuccessful. [A foreign] government unit was trained and
equipped for a similar mission, but has not yet been employed in an operation.

The Afghan Northern Alliance is engaged in civil war with the Taliban. al Qida
has been a major source of the Taliban's success, providing the best fighting unit
(the 55th Brigade) and literally buying the support of provincial leaders. The
Pakistani Army has also provided the Taliban with advisors, intelligence, training,
equipment, and placed personnel in Taliban units. The US has provided very
limited intelligence and non-lethal equipment to the Northern Alliance, in
exchange for intelligence on al Qida. The Northern Alliance has not yet been able
to mount an apprehension operation against al Qida commanders.

o <u>Military Operations</u>: In August, 1998 the US struck al Qida facilities in
Afghanistan and an al Qida associated chemical plant in Sudan. Subsequent to
those attacks, follow-on attacks were considered and military assets deployed on
three occasions when the al Qida commanders were located in Afghanistan by
Humint sources. The Humint sources were not sufficiently reliable and a lack of
second source corroboration prevented US military action. Thus in September,

8

2000 the CIA began covert flights into Afghanistan using the Predator UAV operating out of Uzbekistan. On three occasions, the UAV provided ███ video coverage of what appeared to be gatherings involving the senior al Qida leadership. The UAV operations were suspended ████████████████ but plans are now being developed to allow operations to recommence in late March. The Spring flights may be able to incorporate a new capability: Hellfire anti-tank missiles mounted aboard the Predators. This new capability would permit a "see it/shoot it" option ██ Operational detail, removed at the request of the CIA ███████

o **Better Self-Defense**: Defense, State, and CIA have all taken steps to enhance our capability to defend US installations abroad against al Qida attacks. Physical security measures have been greatly enhanced at likely target facilities. Additional security personnel have been deployed, including covert counter-surveillance units. Intelligence reports indicate that al Qida considered attacks on several facilities, but decided that the enhanced defensive measures would prevent those attacks from succeeding. Ambassadors have been encouraged to take steps, including temporary closing of embassies and consulates, based upon intelligence without waiting for Washington approval. Embassy Dushanbe and Embassy Khartoum have been closed for security reasons. Embassy Doha was relocated on an emergency basis. New, more secure embassies are under construction or planned at several locations as part of a multi-year plan, but further funding is needed.

o **Financing**: Al Qida and several of its affiliates are legally designated Foreign Terrorist Organizations under US law, making it a felony to transfer money to them through US institutions or to raise money for them (or their front organizations) in the US. Moreover, the US can take banking sanctions against foreign banking institutions which facilitate terrorist finances. ████████ CIA has ██ been able to collect numerous reports about alleged al Qida investments, companies, and transactions. Treasury has had pledges of cooperation from several nations, including Saudi Arabia, the UAE, and Kuwait. Based on the absence of actionable intelligence, however, Treasury has not been able to make specific requests to these countries. State has taken action against several Islamic NGOs which appear to be fronts for al Qida ████████████

5. Bringing the Strategy to Completion – The Next Three to Five Years

The programs initiated in the last three years lay the basis for achieving the strategic goal of rendering the al Qida network as a non serious threat to the US,

9

but success can only be achieved if the pace and resource levels of the programs continue to grow as planned.

Continued anti-al Qida operations at the current level will prevent some attacks, but will not seriously attrit their ability to plan and conduct attacks. Absent additional resource, cells that are disrupted will continue to be replaced, the organizational presence in the US will not be uncovered fully, and the overall capability of the al Qida networks may be held in check or may continue to grow, but will not be dismantled.

In order to implement the overall, global strategy while undermining the ability of al-Qa'ida to utilize Afghanistan, CIA has prepared a program that focuses on eliminating it as a safehaven, disrupting the mujahidin support infrastructure that connects Afghanistan to the global network, and changing the operational environment inside Afghanistan.
Possible steps include:

Safehavens

- Massive support to anti-Taliban groups such as the Northern Alliance led by Ahamd Shah Masood. This effort would be intended primarily to keep Islamic extremist fighters tied down in Afghanistan.

- Identify and destroy camps or portions of camps run by known terrorists while classes are in session. To take advantage fully of this initiative, we would need to have special teams ready for covert entry into destroyed camps to acquire intelligence for locating terrorist cells outside Afghanistan. This effort would require either a commitment from JSOC or a liaison force capable of conducting activity on-the-ground inside Afghanistan.

- In order to integrate the above elements and to fully exploit proposed new capabilities, we would need to continue and expand the Predator UAV program. If testing prove successful, we could also introduce armed UAVs into Afghanistan in the Spring.

Mujahidin Support Infrastructure

- Continue and expand efforts to arrest and disrupt recruiter, travel, and false document facilitators, and those who run the waystaions and guesthouses abroad.

10

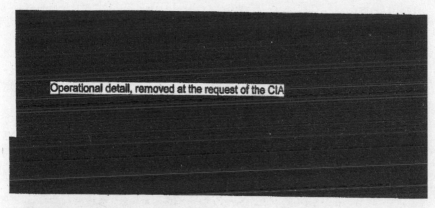

Operational detail, removed at the request of the CIA

## Operational Environment Afghanistan

- Explore possible efforts to remove the more extreme wing of the Taliban from power. This could involved a combination of propaganda and covert action to further divide the Taliban by amplifying and exploiting divisions within the leadership.

CIA's program would require funding ▓▓▓▓▓▓▓▓▓▓▓▓▓ over five years. In addition, other U.S. assets must be incorporated into the effort.

-- State Department programs for Anti-terrorism Assistance and a new information media effort;

-- Treasury's new interagency Terrorist Asset Tracking Center;

--a significant US role in multilateral counter narcotics operations aimed at the Afghan heroin trade, requiring increased State and DEA resources; and

-- FBI's programs to translate and analyze material obtained from domestic surveillance authorized under the Foreign Intelligence Surveillance Act (FISA) and to operate multi-agency Joint Terrorism Task Forces (JTTFs) in major metropolitan areas. And recent funding to support Customs, IRS, and INS participation in the JTTFs must be sustained and expanded.

o Near Term Policy Decisions: In addition to program above, there are also several key policy decisions on steps that hold significant prospects for reducing

██████████████████             II

the al Qida threat. These policy decisions relate to attacking al Qida's center of gravity: sanctuary in Afghanistan under Taliban sponsorship.

-- Covert US assistance to the Northern Alliance to oppose the Taliban militarily. Such assistance could include funding, intelligence support, and ████ ██████████ equipment. █████████ proposed a twelve month program ████ ██████████ that would allow Masood to stay in the fight with the Taliban and al-Qida as a credible, conventional threat;

-- Covert US assistance to Uzbekistan ███████████████████████████
Operational detail, removed at the request of the CIA
██████████████████████████████████████████████████████

--Continued Predator UAV operations, resuming in March.

--Overt US military action to destroy al Qida command/control and infrastructure and Taliban military and command assets.

## Considerations with Pakistan

These decisions involve consideration of US policy toward Pakistan. Like almost all of Pakistan's foreign and security policy, their approach to the Taliban and to terrorism flows from ████ concems ██████████ with seizing Kashmir and redressing its defeat by India in three wars. Support for the Taliban has run through three Pakistani governments – Bhutto, Sharif, and now Musharraf – and is predicated on the concept of "strategic depth," i.e. ensuring a friendly government in Kabul that will not pose a threat in the event of another war with India. The Pakistani military has consistently believed the Taliban was the best means of achieving that goal. Russian and Indian support for the Taliban's only remaining military opponent reinforces Pakistan's tendency to view Afghanistan through an Indo-Pakistani lens.

Pakistan's acquiescence in the Taliban's hosting of terrorist camps and bin Laden is a product of the nexus between Afghanistan and Pakistan's proxy war in Kashmir. ████████████████████████████████████████
Operational detail, removed at the request of the CIA
██████████████████████████████████████████████████████

12

Support for bin Laden comes also from a small but dedicated cadre of Islamist leaders whose electoral influence in Pakistan is minimal but whose street power has intimidated successive governments into fostering Islamic causes. Bin Laden has benefited as he ostentatiously supports Islamic causes as far afield as Bosnia and Chechnya.

As we seek Pakistani cooperation, we need to keep in mind that Pakistan has been most willing to cooperate with us on terrorism when its role is invisible or at least plausibly deniable to the powerful Islamist right wing. Pakistan's rendition to the US of Ramzi Yousef and Mir Aimal Kansi and to Jordan last year of Khalil Deek were sharply criticized by the Islamic parties. Overt Pakistani support for U.S. action against bin Laden, who is a hero especially in the Pushtun-ethnic border areas near Afghanistan, would be so unpopular as to threaten Musharraf's government.

We do have levers with the Pakistanis, despite the deleterious effect of overlapping sanctions (Pressler, Glenn, military coup, MTCR) that we imposed beginning in 1990:
- The blunt instrument of UNSC sanctions – Pakistan wants to be seen as a responsible member of the international community and will attempt to comply, in whole or in part
- Increasing domestic opposition to ███ clandestine campaigns. The Afghan camps train Sunni extremists whose bloody warfare against Pakistan's Shi'a community ultimately threatens the nation's future. Similarly, the fundamentalism fed by the madrassas of Pakistan and by Taliban hard-liners is anathema to the moderate military and civilian leaders of Pakistan
- Economic leverage. As Musharraf implements the economic rescue policies he hopes will pull Pakistan out of its steep decline, he needs our moral and practical support in the IMF for a medium-term economic support package.

We are already pursuing policies that have the effect – but only over a very long term – of encouraging Pakistan's distaste for its Taliban adventure:

- Lending our support to a fair but non-violent settlement of Kashmir;

13

- Demonstrating that there are alternatives to the Taliban (e.g., traditional leaders chosen through the Loya Jirga process) that serve Pakistan's national interests; and
- Helping to build up a secular educational system that ends rural Pakistan's exclusive reliance on the fundamentalist madrassas.

Chief Executive Musharraf has been clear in his discussions with American officials that:

--he opposes terrorism and al Qida and believes that the spread of such fundamentalism threatens Pakistani internal stability;

--Pakistan requires a Pashtun majority government in Afghanistan and the repatriation of refugees, which can best be achieved through support to Taliban;

--but there are influential radical elements in Pakistan that would oppose significant Pakistani measures against al Qida or the Taliban;

--Pakistan has been unable to persuade the Taliban to yield up bin Ladin and close the sanctuary and is unwilling to do more to persuade them.

In the wake of the attack on the USS Cole, Pakistan has called upon the US not to violate Pakistani airspace (again) to launch punitive strikes in Afghanistan.

# PENTAGON NEWS RELEASE CRITICIZING A MEDIA MYTH FEATURED IN THE *NEW YORKER* MAGAZINE

**U.S. Department of Defense**
Office of the Assistant Secretary of Defense (Public Affairs)

# News Release

On the Web:
http://www.defenselink.mil/cgi-bin/dlprint.cgi?
http://www.defenselink.mil/releases/2005/nr20050117-1987.html
Media contact: +1 (703) 697-5131

Public contact:
http://www.dod.mil/faq/comment.html
or +1 (703) 428-0711

No. 046-05
January 17, 2005

**IMMEDIATE RELEASE**

### Statement from Pentagon Spokesman Lawrence DiRita on Latest Seymour Hersh Article

The Iranian regime's apparent nuclear ambitions and its demonstrated support for terrorist organizations is a global challenge that deserves much more serious treatment than Seymour Hersh provides in the *New Yorker* article titled "The Coming Wars."

Mr. Hersh's article is so riddled with errors of fundamental fact that the credibility of his entire piece is destroyed.

Mr. Hersh's source(s) feed him with rumor, innuendo, and assertions about meetings that never happened, programs that do not exist, and statements by officials that were never made.

A sampling from this article alone includes:

- The post-election meeting he describes between the Secretary of Defense and the Joint Chiefs of Staff did not happen.

- The only civilians in the chain-of-command are the President and the Secretary of Defense, despite Mr. Hersh's confident assertion that the chain of command now includes two Department policy officials. His assertion is outrageous, and constitutionally specious.

- Arrangements Mr. Hersh alleges between Under Secretary Douglas Feith and Israel, government or non-government, do not exist. Here, Mr. Hersh is building on links created by the soft bigotry of some conspiracy theorists. This reflects poorly on Mr. Hersh and the *New Yorker*.

- Mr. Hersh cannot even keep track of his own wanderings. At one point in his article, he makes the outlandish assertion that the military operations he describes are so secret that the operations are being kept secret even from U.S. military Combatant Commanders. Mr. Hersh later states, though, that the locus of this super-secret activity is at the U.S. Central Command headquarters, evidently without the knowledge of the commander if Mr. Hersh is to be believed.

By his own admission, Mr. Hersh evidently is working on an "alternative history" novel. He is well along in that work, given the high quality of "alternative present" that he has developed in several recent articles.

Mr. Hersh's preference for single, anonymous, unofficial sources for his most fantastic claims makes it difficult to parse his discussion of Defense Department operations.

Finally, the views and policies Mr. Hersh ascribes to Secretary Rumsfeld, Deputy Secretary Wolfowitz, Under Secretary Feith, and other Department of Defense officials do not reflect their public or private comments or administration policy.

# BIBLIOGRAPHY

*The al-Qaeda Documents, Volume 1*. Alexandria, VA: Tempest Publishing, 2002. A good compendium of primary source materials.

*The al-Qaeda Documents, Volume 2*. Alexandria, VA: Tempest Publishing, 2003.

*The al-Qaeda Documents, Volume 3*. Alexandria, VA: Tempest Publishing, 2003.

Abuza, Zachary. *Militant Islam in Southeast Asia: Crucible of Terror*. Boulder: Lynne Rienner Publishers, 2003. An excellent resource on terrorism in Southeast Asia. The author has regional intelligence sources, a good grasp of history, and writes with authority.

Alexander, Yonah. *Combating Terrorism: Strategies of Ten Countries*. Ann Arbor: University of Michigan Press, 2002. A strong, scholarly study.

Alexander, Yonah and Michael S. Swetnam. *Usama bin Laden's al-Qaida: Profile of a Terrorist Network*. New York: Transnational Publishers, Inc., 2001. A good primer, some dodgy information.

Allison, Graham. *Nuclear Terrorism: The Ultimate Preventable Catastrophe*. New York: Owl Books, 2004. If you worried about nuclear suitcase-sized bombs, this is the book for you.

Al-Rasheed, Madawi. *A History of Saudi Arabia*. Cambridge: Cambridge University Press, 2002. A good introduction to the history of Arabia.

Anonymous. *Through Our Enemies' Eyes: Osama bin Laden, Radical Islam, and the Future of America*. Washington, D.C.: Brassey's, Inc., 2002. The former chief of the CIA's "bin Laden station" gives the agency's institutional view. Very interesting.

Armstrong, Karen. *Islam: A Short History*. New York: Random House, 2000. A good overview from an American liberal scholar. Discussion of the Arab pre-Islamic roots of Islam (especially Islam's pilgrimage to Mecca pre-dating the prophet Mohammed by hundreds of years).

Ashley, Clarence. *CIA SpyMaster*. Graetna, LA: Pelican Publishing Company, 2004. The biography of George Kisevalter, a legendary agency man, who recruited the CIA's first sources inside Soviet military intelligence. Excellent on the Cuban missile crisis.

Avni, Zeev. *False Flag: The Soviet Spy Who Penetrated the Israeli Secret Intelligence Service*. London: St. Ermin's Press, 1999. The story of a Swiss Jewish Communist who became a double agent—against the legendary Mossad. Most interesting, especially given that the author is now a psychiatrist, is the mental states of terrorists and traitors. That self-loathing could be a cause of anti-state violence is a theme that should be further investigated.

Baer, Robert. *See No Evil: The True Story of a Ground Soldier in the CIA's War on Terrorism*. New York: Three Rivers Press, 2002. A very readable account by a CIA officer operating in Lebanon in the 1980s and Iraq in the 1990s. Read the Beirut story about the CIA polygraph operator trying to administer a lie detector test to a source as shells are exploding nearby.

Bahmanyar, Mir. *Afghanistan Cave Complexes 1979–2004: Mountain Strongholds of the Mujahideen, Taliban, and Al Qaeda*. Oxford, UK: Osprey Publishing, 2004.

Bamford, James. *Body of Secrets: Anatomy of the Ultra-Secret National Security Agency*. New York: Anchor Books/Random House, 2002. Bamford is the best kind of critic—one with inside sources. A must read.

Barkey, Henri J. and Graham E. Fuller. *Turkey's Kurdish Question*. New York: Carnegie Corporation, 1998. A dry, thorough treatment of the Kurds inside Turkey. Particularly good on the ideology of the PKK.

Barnett, Thomas P. M. *The Pentagon's New Map: War and Peace in the Twenty-First Century*. New York: G. P. Putnam's Sons, 2004. A fascinating 30,000-foot perspective on America's new strategic landscape. It should bury lingering Cold War notions.

Barone, Michael and Grant Ujifusa. *The Almanac of American Politics 2004*. Washington, D.C.: National Journal Group, 2003. The bible of Washington. Its pithy profiles of senators and congressman are invaluable and well written. The section on Representative Porter Goss is essential background.

Bearden, Milt and James Risen. *The Main Enemy: The Inside Story of the CIA's Final Showdown with the KGB*. New York: Random House, 2003. A masterful account of Cold War intelligence operations against the Soviets. Some of those mentioned here are now directing operations against al Qaeda. Bearden was CIA station chief in Islamabad and Khartoum.

Bell, Stewart. *Cold Terror: How Canada Nurtures and Exports Terrorism around the World*. Canada: John Wiley & Sons Canada Ltd., 2004. A very readable and powerful account of Canada's ties to al Qaeda and other terrorist groups—and why, for internal political reasons, they do little about it.

Benjamin, Daniel and Steven Simon. *The Age of Sacred Terror*. New York: Random House, 2002. One of the very few inside accounts of the Clinton years. The authors were directors on the National Security Council. Though unduly defensive in certain areas, this is an important book.

Bergen, Peter L. *Holy War, Inc.: Inside the Secret World of Osama bin Laden*. New York: Simon and Schuster, 2002. An excellent early account of bin Laden by a veteran CNN producer. Bergen actually interviewed bin Laden in Afghanistan.

Berman, Paul. *Terror and Liberalism*. New York: W. W. Norton & Company, 2003. Academic but interesting.

Bodansky, Yossef. *Bin Laden: The Man Who Declared War on America*. Roseville, CA: Prima Publishing, 2001. Meeting in his hideaway office, a senator on the Intelligence Committee summed it up best: "great book, no footnotes." A treasure trove of information and analysis. Given the nature of his sources, it can be hard to verify some items. The ones that the author has been able to check through intelligence sources have all checked out.

———. *The Secret History of the Iraq War*. New York: ReganBooks/HarperCollins, 2004. Lays out interesting new evidence about Saddam's support for Islamic terrorists following the 1991 Gulf War.

———. *Target America: Terrorism in the U.S. Today*. New York: S.P.I. Books, 1993. Unlike his later works, this was not a bestselling book. But a serious student of terrorism should read it; among other things, it describes terrorist sleeper cells in the United States and gives an interesting account of the terrorist attack outside CIA headquarters in 1993. It also mentions Iran's plans to fly planes into buildings in the 1980s.

Boot, Max. *The Savage Wars of Peace: Small Wars and the Rise of American Power*. New York: Basic Books, 2002. An interesting book by an engaging writer and former *Wall Street Journal* editorial-page features editor. For policymakers and citizens, it provides a good primer for how the U.S. once fought and won small-unit wars. This is probably how the War on Terror will be won. Useful for evaluating U.S. operations in the Philippines, Iraq, Afghanistan, and elsewhere.

Briody, Dan. *The Halliburton Agenda: The Politics of Oil and Money*. Hoboken, N.J.: John Wiley & Sons, Inc., 2004. A careful critique of one of America's hated companies by an able reporter.

————. *The Iron Triangle: Inside the Secret World of the Carlyle Group*. Hoboken, N.J.: John Wiley & Sons, Inc., 2003. Despite some bursts of heavy breathing, a reliable account of the Carlyle Group.

Brisard, Jean-Charles. *Zarqawi: The New Face of Al-Qaeda*. New York: Other Press, 2005. A biography of Zarqawi, which reproduces many interesting documents.

Burke, Jason. *Al-Qaeda: The True Story of Radical Islam*. New York: Penguin Books, 2003, 2004. Burke argues that "al Qaeda" is just a loose grouping of terrorists, not a global organization. Ultimately, Burke is wrong, but the writing is sharp and the observations often sound.

Bush, George W. *We Will Prevail: On War, Terrorism, and Freedom*. New York: The Continuum International Publishing Group Ltd, 2003. A collection of Bush's speeches and documents. A handy reference.

Clarke, Richard A. *Against All Enemies: Inside America's War on Terror*. New York: Simon & Schuster/Free Press, 2004. The first chapter and the last few chapters are worth reading, even though he gets many checkable small facts wrong.

Coll, Steve. *Ghost Wars: A Secret History of the CIA, Afghanistan, and Bin Laden from the Soviet Invasion to September 10, 2001*. New York: The Penguin Press, 2004. An excellent piece of reporting about Central Asia's cauldron of terror.

Cooley, John K. *Unholy Wars: Afghanistan, America, and International Terrorism*. London: Pluto Press, 2000. An energetic critic.

Corbin, Jane. *The Base: Al-Qaeda and the Changing Face of Global Terror*. London: Pocket Books/Simon & Schuster, 2003. A veteran BBC reporter writes a serious, detailed account. A must read.

Coughlin, Con. *Saddam*. London: Macmillan, 2002. An excellent and readable account of the rise and rule of Saddam Hussein. Saddam's early esteem for the Nazis is especially interesting.

Crile, George. *Charlie Wilson's War: The Extraordinary Story of the Largest Covert Operation in History*. New York: Atlantic Monthly Press, 2003. A very lively book that explores U.S. endeavors to drive the Soviets from Afghanistan through the efforts of a colorful, self-destructive congressman.

Dresch, Paul. *A History of Modern Yemen*. Cambridge: Cambridge University Press, 2000. Good, recent books on Yemen are hard to find. This is one.

Elshtain, Jean Bethke. *Just War Against Terror: The Burden of American Power in a Violent World*. New York: Basic Books, 2003. A rare pro-interventionist argument.

Esposito, John L. *Unholy War: Terror in the Name of Islam*. New York: Oxford University Press, 2002. The consensus, establishment view on radical Islam, for better or worse.

Farah, Douglas. *Blood from Stones: The Secret Financial Network of Terror*. New York: Broadway Books, 2004. Good reporting from West Africa.

Friedman, George. *America's Secret War: Inside the Hidden Worldwide Struggle between America and its Enemies*. New York: Doubleday, 2004.

Frum, David and Richard Perle. *An End to Evil: How to Win the War on Terror*. New York: Random House, 2003. The media wasted their time worrying if evil exists or if it could be ended. They should have been reading this fascinating book.

Geraghty, Tony. *Who Dares Wins: The Special Air Service; 1950 to the Gulf War*. London: Time Warner Paperbacks, 1992. A classic account of British special forces.

Gertz, Bill. *Breakdown: How America's Intelligence Failures Led to September 11*. Washington, D.C.: Regnery, 2002. By the dogged *Washington Times* investigative reporter, with excellent intelligence sources. The section on "Project Bojinka" in the Philippines is especially good.

Gold, Dore. *Hatred's Kingdom: How Saudi Arabia Supports the New Global Terrorism*. Washington, D.C.: Regnery, 2003. While academic in tone, it provides many fresh details linking the oil kingdom to terrorism. The history chapters are particularly strong.

———, *Tower of Babel: How the United Nations has Fueled Global Chaos*. New York: Crown Forum, 2004. An interesting critique by someone who saw the UN up close.

Griffin, Michael. *Reaping the Whirlwind: Afghanistan, Al Qa'ida, and the Holy War*. London: Pluto Press, 2003. Good, fresh details on the Taliban.

Gudjonsson, Gisli H. *The Psychology of Interrogations and Confessions: A Handbook*. West Sussex, UK: John Wiley & Sons, Ltd, 2003. The definitive book on how intelligence operatives get information from prisoners. Recommended to me by David Rose of *Vanity Fair* and, as usual, a damn good recommendation.

Gunaratna, Rohan. *Inside Al Qaeda*. New York: Columbia University Press, 2002. Thorough and academic, but a must read. Gunaratna is widely respected in the field, often consulted by intelligence services, and carefully parses his facts. One small example: We learn that bin Laden never got a degree in engineering, as was widely reported.

Hayes, Stephen F. *The Connection: How Al Qaeda's Collaboration with Saddam Hussein Has Endangered America*. New York: HarperCollins, 2004.

Hitz, Frederick P. *The Great Game: The Myths and Reality of Espionage*. New York: Vintage Books, 2004. A CIA veteran writes about the art of "tradecraft." Interesting background.

Hoffman, Bruce. *Inside Terrorism*. New York: Columbia University Press, 1998. Hoffman is a giant in this field. This book shows why.

Hoge, James F. Jr. and Gideon Rose. *How Did This Happen? Terrorism and the New War*. New York: Council on Foreign Relations, Inc., 2001. Authoritative and thorough.

Hoile, David. *Images of Sudan: Case Studies in Propaganda and Misrepresentation*. London: European-Sudanese Public Affairs Council, 2003. A pro-Sudan activist makes his case, with many footnotes. Offers a more nuanced view than usually appears in the Western press.

———. *The Search for Peace in the Sudan: A Chronology of the Sudanese Peace Process 1989–2001*. London: European-Sudanese Public Affairs Council, 2002. A pro-Sudan look at the political situation in Africa's largest country.

Holm, Richard L. *The American Agent: My Life in the CIA*. London: St. Ermin's Press, 2003. A well-written account from a CIA station chief who served in Laos in the 1960s to the capture of Carlos the Jackal in 1994. Holm was also the first head of the Counter-Terrorism Center. Informative and enjoyable reading.

Holt, P. M., and M. W. Daly. *A History of the Sudan: From the Coming of Islam to the Present Day*. Essex, UK: Pearson Education Limited, 2000. A good history of post-1956 Sudan. Important for understanding the various deep currents in Sudanese politics.

Kaplan, Robert D. *The Coming Anarchy: Shattering the Dreams of the Post Cold War*. New York: Vintage Books, 2000. A good tour through many failed states.

Keegan, John. *The Iraq War*. New York: Vintage Books, 2004. One of Britain's finest military historians and writers sheds light on America's most misunderstood war.

Kessler, Ronald. *The Bureau*. New York: St. Martin's Press, 2002. A good, critical history of the FBI. Excellent sources; note the website where agents and retirees grumble.

———. *The CIA at War: Inside the Secret Campaign Against Terror*. New York: St. Martin's Press, 2003. A good read that is obviously the product of many interviews.

Kushner, Harvey with Bart Davis. *Holy War on the Home Front: The Secret Islamic Terror Network in the United States*. New York: Sentinel, 2004.

Lance, Peter. *1,000 Years for Revenge: International Terrorism and the FBI; The Untold Story*. New York: HarperCollins/ReganBooks, 2003. Lance's account of the O'Neill-Bodine dispute is valuable.

Laqueur, Walter. *The New Terrorism: Fanaticism and the Arms of Mass Destruction*. New York: Oxford University Press, 1999. An unblinking look at the root causes of terror.

————, ed. *Voices of Terror: Manifestos, Writings, and Manuals of Al Qaeda, Hamas, and Other Terrorists from Around the World and Throughout the Ages.* New York: Reed Press, 2004. A good collection of primary source documents from a variety of terror groups.

Lesser, Ian O., Bruce Hoffman, John Arquilla, David Ronfeldt, Michele Zanini. *Countering the New Terrorism.* Santa Monica: RAND (Project Air Force), 1999. A collection of essays, some of which are penetrating.

Lewis, Bernard. *The Crisis of Islam: Holy War and Unholy Terror.* London: Weidenfeld & Nicolson, 2003. Clear-eyed and well written, especially chapter three, "From Crusaders to Imperialists."

————. *The Middle East: A Brief History of the Last 2,000 Years.* New York: Touchstone, 1995. Probably the best single-volume history of the Middle East accessible to the layman.

————. *What Went Wrong? Western Impact and Middle Eastern Response.* Oxford: Oxford University Press, 2002. An enlightening essay from one of the premier scholars in the field.

Lewis, Jon E. *The Mammoth Book of SAS & Elite Forces: Graphic Accounts of Military Exploits by the World's Special Forces.* London: Constable and Robinson, Ltd, 2001. More information on the equipment and technologies of the British special forces.

Mackey, Sandra. *The Iranians: Persia, Islam, and the Soul of a Nation.* New York: Plume Books, 1998. A good history of Iran.

Maley, William, ed. *Fundamentalism Reborn? Afghanistan and the Taliban.* New York: New York University Press, 2001. An interesting pre–September 11 assessment.

McInerney, Lt. Gen. Thomas and Maj. Gen. Paul Vallely. *Endgame: The Blueprint for Victory in the War on Terror.* Washington, D.C.: Regnery, 2004.

Mead, Walter Russell. *Power, Terror, Peace, and War: America's Grand Strategy in a World at Risk.* New York: Borzi, 2004. A Council on Foreign Relations fellow offers a "Jacksonian" view on foreign policy. Very interesting. I've read it several times.

Miller, John and Michael Stone. *The Cell: Inside the 9/11 Plot, and Why the FBI and CIA Failed to Stop It.* New York: Hyperion, 2003. Probably the single best account so far. Well documented.

Miniter, Richard. *Losing bin Laden: How Bill Clinton's Failures Unleashed Global Terror.* Washington, D.C.: Regnery, 2003. My first book on terrorism, with accounts from many Clinton insiders including counter-terrorism czar Richard Clarke, former secretary of state Madeleine Albright, former CIA director James

Woolsey, and others. Includes intelligence documents received from Sudanese intelligence on al Qaeda and rare photos of bin Laden's house, office, and plane.

————. *Shadow War: The Untold Story of How America Is Winning the War on Terror*. Washington, D.C.: Regnery, 2004. An account of covert operations against al Qaeda by the Bush administration, including a special section on the many connections between Iraq and al Qaeda.

Moore, Robin. *The Hunt for Bin Laden: Task Force Dagger; On the Ground with the Special Forces in Afghanistan*. New York: Random House, 2003. A solid account that deserves more attention than it got.

Moussaoui, Abd Samad. *Zacarias, My Brother: The Making of a Terrorist*. New York: Seven Stories Press, 2003. Originally published in French. An intimate portrait of an ordinary man who became seduced by terror and why, written by his brother.

The National Commission on Terrorist Attacks Upon the United States. *The 9-11 Commission Report*. New York: W. W. Norton & Company, July 2003.

Nojumi, Neamatollah. *The Rise of the Taliban in Afghanistan: Mass Mobilization, Civil War, and the Future of the Region*. New York: Palgrave, 2002. It was first written as a dissertation and still reads that way. But many valuable facts and insights.

Omrani, Bijan and Matthew Leeming. *Afghanistan: A Companion and Guide*. New York: W. W. Norton & Company, Inc., 2005. A good short history, with many practical details and photos.

Parfrey, Adam, ed. *Extreme Islam: Anti-American Propaganda of Muslim Fundamentalism*. Los Angeles: Feral House, 2001. An examination of the messages of radical Islam. Some interesting details.

Peters, Rudolph. *Jihad in Classical and Modern Islam: A Reader*. Princeton: Markus Wiener Publishers, 1996. An interesting collection of primary sources.

Pollack, Kenneth M. *The Persian Puzzle: The Conflict between Iran and America*. New York: Random House, 2004. Pollack's account of the Clinton administration's apology to Iran for the 1953 "coup"—and how it backfired—is telling.

Pope, Hugh and Nicole. *Turkey Unveiled: A History of Modern Turkey*. London: John Murray, 1997. A reliable, readable history of modern Turkey by a veteran *Wall Street Journal* reporter.

Prados, John. *America Confronts Terrorism: Understanding the Danger and How to Think about It; A Documentary Record*. Chicago: Ivan R. Dee, 2002. A good collection of primary sources.

Qutb, Seyyid. *Milestones*. Damascus: Dar Al-Ilm, undated. The author of *In the Shade of the Koran*, Qutb is one of the founding philosophers of radical Islam.

He is the ideological father of the Muslim Brotherhood (although the group was founded decades before Qutb's prominent involvement), and by extension al Qaeda. As a primary document, it must be read by any serious student of radical Islam.

Rashid, Ahmed. *Jihad: The Rise of Militant Islam in Central Asia*. New Haven: Yale University Press, 2002. An essential guide to the region.

———. *The Taliban: The Story of the Afghan Warlords*. London: Pan Books, 2001. Well written, with a reporter's eye for telling detail. Before the car bomb came the "camel bomb."

Reeve, Simon. *The New Jackals: Ramzi Yousef, Osama bin Laden, and the Future of Terrorism*. Boston: Northeastern University Press, 1999. A very readable reporter's account of the 1993 World Trade Center bombing and its subsequent investigation.

Reich, Walter. *Origins of Terrorism: Psychologies, Ideologies, Theologies, States of Mind*. Washington, D.C.: Woodrow Wilson Center Press, 1998. A good, general text that pays little direct attention to bin Laden.

Ressa, Maria A. *Seeds of Terror: An Eyewitness Account of Al-Qaeda's Newest Center of Operations in Southeast Asia*. New York: Free Press/Simon & Schuster, 2003. By a CNN reporter with excellent sources. Especially good on the Philippines and Indonesia.

Robins, Christopher. *Air America: From World War II to Vietnam*. Bangkok, Asia Books, 2002. The history of the CIA-operated airline. A good contrast with today's CIA. Very readable. The section on a pilot named "Shower Shoes" is fun and ultimately sad.

Robinson, Adam. *Bin Laden: Behind the Mask of the Terrorist*. New York: Arcade Publishing, 2001. Hard to verify, especially with respect to bin Laden's teenage years. But interesting.

Royal Embassy of Saudi Arabia. *Initiatives and Actions Taken by the Kingdom of Saudi Arabia in the War on Terrorism*. Washington, D.C., 2003. The oil-rich kingdom presents the evidence that it is actively fighting al Qaeda.

Sageman, Marc. *Understanding Terror Networks*. Philadelphia: University of Pennsylvania Press, 2004. Interesting. Perhaps the single best account of the demographics of terrorists that I have seen.

Scarborough, Rowan. *Rumsfeld's War: The Untold Story of America's Anti-Terrorist Commander*. Washington, D.C.: Regnery, 2004. A *Washington Times* reporter takes a fresh look at Rumsfeld.

Scheuer, Michael. *Imperial Hubris: Why the West Is Losing the War on Terror*. Washington, D.C.: Potomac Books, 2004. An analyst argues that America bears some blame for bin Laden's ire. Worth reading.

Schroen, Gary C. *First In: An Insider's Account of How the CIA Spearheaded the War on Terror in Afghanistan*. New York: Ballantine Books, 2005. Probably the best account, by a participant of a recent CIA field operation.

Sciolino, Elaine. *Persian Mirrors: The Elusive Face of Iran*. New York: Touchstone, 2000. A well-written history.

Seierstad, Asne. *The Bookseller of Kabul*. New York: Little, Brown and Co., 2003. A Norwegian woman moves in with a Kabul family and discovers a lot about Afghan life.

Sharp, Gene. *From Dictatorship to Democracy: A Conceptual Framework for Liberation*. Boston: Albert Einstein Institution, 2003. A blueprint for overthrowing dictators without violence. I am reliably informed that it was translated into Farsi and distributed inside Iran.

Sifaoui, Mohamed. *Inside Al Qaeda: How I Infiltrated the World's Deadliest Terrorist Organization*. New York: Thunder's Mouth Press, 2003. A Luxembourg journalist, born in Algeria, worms his way inside an al Qaeda cell. An interesting perspective that reveals how terrorists are drawn in and how tawdry their lives truly are.

Silvers, Robert B. and Barbara Epstein, eds. *Striking Terror: America's New War*. New York: *New York Review of Books*, 2001. A good anthology of writing from the Left.

Smucker, Philip. *Al Qaeda's Great Escape: The Military and the Media on Terror's Trail*. Washington, D.C.: Brassey's, Inc., 2004. A *Christian Science Monitor* reporter tells an engaging story. Helpful in establishing bin Laden's movements prior to the battle in Tora Bora.

Stern, Jessica. *Terror in the Name of God: Why Religious Militants Kill*. New York: HarperCollins, 2003. Well documented.

Thesiger, Wilfred. *Arabian Sands*. London: HarperCollins Publishers, Ltd., 1959. Thesiger's experiences among Yemeni and other Arabs. Beautifully written.

———. *The Danakil Diary: Journeys through Abyssinia, 1930–34*. London: Harper Collins Publishers, 1996. I found the chapters on Sudan particularly interesting.

———. *The Life of My Choice*. New York: William Collins Sons & Co. Ltd., 1987. Thesiger's biography. Worth reading.

————. *The Marsh Arabs*. London: HarperCollins Publishers, 1964. Thesiger's time among the Marsh Arabs in 1950s and 1960s Iraq—decades before Saddam Hussein blocked their water and tried to end their way of life. A porthole on a lost world.

Venzke, Ben and Aimee Ibrahim. *The al-Qaeda Threat: An Analytical Guide to al-Qaeda's Tactics and Targets*. Alexandria, VA: Tempest Publishing, 2003. Demonstrates that al Qaeda's tactics have evolved due to U.S. pressure.

Verton, Dan. *Black Ice: The Invisible Threat of Cyber-Terrorism*. Emeryville, IL: McGraw-Hill/Osborne, 2003. The definitive book on the subject. To those who say cyber-terror will never be a threat, I say read *Black Ice*.

Weaver, Mary Anne. *Pakistan: In the Shadow of Jihad and Afghanistan*. New York: Farrar, Straus and Giroux, 2002. A well-reported account. The bits about Bhutto and Musharif are interesting.

————. *A Portrait of Egypt: A Journey through the World of Militant Islam*. New York: Farrar, Straus and Giroux, 2000. Beautifully written and penetrating, by a writer who lived in Egypt during the pivotal late 1970s.

Weiss, Murray. *The Man Who Warned America: The Life and Death of John O'Neill, the FBI's Embattled Counterterror Warrior*. New York: HarperCollins/Regan Books, 2003. By a distinguished police reporter who knew O'Neill well. Very readable with many fresh facts.

Weldon, Curt. *Countdown to Terror*. Washington, D.C.: Regnery, 2005. A series of memos to the congressman from a well-placed Iranian source.

West, Bing and Maj. Gen. Ray L. Smith. *The March Up: Taking Baghdad with the 1st Marine Division*. New York: Bantam Dell, 2003. Two Vietnam-era commanders ride along with the troops. Incidentally demolishes the comparisons between the Iraq and Vietnam wars.

Williams, Paul L. *Al Qaeda: Brotherhood of Terror*. New York: Alpha, 2002. An early account. The description of bin Laden rejoicing at the 1993 World Trade Center bombing is a first, if true.

# ACKNOWLEDGMENTS

### Afghanistan
Amrullah Saleh, head of Afghan intelligence; Ottilie English, one-time lobbyist for the Northern Alliance who knows more about Afghanistan than the State Department; Gay Leclare Qaderi, an American living in Kabul; Dr. Barnett Rubin at New York University; Ambassador Syeed Tyeb Jawad, ambassador from Afghanistan to the U.S.; Professor John F. Shroder, a geology professor at the University of Nebraska; Mir Bahmanyar, former member of U.S. special forces; and Lt. Gen. Mike "Rifle" DeLong, deputy commander of CentCom during the Afghan War in 2001–2003.

### United States
Peter Bergen, Sam Dealey, Eli Lake, Christopher Hitchens (whose fine eye caught many small errors or omissions), Philip Smucker, Richard Perle, Kenneth Adelman, P. J. Crowley, David Ignatius, Viet Dinh, and Captain Frank Thorp.

### Israel
Moshe Weiss, Caroline Glick of the *Jerusalem Post*, former Israeli ambassador to Iran Uri Lehrani, Colonel Itzak, and Israel's former UN ambassador Dore Gold.

### Saudi Arabia
David Bass, for introducing me to Saudi sources and always staying for one more at the Palm, and Adel al-Jubeir.

## Belgium

Kalle Isakson, Cecilia Kindstrand, Jeremy Slater, and Paul Belien, who edits www.brusselsjournal.com.

## France

Christian de Fouloy and several sources in French intelligence.

## United Kingdom

Stephen Grey, who kindly put me up in his new house and gave me the private phone numbers of some die-hard Islamists, as well as several sources in British intelligence.

# STAFF

I'd also like to thank my researcher, the indefatigable Martin Morse Wooster; my excellent transcriber in Hong Kong, Carol Hopkins; and Winfred J. "Skip" Keats II, of nextstrategy.com, who developed www.richardminiter.com. I'd also like to thank Dan Darling, the counter-terrorism wunderkind who sent me a number of valuable and interesting documents.

# INSPIRATIONAL PEOPLE

I'd like to thank the owners and staff of Portner's in Alexandria, Virginia, and Havana Corner in Brussels. They let me work for hours in their fine establishments and never complained about the cigars or the dog, Boxer. I'd also like to thank Laurent Menoud of Café Milano, who always found me a last-minute table to entertain a source.

Hats off to Mel Berger, my agent at William Morris; Harry Crocker, a great book editor; James Taranto (sorry about ditching you in Brussels); Brett Decker, who is so well connected in the Philippines that he should be made U.S. ambassador there (sorry about the flood); Doug Heye, who persuaded me to join him at bullfights and to run with the bulls at Pamplona; and Kevin Washington, a true gentleman whose impeccable taste should rub off on me someday.

# ABOUT THE AUTHOR

RICHARD MINITER is the author of two *New York Times* bestsellers, *Shadow War* and *Losing bin Laden*. A veteran investigative journalist, he was a member of the award-winning *Sunday Times* (of London) investigative team and an editorial page writer at the *Wall Street Journal Europe*.

Miniter's articles have appeared in the *Wall Street Journal*, the *New York Times*, the *Washington Post*, the *Christian Science Monitor*, the *Atlantic Monthly*, the *New Republic*, *National Review*, and *Reader's Digest*.

As a recognized expert on international terrorism, Miniter has appeared over the past three years nearly 200 times on CNN, C-SPAN, FOX News Channel, and MSNBC, and has been featured on more 2,000 radio programs in the past three years.
Miniter's reporting has been cited by NBC's Tim Russert on *Meet the Press* and by columnists Steve Forbes, Robert Novak, and George Will.

An active speaker, Miniter has addressed audiences as wide-ranging as NATO officers at the Royal Military College of Belgium, legislators at the European Parliament, journalists at the Hong Kong Foreign Correspondents' Club, business leaders at the Young Presidents' Organization, and activists at CPAC in Washington, D.C.

Miniter has reported from war zones in Afghanistan and Iraq as well as from Egypt, Kuwait, Israel, Sudan, Thailand, Vietnam, and elsewhere.

A graduate of Vassar College, he divides his time between his homes in Brussels, Belgium, and Alexandria, Virginia. His website and terrorism blog can be found at www.RichardMiniter.com.

# NOTES

## Introduction

1. This is an oft-repeated aphorism generally attributed to Senator Daniel Patrick Moynihan. Senator Moynihan's famous line is similar to one uttered by financier Bernard M. Baruch: "Every man has a right to his opinion, but no man has a right to be wrong in his facts."

2. This is a paraphrase of her question, in order to shield her identity in this world of blogging sleuths. The point of this anecdote is her question and belief, not to single her out specifically. For the same reason, I am keeping her name and network to myself.

3. Richard Hofstadter, "The Paranoid Style in American Politics," *Harper's Magazine*, November 1964.

4. Richard Hofstadter, "The Paranoid Style in American Politics," *Harper's Magazine*, November 1964.

5. http://usinfo.state.gov/media/Archive/2005/Apr/08-205989.html.

6. This *Commentary* article is most easily viewed at http://www.commentarymagazine.com/production/files/epsteinwatergate.html. There are a few typos.

## Myth #1: Bin Laden was trained or funded by the CIA

1. Mary Anne Weaver, "The Real Bin Laden," *New Yorker*, January 24, 2000. What is interesting about this article is that it also presents a lot of evidence against the myth that the CIA funded bin Laden.

2. Robert Fisk, "Anti-Soviet Warrior Puts His Army on the Road to Peace," *Independent*, December 6, 1993.

3. Robert Fisk, "Why We Reject the West, by the Saudis' Fiercest Arab Critic," *Independent*, July 10, 1996.

4. One variant of the CIA-funded-bin Laden argument is that the CIA created the conditions that made bin Laden's rise possible by bankrolling the anti-Soviet

resistance in Afghanistan. This argument is also implausible. The chaos in Afghanistan was caused by the Soviets, who invaded in 1979. And bin Laden's ideology—which turned him against the U.S.—was forged in the 1970s.

5.   Ayman al-Zawahiri, *Knights Under the Prophet's Banner*, part two (translated FBIS), *Al-Sharq al-Awsat*, December 3, 2001. Contrast this text with the censored State Department version.

6.   As cited in "Did the U.S. 'Create' Osama bin Laden?" http://www.usinfo.state.gov.

7.   Ahmed Rashid, "The Making of a Terrorist" (excerpted from *Taliban*), *Straits Times*, (Singapore), September 23, 2001.

8.   Peter Bergen, *Holy War Inc.: Inside the Secret World of Osama bin Laden* (New York: The Free Press, 2001), 64–66.

9.   As cited in "Did the U.S. 'Create' Osama bin Laden?"

10.  Weaver, "The Real Bin Laden."

11.  Weaver, "The Real Bin Laden."

12.  Author interview, June 2003.

13.  Milt Bearden's latest book is *The Main Enemy*. His novel on Afghanistan is called *The Black Tulip*.

14.  Interview with a CIA station chief who spoke on the condition of anonymity. The e-mail in question was sent to the author in June 2003.

15.  Author interview in Rohrabacher's Capitol Hill office, January 2002.

16.  "Did the U.S. 'Create' Osama bin Laden?"

17.  Weaver, "The Real Bin Laden."

18.  BBC.com.

19.  Abdullah Azzam, speaking in Oklahoma City in 1988, as cited by Steven Emerson in *American Jihad: The Terrorists Living Among Us* (New York: Free Press, 2002). Though this quote comes more than ten years after bin Laden first heard Azzam speak, and in a forum some 10,000 miles from Saudi Arabia, it is remarkably similar in spirit and tone to the late 1970s speeches of Azzam. Azzam had a consistent theme and repeated it, by all accounts, throughout the 1970s and 1980s.

20.  Dore Gold, *Hatred's Kingdom: How Saudi Arabia Supports the New Global Terrorism* (Washington, D.C.: Regnery, 2003), 94.

21.  As quoted by Jane Corbin in *The Base* (London: Simon & Schuster, 2002), 13. Strangely, Corbin does not cite Fisk by name.

22.  Sometimes translated as the "office of services."

23.  According to an informal estimate by a retired CIA official who worked in Afghanistan.

## Myth #2: Bin Laden has a vast fortune and is able to finance terrorism out of his own pocket

1.  Nimrod Raphaeli, "Financing of Terrorism: Sources, Methods, and Channels," *Terrorism and Political Violence*, Vol. 15, Nov. 4, winter 2003.

2.  As cited in the National Commission on Terrorist Attacks Upon the United States Staff Report to the 9-11 Commission, "Monograph on Terrorist Financing."

3.  *Sunday Times* (London), November 29, 2001. Also cited on http://www.edward-jayepstein.com/nether_fictoid3.htm.

4.  "Monograph on Terrorist Financing."

5.  "Monograph on Terrorist Financing."

6.  Author interview, August 19, 2005.

7.  Author interview, March 2002.

8.  "Monograph on Terrorist Financing."

9.  "Monograph on Terrorist Financing."

10.  "Monograph on Terrorist Financing."

11.  "Monograph on Terrorist Financing."

12.  "Monograph on Terrorist Financing."

13.  Stephen Fidler, "Al Qaeda Outsmarts Sanctions, Says UN," *Financial Times*, August 28, 2004.

14.  Author interview with an American intelligence source, May 2005.

15.  Raphaeli, "Financing of Terrorism."

16.  Raphaeli, "Financing of Terrorism."

17.  Raphaeli, "Financing of Terrorism."

18.  "Monograph on Terrorist Financing."

19.  "Monograph on Terrorist Financing."

20.  "Monograph on Terrorist Financing."

21.  "Monograph on Terrorist Financing."

22.  "Monograph on Terrorist Financing."

23.  "Monograph on Terrorist Financing."

24.  Dirk Laabs, "A Dwarf Known as Al-Qaeda," *Los Angeles Times*, November 30, 2004.

25.  Dirk Laabs, "A Dwarf Known as Al-Qaeda," *Los Angeles Times*, November 30, 2004.

26.  Raphaeli, "Financing of Terrorism."

27. "Monograph on Terrorist Financing."

28. "Monograph on Terrorist Financing."

29. "Monograph on Terrorist Financing."

30. "Material Aid for Terrorists." Testimony of Assistant Attorney General Christopher Wray before the Senate Judiciary Committee, May 5, 2004.

31. "Monograph on Terrorist Financing."

32. Author interview, May 2005.

## Myth #3: Bin Laden is on dialysis

1. Thom Shanker, "Touring with the U.S.O. in '04; it's still thanks for the memories," *New York Times*, December 26, 2004.

2. William Safire, "Prague Connection," *New York Times*, November 12, 2001.

3. http://www.snopes.com/rumors/kidney.htm. Last updated November 20, 2001.

4. http://www.snopes.com/rumors/kidney.htm. Last updated November 20, 2001.

5. http://www.snopes.com/rumors/kidney.htm. Last updated November 20, 2001.

6. "Pakistani president thinks bin Laden 'most likely dead; due to kidney ailment,'" *(Islamabad) News*, January 19, 2002. The *News* is an English-language newspaper.

7. *CNN Late Edition with Wolf Blitzer*, broadcast December 5, 2004. Transcript 120501CN.V47.

8. *CNN Impact*, broadcast August 10, 1997. Transcript 97081000V55.

9. Author interview, August 22, 2005.

10. Magnus Clarke, "The Osama I Knew, by His Boyhood Pal," *Sunday Tasmanian*, April 21, 2002.

11. Author interview, August 19, 2005.

12. Author interview, March 2002.

13. Author interview.

14. Hamid Mir, "Osama claims he has nukes: If U.S. uses nuclear arms it will get same response," *Dawn*, November 10, 2001.

15. Olivia Ward, "Anti-U.S. sentiment festers in Pakistan," *Toronto Star*, December 21, 2002.

16. Carlotta Gall, "Threats and Responses: The Qaeda Trail, Pakistani who treated bin Laden is questioned by U.S.," *New York Times*, November 28, 2002.

17. There is a second Amer Aziz, who was arrested by Spanish authorities in 2004 as part of the Madrid plot. This is a different person.

18. Rory McCarthy, "Doctors held for treating al-Qaida sick," *Guardian*, January 20, 2003.

19. Thomas M. DeFrank and Corky Siemaszko, "Doc says Osama is alive and well," *New York Daily News*, November 28, 2002. The story cites the Associated Press.

20. Thomas M. DeFrank and Corky Siemaszko, "Doc says Osama is alive and well," *New York Daily News*, November 28, 2002. The story cites the Associated Press.

21. Thomas M. DeFrank and Corky Siemaszko, "Doc says Osama is alive and well," *New York Daily News*, November 28, 2002. The story cites the Associated Press.

22. Paul Haven, "Bin Laden healthy: MD," *(Montreal) Gazette*, November 28, 2002.

23. Gall, "Threats and Responses."

## Myth #4: Before September 11, no one had heard of bin Laden

1. According to an interview with a intelligence community source.

2. For more information on this point, please see Richard Miniter, *Losing bin Laden* (Washington, D.C.: Regnery, 2003).

3. Kenneth R. Timmerman, "This Man Wants You Dead," *Reader's Digest*, July 1998.

4. Robert Fisk, "Talks with Osama bin Laden," *The Nation*, August 21, 1998.

5. Peter Bergen and Frank Smyth, "Holy Warrior," *New Republic*, August 31, 1998.

6. John Miller, "Greetings, America. My Name is Osama bin Laden," *Esquire*, February 1999.

7. John Barry et al., "Making a Symbol of Terror," *Newsweek*, March 1, 1999.

8. Rahimullah Yusufzai, "Conversations with Terror," *Time*, January 11, 1999.

9. Warren P. Strobel et al., "A War in the Shadows," *U.S. News & World Report*, January 8, 2001.

## Myth #5: The U.S. government had many warnings about bin Laden prior to September 11 but failed to act on them

1. This was a front-page headline appearing on May 16, 2002.

2. Richard Miniter, *Shadow War* (Washington, D.C.: Regnery, 2004), 54.

3. Richard Miniter, *Shadow War* (Washington, D.C.: Regnery, 2004), 54.

4. Richard Miniter, *Shadow War* (Washington, D.C.: Regnery, 2004), 54.

5. Testimony of Condoleezza Rice before the 9-11 Commission, April 6, 2004, as excerpted on the National Security Archive website.

6. Steve Coll, *Ghost Wars: The Secret History of the CIA, Afghanistan, and Bin Laden, from the Soviet Invasion to September 10, 2001* (New York: Penguin Press, 2004), 562.

7.   As cited in the 9-11 Commission Report, 345.

8.   Richard A. Clarke, *Against All Enemies: Inside America's War on Terror* (New York: Free Press, 2004), 238.

9.   Kevin Michael Derksen, "Commentary: The Logistics of Actionable Intelligence Leading to 9-11," *Studies in Conflict & Terrorism*, Vol. 28, 255.

10.  Bill Gertz, *Breakdown: How America's Intelligence Failures Led to September 11* (Washington, D.C.: Regnery, 2002), 146–47.

11.  "Transcript of Usama Bin Laden Videotape," www.cnn.com, December 13, 2001, cited by Anonymous in *Imperial Hubris* (Washington, D.C.: Brassey's Inc., 2004), 136.

12.  Bin Laden wanted it to occur on the seven-month anniversary of the attack on the USS *Cole*, according to the 9-11 Commission.

13.  Ramsi Yousef's uncle, Khalid Sheikh Mohammed (KSM), also contributed to the Bojinka plot. The 9-11 Commission Report described KSM as the "mastermind" of the 2001 attacks on New York and Washington.

14.  Gertz, 44.

15.  Walter Pincus and Dana Priest, "NSA Intercepts on Eve of 9/11 Sent a Warning," *Washington Post*, June 20, 2002.

16.  Patrick Martin, "The Strange Case of Zacarias Moussaoui: FBI Refused to Investigate Man Charged in September 11 Attacks," *World Socialist*, January 5, 2002. Available at ⟨http://www.wsws.org/articles/2002/jan2002/mousj05.shtml⟩.

17.  Derksen, "Commentary: The Logistics of Actionable Intelligence Leading to 9-11."

18.  Heather Mac Donald, "Why the FBI Didn't Stop 9/11," *City Journal*, Autumn 2002.

19.  Dan Verton, "IT Deficiencies Blamed in Part for Pre–9/11 Intelligence Failure," *Computerworld*, July 18, 2003.

20.  David E. Kaplan, Kevin Whitelaw, Edward T. Pound, and Chitra Ragravan, "Pieces of the 9/11 Puzzle," *U.S. News & World Report*, March 15, 2004.

21.  Sophie Goodchild and Zachary Mesenbourg, "FBI Admits It Failed to Act on 9/11 Tip-Off," *Independent on Sunday*, June 6, 2004.

22.  Susan Schmidt, "9/11 Hijackers' San Diego Contacts Detailed by Lawmakers' Report," *Washington Post*, July 23, 2003.

23.  Gail Russell Chaddock, "Was There Enough Intel to Act?" *Christian Science Monitor*, April 15, 2004.

24.  Joseph E. Persico, "What Did He Know, and When?" *New York Times*, April 18, 2004.

## Myth #6: Warned by the Mossad, there were no Jews at the World Trade Center on September 11

1.   As cited in Bryan Curtis, "4,000 Jews, 1 Lie: Tracking an Internet Hoax," Slate.com, October 5, 2001.

2.    As cited in Bryan Curtis, "4,000 Jews, 1 Lie: Tracking an Internet Hoax," Slate.com, October 5, 2001.

3.    Gil Rudawsky, "At 29, a Billionaire; at 31, a Casualty," *Rocky Mountain News*, September 4, 2002.

4.    Jack Schofield, "Daniel Lewin," *Guardian* (London), September 15, 2001.

5.    Richard Sisk and Monique El-Faizy, "First Victim died a hero on Flt. 11; Ex-Israeli Commando tried to halt unfolding hijacking," *New York Daily News*, July 24, 2004.

6.    Richard Sisk and Monique El-Faizy, "First Victim died a hero on Flt. 11; Ex-Israeli Commando tried to halt unfolding hijacking," *New York Daily News*, July 24, 2004.

7.    Richard Sisk and Monique El-Faizy, "First Victim died a hero on Flt. 11; Ex-Israeli Commando tried to halt unfolding hijacking," *New York Daily News*, July 24, 2004.

8.    "Five Israeli Victims Remembered in Capital," *Jerusalem Post*, September 12, 2002.

9.    "A Dad's Inner Artist, An Irresistible Friend and a Distinctive Vocabulary," *New York Times*, November 19, 2001.

10.   "Shay Levinhar, 29," Haaretz.com, accessed June 17, 2005.

11.   "Haggai Sheffi, 34," Haaretz.com, accessed June 17, 2005. Ori Golan, "Hagay, What a Guy!" *Jerusalem Post*, September 13, 2002.

12.   *The Resuscitation of Anti-Semitism: An American Perspective; An Interview with Abraham Foxman* (Jerusalem Center for Public Affairs, 2003).

13.   Adam Dickter, "The Lives They Led," *Jewish Week*, September 5, 2002.

14.   "The 4,000 Jews Disinformation. The 4,000 Jews Rumor: Rumor Surrounding Sept. 11th Proved Untrue," http://www.middleast.org/forum/fb-public/1/4390.shtml.

15.   "The 4,000 Jews Disinformation. The 4,000 Jews Rumor: Rumor Surrounding Sept. 11th Proved Untrue," http://www.middleast.org/forum/fb-public/1/4390.shtml.

16.   Curtis, "4,000 Jews, 1 Lie."

17.   Caroline Glick, "Our Egyptian Friends," *Jerusalem Post*, July 25, 2005.

## Myth #7: The post–September 11 world is more dangerous for Americans than ever before

1.    E. B. White, *Here is New York* (New York: Harper & Brothers, 1949), 51.

2.    Ibid., 50–51.

3.    These paragraphs first appeared in book form in 1949. E. B. White's text first appeared in a now-defunct magazine called *Holiday*.

4.    *Spectator* (London), Issue 7, April 2, 2005, http://www.spectator.co.uk/article_archive. php?id=5911&issue=2005-04-02.

5.    Russell Seitz, "Weaker Than We Think," *American Conservative*, December 6, 2004.

6.    Russell Seitz, "Weaker Than We Think," *American Conservative*, December 6, 2004.

7.    Boris Melnikov, "Professor Finds New Terrorism Statistics," *Daily Trojan*, October 18, 2004.

8.    Boris Melnikov, "Professor Finds New Terrorism Statistics," *Daily Trojan*, October 18, 2004.

9.    Boris Melnikov, "Professor Finds New Terrorism Statistics," *Daily Trojan*, October 18, 2004.

10.   Todd Sandler, "Collective Action and Transnational Terrorism," Leverhulme Centre at Nottingham University (UK), Research Paper 2003/13.

11.   Todd Sandler, "Collective Action and Transnational Terrorism," Leverhulme Centre at Nottingham University (UK), Research Paper 2003/13.

12.   Todd Sandler, "Collective Action and Transnational Terrorism," Leverhulme Centre at Nottingham University (UK), Research Paper 2003/13.

13.   Martin Wolf, "The frightening flexibility of international terrorism," *Financial Times*, June 4, 2003.

14.   Martin Wolf, "The frightening flexibility of international terrorism," *Financial Times*, June 4, 2003.

15.   Sandler, "Collective Action and Transnational Terrorism." Sandler is citing the research of respected terrorist scholar and Rand Institute researcher Bruce Hoffman.

16.   Sandler, "Collective Action and Transnational Terrorism."

17.   John Mueller, "A False Sense of Insecurity?" *Regulation*, fall 2004.

18.   John Mueller, "Simplicity and Spook: Terrorism and the Dynamics of Threat Exaggeration." Paper presented at Harvard University, October 2004.

19.   Mueller, "A False Sense of Insecurity?"

20.   Mueller, "A False Sense of Insecurity?"

21.   Mueller, "A False Sense of Insecurity?"

22.   Mueller, "A False Sense of Insecurity?"

23.   Mueller, "A False Sense of Insecurity?"

24.   Mueller, "A False Sense of Insecurity?"

25.   Brendan Miniter, "What a Bastard: Every day in every way, I hate Osama more," OpinionJournal.com, Monday, July 8, 2002.

## Myth #8: The Iraq war is another Vietnam

1.    As quoted in "Auteur Is Born: Star Wars looks to France for respect," *Wall Street Journal*, May 20, 2005.

2.    Author interview.

3.  This was widely reported.  See, for example, Patrick J. Buchanan, "Soldier on, escalate or get out," syndicated column, April 14, 2003.

4.  Patrick J. Buchanan, "Iraq & Tet, George W. Bush, Lyndon B. Johnson," syndicated column, September 29, 2003.

5.  Staff Sergeant Barry Sadler, "The Ballad of the Green Beret."

6.  In a 1999 trip to Vietnam, I interviewed North Vietnam's former ambassador to Moscow. Now a prosperous commissar, he regretted that when the U.S. returned to Vietnam, it tore down the old embassy. He though the loss of tourist revenue was incalculable.

7.  See, for example, Richard Miniter, "Vindication in Swift Victory," *Australian*, available at www.richardminiter.com/articles.

8.  See, for example, Richard Miniter, "Vindication in Swift Victory," *Australian*, available at www.richardminiter.com/articles.

9.  See, for example, Richard Miniter, "Vindication in Swift Victory," *Australian*, available at www.richardminiter.com/articles.

10. See, for example, Richard Miniter, "Vindication in Swift Victory," *Australian*, available at www.richardminiter.com/articles.

11. See, for example, Richard Miniter, "Vindication in Swift Victory," *Australian*, available at www.richardminiter.com/articles.

12. See, for example, Richard Miniter, "Vindication in Swift Victory," *Australian*, available at www.richardminiter.com/articles.

13. See, for example, Richard Miniter, "Vindication in Swift Victory," *Australian*, available at www.richardminiter.com/articles.

14. Jeffrey Record and W. Andrew Terrill, *Iraq and Vietnam: Differences, Similarities, and Insights* (Carlisle, PA:  Strategic Studies Institute, U.S. Army War College, 2004), vii.

15. Iraq has not conducted a census since the 1970s.  Today, the Sunni population could be anywhere from 25 to 99 percent of the total population.

16. Record and Terrill.

17. Record and Terrill, 10.

18. Record and Terrill, 13.

19. Record and Terrill, 13.

20. Record and Terrill, 6.

21. Record and Terrill, 7.

22. Record and Terrill, 11.

23. Record and Terrill, 17.

24. James Kitfield, "No, It's Not Vietnam," *National Journal*, November 22, 2003.

25.   Interview on ABC's "This Week with George Stephanopoulos," September 13, 2004

26.   Kitfield, "No, It's Not Vietnam."

27.   Kitfield, "No, It's Not Vietnam."

28.   Kitfield, "No, It's Not Vietnam."

29.   Andrew England, "Iraq's insurers hedge bets on a brighter future," *Financial Times*, May 17, 2005.

30.   Andrew England, "Iraq's insurers hedge bets on a brighter future," *Financial Times*, May 17, 2005.

31.   Andrew England, "Iraq's insurers hedge bets on a brighter future," *Financial Times*, May 17, 2005.

32.   Andrew England, "Iraq's insurers hedge bets on a brighter future," *Financial Times*, May 17, 2005.

## Myth #9: The U.S. military killed 100,000 civilians in Iraq

1.    Les Roberts et al., "Mortality Before and After the 2003 Invasion of Iraq:  Cluster-Sample Survey," *Lancet*, November 20, 2004.

2.    Lila Guterman, "Researchers Who Rushed into Print a Study of Iraqi Civilian Deaths Now Wonder Why It Was Ignored," *Chronicle of Higher Education*, January 27, 2005.

3.    William Tinning, "Dispute Over Toll of Casualties," *Glasgow Herald*, December 8, 2004.

4.    Shaoni Battacharya, "Civilian Death Toll in Iraq Exceeds 100,000," Newscientist.com, October 29, 2004.

5.    As cited in NationalJournal.com's "2004 Tip Sheets: Electoral Scoreboard." Associated Press, November 23, 2004.

6.    Guterman, "Researchers Who Rushed into Print a Study of Iraqi Civilian Deaths Now Wonder Why It Was Ignored;" Edward Ericson, Jr., "A Controversial Report from Johns Hopkins Researchers Estimates Iraq Civilian Toll," *Baltimore City Paper*, November 17, 2004.

7.    Michael Fumento, "Lancet Civilian Death Report Kills the Truth," Techcentralstation.com, November 1, 2004.

8.    Stephen Apfelroth, "Mortality in Iraq," *Lancet*, March 26, 2005.

9.    Fred Kaplan, "100,000 Dead—or 8,000," Slate.com, October 29, 2004.

10.   Apfelroth, "Mortality in Iraq."

11.   Fumento, "Lancet Civilian Death Report Kills the Truth."

12.   Kaplan, "100,000 Dead—or 8,000."

13.   Iraq Body Count Project, http://www.iraqbodycount.net, accessed June 13, 2005.

## Myth #10: Wolfowitz told Congress that oil would pay for the Iraq war

1. House Committee on the Budget, *Department of Defense Budget Priorities for Fiscal Year 2004*. Hearing held on February 27, 2003. Page 37 of transcript.

2. Defense Subcommittee, House Appropriations Committee, *Administration's FY 2003 Supplemental Budget Request*. Hearing held March 27, 2003. Pages 20–21 of transcript.

3. Paul Blustein, "Wolfowitz Strives to Quell Criticism," *Washington Post*, March 21, 2005. A transcript of the Jon Stewart segment is found on http://www.worldbankpresident.org.

## Myth #11: There is no evidence that Iraq had weapons of mass destruction

1. As cited by William Kristol, "About Those Iraqi Weapons…" *Weekly Standard*, May 31, 2004.

2. As cited in "Apparatus of Lies: Saddam's Disinformation and Propaganda 1990–2003" on http://www.whitehouse.gov/ogc/apparatus/apparatus-of-lies.pdf.

3. "US reveals Iraq nuclear operations," BBC News, July 7, 2004.

4. "US reveals Iraq nuclear operations," BBC News, July 7, 2004.

5. "Troops 'foil Iraq nerve gas bid,'" BBC News, July 2, 2004.

6. "Troops 'foil Iraq nerve gas bid,'" BBC News, July 2, 2004.

7. "Troops 'foil Iraq nerve gas bid,'" BBC News, July 2, 2004.

8. Ellen Knickmeyer, "Iraqi chemical stash uncovered," *Washington Post*, August 14, 2005. Yes, this was reported almost a week after the fact, and on page A18.

9. As cited in "Apparatus of Lies: Saddam's Disinformation and Propaganda 1990–2003."

10. "Sarin, mustard gas discovered separately in Iraq," FOX News, May 17, 2004.

11. Amatzia Baram, "An Analysis of Iraqi WMD Strategy," *Nonproliferation Review*, Summer 2001.

12. "Iraq's National Security Goals: An Intelligence Assessment," (CIA, 1988), iv. Obtained by National Security Archive (Electronic Briefing Book item 4).

13. Hans Blix, "An Update on Inspection," speech to the UN Security Council, January 27, 2003.

14. Richard Butler, *The Greatest Threat: Iraq, Weapons of Mass Destruction, and the Crisis of Global Security* (New York: PublicAffairs, 2000), 13.

15. Richard Butler, *The Greatest Threat: Iraq, Weapons of Mass Destruction, and the Crisis of Global Security* (New York: PublicAffairs, 2000), 159–60.

16. Richard Butler, *The Greatest Threat: Iraq, Weapons of Mass Destruction, and the Crisis of Global Security* (New York: PublicAffairs, 2000), 79–85.

17.   Richard Butler, *The Greatest Threat: Iraq, Weapons of Mass Destruction, and the Crisis of Global Security* (New York: PublicAffairs, 2000), 81.

18.   Richard Butler, *The Greatest Threat: Iraq, Weapons of Mass Destruction, and the Crisis of Global Security* (New York: PublicAffairs, 2000), 181.

19.   Richard Butler, *The Greatest Threat: Iraq, Weapons of Mass Destruction, and the Crisis of Global Security* (New York: PublicAffairs, 2000), 206.

20.   As cited in "Apparatus of Lies: Saddam's Disinformation and Propaganda 1990–2003."

21.   Kenneth Katzman, "Iraq: Weapons Threat, Compliance, Sanctions, and U.S. Policy," Congressional Research Service, 2002.

22.   Anthony R. Cordesman, *The Iraq War: Strategy, Tactics, and Military Lessons* (CSIS/Praeger, 2004), 425.

23.   Anthony R. Cordesman, *The Iraq War: Strategy, Tactics, and Military Lessons* (CSIS/Praeger, 2004), 432–33.

24.   Testimony of Charles Duelfer before the Senate Armed Services Committee, October 6, 2004.

25.   Rolf Ekeus, "Iraq's Real Weapons Threat," *Washington Post*, June 29, 2003.

26.   Testimony of David Kay before the House and Senate Intelligence Committees, October 2, 2003.

27.   Yossef Bodansky, *The Secret History of the Iraq War* (Regan Books/HarperCollins, 2004), 496.

28.   Kenneth M. Pollack, *The Threatening Storm: The Case for Invading Iraq* (Random House, 2002), 103.

29.   Kenneth M. Pollack, *The Threatening Storm: The Case for Invading Iraq* (Random House, 2002), 169.

30.   Kenneth M. Pollack, *The Threatening Storm: The Case for Invading Iraq* (Random House, 2002), 171.

31.   Kenneth M. Pollack, *The Threatening Storm: The Case for Invading Iraq* (Random House, 2002), 174.

32.   Kenneth M. Pollack, *The Threatening Storm: The Case for Invading Iraq* (Random House, 2002), 175.

33.   Kenneth M. Pollack, *The Threatening Storm: The Case for Invading Iraq* (Random House, 2002), 176.

34.   Stuart A. Cohen, "Iraq's WMD Programs: Culling Hard Facts from Soft Myths," National Security Council, November 28, 2003.

## Myths #12, #13, # 14, #15: There is no connection between Iraq and al Qaeda

1.    Shaun Waterman, "White House 'delayed 9-11 Report'," UPI, July 25, 2003.

2.   *New York Post*, March 27, 2003.

3.   Deroy Murdock, "Saddam Hussein's Philanthropy of Terror." Published for the Hoover Institution at Stanford University, September 22, 2004. Also seen on www.husseinandterror.com.

4.   Stephen Hayes, "The Connection," *Weekly Standard*, June 7, 2004.

5.   Stephen Hayes, "Nothing: What Michael Scheuer has to say about bin Laden and Saddam—and what that says about the CIA's performance," *Weekly Standard*, November 21, 2004.

6.   Stephen Hayes, "Nothing: What Michael Scheuer has to say about bin Laden and Saddam—and what that says about the CIA's performance," *Weekly Standard*, November 21, 2004.

7.   Transcript of Secretary of State Colin L. Powell's Address on "'Deeply Troubling' Evidence on Iraq" to the United Nations Security Council, Federal News Service, February 6, 2003.

8.   Transcript of Secretary of State Colin L. Powell's Address on "'Deeply Troubling' Evidence on Iraq" to the United Nations Security Council, Federal News Service, February 6, 2003.

9.   http://en.wikipedia.org/wiki/Iraq-al_Qaeda_Connection/9-11 Commission Report; http://www.9-11commission.gov/report/911Report.pdf.

10.  Stephen Hayes, "Body of evidence: A CNN anchor gets Iraq and al Qaeda wrong. But will the network issue a correction?" *Weekly Standard*, June 30, 2005.

11.  Stephen Hayes, "Body of evidence: A CNN anchor gets Iraq and al Qaeda wrong. But will the network issue a correction?" *Weekly Standard*, June 30, 2005.

12.  Jeffrey Goldberg, "The Great Terror," *New Yorker*, March 25, 2002.

13.  Stephen Hayes, *The Connection: How al Qaeda's Collaboration with Saddam Hussein Has Endangered America* (New York: HarperCollins, 2004), 43.

14.  Stephen Hayes, *The Connection: How al Qaeda's Collaboration with Saddam Hussein Has Endangered America* (New York: HarperCollins, 2004), 43.

15.  "Iraq: Former PM Reveals Secret Service Data on Birth of al-Qaeda in Iraq," *Al-Hayat*, May 23, 2005.

16.  "Iraq: Former PM Reveals Secret Service Data on Birth of al-Qaeda in Iraq," *Al-Hayat*, May 23, 2005.

17.  Powell, Address on "'Deeply Troubling' Evidence on Iraq."

18.  Stephen Hayes and Thomas Joscelyn, "Another Link in the Chain: The role of Saddam and al Qaeda in the creation of Ansar al-Islam," *Weekly Standard*, July 22, 2005.

19.  Stephen Hayes and Thomas Joscelyn, "Another Link in the Chain; The role of Saddam and al Qaeda in the creation of Ansar al-Islam," *Weekly Standard*, July 22, 2005.

20.  Stephen Hayes and Thomas Joscelyn, "Another Link in the Chain; The role of Saddam and al Qaeda in the creation of Ansar al-Islam," *Weekly Standard*, July 22, 2005.

21.  Stephen Hayes, "Why Can't the CIA Keep Up with the *New Yorker*? Good reporting has been done in the media on links between Saddam and al Qaeda, and the CIA still hasn't acted on it," *Weekly Standard*, September 13, 2002.

22.  Hayes, "Body of evidence: A CNN anchor gets Iraq and al Qaeda wrong."

23.  Hayes, *The Connection*, 37–38.

24.  Hayes, *The Connection*, 37–38.

25.  Ravi Nessam, "Marines capture camp suspected as Iraqi training base for terrorists," Associated Press, April 6, 2003.

26.  Ravi Nessam, "Marines capture camp suspected as Iraqi training base for terrorists," Associated Press, April 6, 2003.

27.  Murdock, "Saddam Hussein's Philanthropy of Terror."

28.  Murdock, "Saddam Hussein's Philanthropy of Terror."

29.  Stephen Hayes, "There They Go Again," *Weekly Standard*, June 28, 2004.

30.  Powell, Address on "'Deeply Troubling' Evidence on Iraq."

31.  Senate Intelligence Committee, "Report on the U.S. Intelligence Community's Pre-War Intelligence Assessments on Iraq," 339.

32.  "Iraq's Capability: Let's not wait for a mushroom cloud," National Review Online, September 24, 2002.

33.  "Germany Arrests Two Iraqis Suspected of Spying," Reuters, March 1, 2001.

34.  "Germany Arrests Two Iraqis Suspected of Spying," Reuters, March 1, 2001.

35.  Edward Morrissey, "The Omission Commission: The 9-11 Commission Report failed to make any mention of Iraqi operations in Germany that might have been connected to al Qaeda," *Weekly Standard*, August 17, 2005.

36.  Stephen Hayes, "The Rice Stuff: Susan Rice talks about Abu Musab al-Zarqawi. Does she know what's going on in Iraq?" *Weekly Standard*, October 20, 2004.

37.  Powell, Address on "'Deeply Troubling' Evidence on Iraq."

38.  Powell, Address on "'Deeply Troubling' Evidence on Iraq."

39.  Powell, Address on "'Deeply Troubling' Evidence on Iraq."

40.  Powell, Address on "'Deeply Troubling' Evidence on Iraq."

41.  Powell, Address on "'Deeply Troubling' Evidence on Iraq."

42.  Powell, Address on "'Deeply Troubling' Evidence on Iraq."

43.   Powell, Address on "'Deeply Troubling' Evidence on Iraq."

44.   Murdock, "Saddam Hussein's Philanthropy of Terror."

45.   Murdock, "Saddam Hussein's Philanthropy of Terror."

46.   Hayes, *The Connection*, 17.

47.   Hayes, *The Connection*, 21.

48.   Powell, Address on "'Deeply Troubling' Evidence on Iraq."

49.   Powell, Address on "'Deeply Troubling' Evidence on Iraq."

50.   Murdock, "Saddam Hussein's Philanthropy of Terror."

51.   U.S. Department of State, Office of the Coordinator to Counter-terrorism, "1968–2003: Total Persons Killed/Wounded—International and Accepted Incidents." Figures prepared for author November 17, 2003.

52.   Statistics on Ansar al-Islam: Jonathan Landsay, "Islamic militants kill senior Kurdish general," Knight-Ridder News Service, February 11, 2003; Catherine Taylor, "Saddam and bin Laden help fanatics, says Kurds," *Times* (London), March 28, 2002.

53.   Murdock, "Saddam Hussein's Philanthropy of Terror."

54.   Murdock, "Saddam Hussein's Philanthropy of Terror."

55.   Murdock, "Saddam Hussein's Philanthropy of Terror."

56.   Murdock, "Saddam Hussein's Philanthropy of Terror."

57.   Murdock, "Saddam Hussein's Philanthropy of Terror."

58.   Hayes, *The Connection*, 46–47.

59.   Hayes, *The Connection*, 47.

60.   Hayes, *The Connection*, 36.

## Myth #16: Terrorism is caused by poverty

1.   This is drawn from the president's remarks on March 22, 2002, in Monterrey, Mexico. See http://whitehouse.gov/news/releases/2002/03/200203221.html.

2.   This is drawn from the president's remarks on March 22, 2002, in Monterrey, Mexico. See http://whitehouse.gov/news/releases/2002/03/200203221.html.

3.   *BusinessWeek*, December 2001.

4.   Alan B. Krueger and Jitka Maleckova, "Education, Poverty, and Terrorism: Is there a causal connection?" *Journal of Economic Perspectives*, Vol. 17, Number 4, Fall 2003.

5.   Marc Sageman, *Understanding Terror Networks,* (Philadelphia: University of Pennsylvania Press, 2004), viii.

6.   Marc Sageman, *Understanding Terror Networks,* (Philadelphia: University of Pennsylvania Press, 2004), viii.

7.    Marc Sageman, "Understanding Terror Networks," Foreign Policy Research Insti-
      tute, November 1, 2004.

8.    Marc Sageman, "Understanding Terror Networks," Foreign Policy Research Insti-
      tute, November 1, 2004.

9.    Marc Sageman, "Understanding Terror Networks," Foreign Policy Research Insti-
      tute, November 1, 2004.

10.   Marc Sageman, "Understanding Terror Networks," Foreign Policy Research Insti-
      tute, November 1, 2004.

11.   Marc Sageman, "Understanding Terror Networks," Foreign Policy Research Insti-
      tute, November 1, 2004, 74.

12.   In fact, the whole phenomenon of Christians converting to radical Islam has
      received too little attention by analysts and scholars. At the moment, this subset
      of the terrorist population is too small to establish a general rule. In any event, it
      may be that (material and spiritual) poverty drives Europeans to convert to Islam
      in prison or outside. It should be remembered that very few Muslims or Muslim
      converts become terrorists.

13.   Sageman, "Understanding Terror Networks," 78.

14.   Sageman, "Understanding Terror Networks," 78.

15.   Sageman, "Understanding Terror Networks," 78.

16.   Nasra Hassan, "An Arsenal of Believers," *New Yorker*, November 19, 2001.

17.   Krueger and Maleckova, "Education, Poverty, and Terrorism."

18.   Krueger and Maleckova, "Education, Poverty, and Terrorism."

19.   Krueger and Maleckova, "Education, Poverty, and Terrorism."

20.   Susan B. Glasser, "Martyrs in Iraq Mostly Saudis," *Washington Post*, May 15, 2005.

21.   Susan B. Glasser, "Martyrs in Iraq Mostly Saudis," *Washington Post*, May 15, 2005.

22.   Susan B. Glasser, "Martyrs in Iraq Mostly Saudis," *Washington Post*, May 15, 2005.

23.   Krueger and Maleckova, "Education, Poverty, and Terrorism."

24.   Charles Russell and Bowman Miller, "Profile of a Terrorist," *Perspectives on Ter-
      rorism* (Wilmington, DE: Scholarly Resources, Inc., 1983), 45–60.

25.   Krueger and Maleckova, "Education, Poverty, and Terrorism."

26.   Sageman, "Understanding Terror Networks."

27.   Sageman, "Understanding Terror Networks."

28.   Sageman, "Understanding Terror Networks."

29.   Sageman, "Understanding Terror Networks."

30.   Hassan, "An Arsenal of Believers."

31.   As cited by Michael Bond in "The Making of a Suicide Bomber," *New Scientist*,
      May 15, 2004.

## Myth #17: Suitcase nukes are a real threat

1.  As cited by Bob Port and Greg B. Smith, "Iraqi's Mission to Get bin Laden a Nuke," *New York Daily News*, October 1, 2001.

2.  As cited by Gary Milhollin, "Can Terrorists Get the Bomb," *Commentary*, February 2002.

3.  Michael Ryan, "Wondering What's Next: What We Know for Sure Is That We Don't Know for Sure," *Boston Globe Magazine*, December 30, 2001.

4.  Graham Allison, *Nuclear Terrorism: The Ultimate Preventable Catastrophe* (New York: Henry Holt & Company, 2004), 1.

5.  Robert D. McFadden, "A Nation Challenged: Threat: Tip on Nuclear Attack Risk Was Kept from New Yorkers," *New York Times*, March 4, 2002. Also see the related article in *Time* magazine, March 4, 2002. Interestingly, no one has asked Bush or his top officials what role this report played in moving their minds toward war with Iraq.

6.  McFadden, "A Nation Challenged."

7.  Ryan, "Wondering What's Next."

8.  David Hoffman, "Suitcase nuclear weapons safely kept, Russian says: but former republics may still have bombs," *Washington Post*, September 14, 1997.

9.  Transcript of CBS *60 Minutes* story, "The Perfect Terrorist Weapon; A Large Number of Small Nuclear Devices in the Shape of Suitcases Appear to be Missing from the Russian Nuclear Stockpile," September 7, 1997.

10. Hoffman, "Suitcase nuclear weapons safely kept, Russian says."

11. Alexander Golts, "What the Papers Say. Part B (Russia): Could al Qaeda Buy a Bomb?" *Ezhenedelny Zhurnal*, No. 12, March 29–April 4, 2004.

12. David Filipov, "Nuclear Shadow: Russia's Scattered Tactical Arms a Temptation for Terrorists," *Boston Globe*, June 18, 2002.

13. Hoffman, "Suitcase nuclear weapons safely kept, Russian says."

14. Golts, "Could al Qaeda Buy a Bomb?"

15. Golts, "Could al Qaeda Buy a Bomb?"

16. Shekhar Shatia and Tim Shipman, "Britain On Alert at Al Qaeda Suicide Bomb Threat," *Sunday Express*, December 15, 2002.

17. Allison, 227. This claim is also made on page 71.

18. Allison, 45.

19. Joseph C. Anselmo, "Defector details plans to plant nukes in U.S.," *Aviation Week and Space Technology*, August 17, 1998.

20. Graham Allison, "Nuclear Terrorism: The Ultimate Preventable Catastrophe." Panel held at the Council on Foreign Relations, September 27, 2004.

21. Allison, 213.

22. Allison, 213.

23. Port and Smith, "Iraqi's Mission: To Get Bin Laden a Nuke."

24. Allison, 23.

25. Michael Crowley and Eric Adams, "Can Terrorists Build the Bomb?" *Popular Science*, February 2005.

26. Dafna Linzer, "Nuclear capabilities may elude terrorists, experts say," *Washington Post*, December 29, 2004.

27. Christopher Helman and Chana R. Schoenberger, "Nukes are Back: Stopping the Bad Guys," *Forbes*, January 31, 2005.

28. Christopher Helman and Chana R. Schoenberger, "Nukes are Back: Stopping the Bad Guys," *Forbes*, January 31, 2005.

29. Linzer, "Nuclear capabilities may elude terrorists, experts say."

30. Linzer, "Nuclear capabilities may elude terrorists, experts say."

31. Allison, 23.

32. David Albright, "Al Qaeda's Nuclear Program: Through the Window of Seized Documents," Nautilus Institute Paper #47, published 2002.

33. David Albright, "Al Qaeda's Nuclear Program: Through the Window of Seized Documents," Nautilus Institute Paper #47, published 2002.

## Myth #18: Oliver North warned us about al Qaeda in the 1980s

1. As cited in "Oliver Twisted" on http://www.snopes.com/rumors/north.htm.

## Myth #19: President Bush said Iraq was an "imminent threat" to America

1. Speech outlining Iraqi threat at the Cincinnati Museum Center, Cincinnati Union Terminal, Cincinnati, Ohio, October 7, 2002.

2. Sydney H. Schanberg, "Bush Still Playing with Truth on Iraq," *Village Voice*, August 20, 2003.

3. Bill Moyers, interview with Buzzflash.com, October 29, 2003, accessed at http://www.workingforchange.com, June 27, 2005.

4. 2003 State of the Union Address.

5. Ben Fritz, "Sorting out the 'Imminent Threat' Debate," Spinsanity.org, November 3, 2003.

6. Ben Fritz, "Sorting out the 'Imminent Threat' Debate," Spinsanity.org, November 3, 2003.

7. National Security Strategy of the United States.

8. Fritz, "Sorting out the 'Imminent Threat' Debate."

9. Jonah Goldberg, "'Imminent Threat' is Revisionist Spin." Syndicated column appearing October 17, 2003.

10. As cited by Fritz, "Sorting out the 'Imminent Threat' Debate."

## Myth #20: Halliburton made a fortune in Iraq

1. As cited by Dan Briody in *The Halliburton Agenda: The Politics of Oil and Money* (New York: John Wiley & Sons, Inc., 2004), vii.

2. Jackie Spinner and Mary Pat Flaherty, "Halliburton Reports $85 Million Profit from Iraq Operations," *Washington Post*, March 9, 2004.

3. Stephanie Anderson Forest and Stan Crock, " A Thorn in Halliburton's Side," *BusinessWeek*, October 4, 2004.

4. Stephanie Anderson Forest, "A Thorn in Halliburton's Side," *Businessweek Online*, September 24, 2004.

5. Mergent analysis, accessed June 2, 2005.

6. Allan Sloan, "Halliburton Pays Dearly but Finally Escapes Cheney's Asbestos Mess," *Washington Post*, January 11, 2005.

7. Peter Elkind, "The Truth About Halliburton," *Fortune*, April 18, 2005.

8. P. W. Singer, *Corporate Warriors: The Rise of the Privatized Military Industry* (Ithaca, NY: Cornell University Press, 2001), 140.

9. Elkind, "The Truth About Halliburton."

10. Joshua Chaffin, "Halliburton Feels Financial Strain of Iraq Contracts," *Financial Times*, June 22, 2004.

11. Dave Lesar, "A Tough Job, and Halliburton Does It," *Los Angeles Times*, October 10, 2004.

12. Reuters, "Halliburton Is Awarded $72 Million in Bonuses," *Los Angeles Times*, May 11, 2005.

13. Briody, xi.

14. Briody, 186–87.

15. Briody, 184.

16. Briody, 185.

17. Briody, 185.

18. Stan Crock, "Halliburton's Rising Cost for Bush," *BusinessWeek Online*, February 20, 2004.

19. Briody, 185.

20. Briody, 188.

21. Briody, 187.

## Myth #21: Racial profiling of terrorists works

1.  Heather Mac Donald, "Looking the Wrong Way: New York City's New Search Policy is a Waste," National Review Online, July 22, 2005.

2.  As cited by Daniel Pipes, "What kind of airport profiling," *Jerusalem Post*, October 6, 2004.

3.  As cited by Daniel Pipes, "What kind of airport profiling," *Jerusalem Post*, October 6, 2004.

4.  Heather Mac Donald, "King Folly: Taking Osama bin Laden at his word is a good place to start in fighting terrorism," National Review Online, August 11, 2005.

5.  Bret Stephens and Joseph Rago, "Stars, Stripes, Crescent," *Wall Street Journal*, August 24, 2005.

6.  "We the People of Arab Ancestry in the United States," Census 2000 Special Report, issued March 2005.

7.  "Muslim Life in America," Office of International Information Programs, U.S. Department of State. See http://usinfo.state.gov.

8.  "We the People of Arab Ancestry in the United States."

9.  "We the People of Arab Ancestry in the United States."

10. "We the People of Arab Ancestry in the United States."

11. Mac Donald, "Looking the Wrong Way."

12. Pipes, "What kind of airport profiling."

13. Pipes, "What kind of airport profiling."

14. Edward Epstein, "Lindh in Many Ways Still a Mystery," *San Francisco Chronicle*, October 4, 2002.

15. Richard Leiby, "Taliban from down under," *Washington Post*, March 10, 2002.

16. Richard Leiby, "Taliban from down under," *Washington Post*, March 10, 2002.

17. "Branded a traitor and now facing life in jail," *Sydney Daily Telegraph*, June 12, 2004.

18. Phillip Coorey, "Traitor's Choice," *Telegraph* (Sydney), June 12, 2004.

19. Leiby, "Taliban from down under."

20. Josh Lefkowitz and Lorenzo Vidino, "Al Qaeda's new recruits," *Wall Street Journal Europe*, August 28, 2003.

21. "Branded a traitor and now facing life in jail."

22. Cameron Stewart, "Odd Man Out," *Weekend Australian Magazine*, September 25, 2004. Colleen Egan, "The Bizarre Story of Jack Roche," *Sunday Mail* (Australia), June 6, 2004.

23. Padraic Murphy and Martin Chulov, "Taxi Driver becomes Fifth Australian Charged Under Terror Laws," *Australian*, November 19, 2004. Martin Chulov, "Agents Finally Come Calling for Jihad Jack," *Australian*, November 19, 2004.

24. Alisa Roth, "Total Recall: Why the new computer surveillance will probably come up empty," *Boston Globe*, January 26, 2003.

25. Alisa Roth, "Total Recall: Why the new computer surveillance will probably come up empty," *Boston Globe*, January 26, 2003.

## Myth #22: The U.S. border with Mexico is the most likely place for al Qaeda terrorists to sneak into the homeland

1. Jerry Seper, "Al Qaeda Seeks Tie to Local Gangs," *Washington Times*, September 28, 2004.

2. Dennis Wagner, "Border No Terror Corridor—So Far," *Arizona Republic*, August 22, 2004.

3. Dennis Wagner, "Border No Terror Corridor—So Far," *Arizona Republic*, August 22, 2004.

4. Dennis Wagner, "Border No Terror Corridor—So Far," *Arizona Republic*, August 22, 2004.

5. Robert S. Leiken, *Bearers of Global Jihad? Immigration and National Security After 9/11* (Washington, D.C.: Nixon Center, 2004), 6.

6. Robert S. Leiken, *Bearers of Global Jihad? Immigration and National Security After 9/11* (Washington, D.C.: Nixon Center, 2004), 116.

7. Ramon J. Miro, *Organized Crime and Terrorist Activity in Mexico, 1999–2002* (Washington, D.C.: Library of Congress Federal Research Division, 2003), 43–46.

8. Seper, "Al Qaeda seeks tie to local gangs."

9. Seper, "Al Qaeda seeks tie to local gangs."

10. "Adnan El Shukrijumah Is Not a Saudi Citizen," Saudi Embassy press release, September 5, 2003. See also Seper, "Al Qaeda seeks tie to local gangs."

11. Seper, "Al Qaeda seeks tie to local gangs."

12. Wilfredo Salamanca, "Salvadoran Police Doubt About Al-Qa'ida Link With Mara Salvatrucha," *El Diario de Hoy*, September 30, 2004 (translated by Foreign Broadcast Information Service (FBIS)). See also Maria Jose Uruarte, "Central American Presidents Secretly Meet to Review Al Qa'ida Presence in Region." *La Prensa*, September 30, 2004 (translated by FBIS).

13. "Witnesses Saw Suspect at Subway," NBC6.net, March 25, 2003.

14. Dudley Althaus, "Mexican Officials Question Briton Linked to al-Qaida," *Houston Chronicle*, June 23, 2005. Also see Sandra Dibble, "Mexico Releases Man Held on Terror Suspicion," *San Diego Union-Tribune*, June 24, 2005.

15. As cited by Stewart Bell in *Cold Terror: How Canada Nurtures and Exports Terrorism Around the World* (Mississauga, Ontario, CA: John Wiley & Sons Canada Ltd., 2004), xii–xiii.

16. As cited by Stewart Bell in *Cold Terror: How Canada Nurtures and Exports Terrorism Around the World* (Mississauga, Ontario, CA: John Wiley & Sons Canada Ltd., 2004), xiii.

17. As cited by Stewart Bell in *Cold Terror: How Canada Nurtures and Exports Terrorism Around the World* (Mississauga, Ontario, CA: John Wiley & Sons Canada Ltd., 2004), xvi.

18. As cited by Stewart Bell in *Cold Terror: How Canada Nurtures and Exports Terrorism Around the World* (Mississauga, Ontario, CA: John Wiley & Sons Canada Ltd., 2004), 133.

19. As cited by Stewart Bell in *Cold Terror: How Canada Nurtures and Exports Terrorism Around the World* (Mississauga, Ontario, CA: John Wiley & Sons Canada Ltd., 2004), 133.

20. Hal Bernton, Mike Carter, David Heath, and James Neff, "Chapter 8: Going to Camp," *Seattle Times*, *Seattle Times* Special Report, June 23–July 7, 2002.

21. Hal Bernton, Mike Carter, David Heath, and James Neff, "Chapter 8: Going to Camp," *Seattle Times*, *Seattle Times* Special Report, June 23–July 7, 2002.

22. Bell, 135.

23. Bernton, et al, "Chapter 8: Going to Camp."

24. Hall Bernton and Sara Jean Green, "Ressam judge decries U.S. tactics," *Seattle Times*, July 28, 2005.

25. Bell, 138.

26. Bell, xx.

27. Bell, 157.

28. Bell, 165.

29. Bell, 159.

30. Bell, 159–60.

31. Bell, 161.

32. Bell, 163.

33. Bell, xv–xvi.

34. Bell, 186.

35. Bell, xxi.

36. Bell, xxii.

37. Bell, xxii.

38. Bell, 209–210.

# INDEX

# I

# N